The Descendants of Simon zu Ohrndorff

The Descendants of Simon zu Ohrndorff

A FAMILY HISTORY

Stephen Orendorff

greatunuplished.com
2003

The Descendants of Simon zu Ohrndorff

To My Aunt Nancy, Without Whom This Work Would Not Have Been Completed. Your Intellect And Steadfast Loyalty To Our Great Family Have Had A Profound Impact In My Life. Meine Ehre Heisst Treue.

CHAPTER ONE

GENERATION NO. I

I. SIMON DER HOFFMAN ZU [1] **ORENDORFF** was born in the early 1500's. The name of his spouse is not known.

They had at least 1 child:

+ 2.   m   i.   **HENNE ZU ORENDORFF**, born 1560, died 11 June 1616.

Notes for Simon:

Simon is the earliest known Orendorff; he appears in a 1544 record from Fruedenburg Germany as being appointed guardian of some children. In that record his name appears spelled as "Ohrndorff". He appears in a 1577 tax list from the Freudenburg district, it names "a widow, Barbara zu Ohrndorff, and Simon der Hofmann zu Ohrndorff" as occupants of the Hof Ohrndorff. A Hoffmann was the principle tenant or occupant of a Hof or manor. This record would indicate that Barbara and Simon were probably a mother and son. In 1594 another tax list of the district names the Hoffman at Ohrndorff as Henn zu Ohrndorff indicating that Simon was deceased and that his son Henn had inherited his title. Prior to this Simon probably did not have a last name and was most likely a landless serf. How he came to oversee Hof Ohrndorff (thus acquiring the last name) is unknown.

CHAPTER TWO

GENERATION NO. 2

2. HENNE ZU² ORENDORFF (1.SIMON¹) was born in 1560 at HOF ORENDORFF PRUSSIA, GERMANY. HENNE died 11 June 1616 at HOF OHRNDORFF, PRUSSIA, GERMANY, at the age of 56. The name of his spouse is not known.

They had 6 children:

+ 3.   m   i.   **HUBERT (HUPERT) ORENDORFF**, born 1610, died 12 December 1662.

4.   m   ii.   **DANIEL ORENDORFF**, born 1615. He married ELIZABETH HORLY 1650 in GERMANY.
BORN BEFORE 1616 DANIEL'S NAME APPEARS AS "ORNDORFF" AND "OHRENDORFF", HIS MOTHER WAS CATHARINA.

5.   m   iii.   **JOHAN ORENDORFF**, born 1590 at FREUDENBERG, GERMANY.
BORN BETWEEN 1586-1590, 1ST BORN JOHAN'S NAME APPEARS AS "OHRNDORFF".

6.   f   iv.   **ELSCHEN ORENDORFF**, born circa 1594 at FREUDENBERG, GERMANY.
ELSCHEN WAS THE 2ND CHILD BORN. SHE WAS STILL LIVING IN 1613, HER NAME IS LISTED AS "OHRNDORFF".

+ 7.   m   v.   **STEPHEN ORENDORFF**, born 1597, died 1632.

8.   m   vi.   **HEINRICH ORENDORFF**, born circa 1602

at FREUDENBERG GERMANY, died at FREUDENBERG, GERMANY.
5TH CHILD BORN HEINRICH'S NAME APPEARS AS "OHRNDORFF".

Notes for Henne:

Henne married a woman named Catherina ("Trin") in Prussia in the early 1600's. She died sometime before 1612. He had another wife named Gela who died at Hof Ohrndorff on Feb 19, 1640. His name is listed in a record also as Henn zu Ohrndorff. Henn was listed in a 1594 tax list as the "Hoffman" at Ohrndorff, indicating that he had inherited title and tenancy of the farm by that date. Since the parish records at Fruedenburg only begin in 1612, the names of his children were determined by later references to them in additional church records. There were other Ohrndorffs in the record whose relationship to Henne could not be determined. Henne was buried at Hof Ohrndorff on 06-12-1616, most likely he died on the previous day.

CHAPTER THREE

GENERATION NO. 3

3. HUBERT (HUPERT)[3] **ORENDORFF** (2.HENNE[2], 1.SIMON[1]) was born in 1610 at HOF ORENDORFF, PRUSSIA GERMANY. HUBERT died 12 December 1662 at HOF OHRNDORFF, PRUSSIA GERMANY, at the age of 53. He married **MARGARETHA SCHNEIDER** 6 June 1641 at FRUEDENBERG, GERMANY. She was born 6 December 1617 at BUCHEN, WESTFALLEN PRUSSIA. MARGARETHA died December 1671 at HOF OHRNDORFF GERMANY, at the age of 54.

They had 15 children:

+ 9.   m   i.   **LUDWIG ORENDORFF**, born 2 November 1656, died 1715.

+ 10.   m   ii.   **GEORG ORENDORFF.**

+ 11.   m   iii.   **HENRICH ORENDORFF.**

12.   f   iv.   **JACOBI ORENDORFF**, born in GERMANY, PROBABLY PRUSSIA. JACOBI MARRIED ADOLPH HYCIMONGUES. NAME APPEARS AS "OHRNDORFF".

13.   f   v.   **BARBARA ORENDORFF**, born 14 September 1642 at HOF OHRNDORFF GERMANY. 1ST BORN BARBARA WAS MARRIED TO JOHANNES SCHMIDT, HER NAME APPEARS AS "OHRNDORFF".

+ 14.   m   vi.   **CHRISTIAN ORENDORFF**, born 27 February 1644.

+ 15.   m   vii.   **GERLACH ORENDORFF**, born 24 May

1644.

+ 16.   m   viii.   **PETER ORENDORFF**, born 12 March 1649, died 13 January 1685.

17.   m   ix.   **MATTHIAS ORENDORFF**, born 21 March 1652 at HOF OHRNDORFF, GERMANY. 5TH CHILD BORN MATTHIAS' NAME APPEARS AS "OHRNDORFF", BAPTISM LISTED AS 03-21-1652.

18.   m   x.   **MATTHIAS ORENDORFF**, born 10 May 1653 at HOF OHRNDORFF, GERMANY. He married Adelheidt Ficke Jan 19, 1679 in Germany/first marriage. Adelheidt died circa 1680 in Germany. Notes for Adelheidt: 1st wife Adelheidt Ficke was the daughter of Conrad Ficke. She was the first wife of Matthias and died soon after they married, sometime before May 23, 1681. Matthias died 1682 in Oberheuslingen, Germany, at the age of 28. 9th child born/married twice Matthias' name appears as "Ohrndorff", his baptism was on 05-10-1653. He married first Adelheidt Ficke on 01-19-1679, then secondly to Anna Catherina Halm on May 23 1681. A son named Christian was born shortly after the death of Matthias. Source-Parish records.

19.   m   xi.   **HERMANN ORENDORFF**, born 20 July 1661 at HOF OHRNDORFF GERMANY. 8TH CHILD BORN HERMAN'S NAME APPEARS AS "OHRNDORFF". HE WAS BAPTIZED ON 07-20-1661. Source-Parish record.

20.   f   xii.   **ANNA CATHARINA ORENDORFF**, born 11 April 1663 at HOF OHRNDORFF, GERMANY. Source-Parish record.

9TH CHILD BORN ANNA CATHARINA'S NAME APPEARS AS "OHRNDORFF".

21.   f   xiii.   **FREUCHE ORENDORFF**, born 2 February 1628 at HOF OHRNDORFF, GERMANY, probably died in HOF OHRNDORFF, GERMANY.
1ST CHILD BORN, WAS A TWIN. DATE GIVEN FOR BAPTISM IS 02-02-1628. HER NAME IS LISTED AS "OHRNDORFF". Source-Parish record.

22.   f   xiv.   **MARIA ORENDORFF**, born 2 February 1628 at HOF OHRNDORFF, GERMANY.
2ND CHILD BORN, WAS A TWIN. MARIA'S NAME IS LISTED AS "OHRNDORFF". Source-Parish record.

23.   m   xv.   **STEPHEN ORENDORFF**, born 3 March 1630 at HOF OHRNDORF, GERMANY.
3RD CHILD BORN, STEPHEN'S NAME APPEARS AS "OHRNDORFF". HIS BAPTISM IS LISTED AS 03-03-1630. Source-Parish record.

Notes for Margaretha:

Margaretha Schneider was buried on 01-01-1672. She appears to have had 9 children. Her father was Jacob Schneider of Buschen.

Notes for Hubert:

4th child born, Hupert's mother was named Catherine. He was buried at Hof Ohrndorff on 12-16-1662. A possible birth date for him is circa 1600. Married in 1627 to a woman named Catherine who was his 1st wife, she was buried at Hof Ohrndorff on Feb 25, 1640. He fathered eight children by his first wife and nine by his second. The first record of Hubert (name also appears as Hupper) is sponsor at the baptism of a child at Freudenburg in 1621. By 1624 he had inherited the Hof Ohrndorff and appears on a tax account as the tenant. He is referred to in a number of instances in the parish register as "Huppert, Hofman zu Ohrndorff" but this usage seems to have died out by the end of the thirty years war and he was referred to as simply Huppert or Hubert Ohrndorff in later years. There are several items from the state archives of Nordhein-Westphalen relating to Hubert Ohrndorff's woodcutting rights and meadowland rights from the town of Buschen. In 1647 he purchased woodcutting rights and meadowland rights from Mathias Muller of (hof) Ohrndorff and in 1856 purchased "mountainland" cutting rights from Johannes Sohler at Buschen (researched by Hanns Schmeck of Siegen, Germany 1982). Hubert Ohrndorff was buried at Hof Ohrndorff Dec 16, 1662 probably having died the previous day. Source-Parish records, tax records.

- - - - - - - - - - -

7. **STEPHEN**[3] **ORENDORFF** (2.HENNE[2], 1.SIMON[1]) was born 1597 in HOF OHRNDORFF, FREUDENBERG GER. STEPHEN died 1632 in BOCKSEIFEN GERMANY, at the age of 35. He married **GELA WAGONER** 3 April 1625 in POSS. BOCKSEIFEN GERMANY. GELA died 6 July 1634 in BOCKSEIFEN GERMANY.

They had 2 children:

24.   m   i.   **JOHANNES ORENDORFF**, born 15 August 1627 in BOCKSEIFEN, PRUSSIA. He married GELA SCHNEIDER August 1650 in POSS. BOCKSEIFEN. She was born June 1626 in BUSCHEN, PRUSSIA, GERMANY. GELA died in BOCKSEIFEN, PRUSSIA, GERMANY. Notes for Gela:
1st wife
Johannes died January 10, 1676 in Bockseifen, Prussia, at the age of 48. Notes for Johannes:
Married twice. Johannes married Gela first, married 2nd Catherina Baumer (not to be confused with other by same name) 09-12-1667.

He lived in the farm hamlet of Bockseifen in the Buschengrund area that had been his fathers home. His first wife Gela was the younger sister of Margaretha Schneider, 2nd wife of Hupert Ohrndorff.

+ 25.   m   ii.   **HERMANN ORENDORFF**, born I January 1632, died 3 January 1676.

Notes for Gela:

Gela was the daughter of Johan Wagoner of Bockseifen. When she died in 1634 she was named as "widow" of Stephen Ohrndorff.

Notes for Stephen:

3rd born between 1596-1598 Stephen's name appears as "Ohrndorff". He was specifically named as a son of "Henn hofman zu Ohrndorff" in the record of his marriage. He lived at Bockseifen, a nearby farm hamlet and died about 1632. He was listed as "Hubert's brother" at a baptism in 1630 when he sponsored Hubert's son. Source-Parish record.

CHAPTER FOUR

GENERATION NO. 4

9. LUDWIG[4] **ORENDORFF** (3.HUBERT[3], 2.HENNE[2], 1.SIMON[1]) was born 2 November 1656 at BUSCHEN, WESTFALLEN PRUSSIA. LUDWIG died 1715 in BUSCHEN, WESTFALLEN PRUSSIA, at the age of 58. He married **CATHERINA BAUMER** 24 November 1687 in PRUSSIA, GERMANY. She was born 1664. CATHERINA died July 1735 at BUSCHEN, WESTFALLEN PRUSSIA, at the age of 71.

They had 5 children:

+ 26.   m i.   **THEISS (MATHIAS) ORENDORFF**, born 13 February 1681.

27.   f ii.   **ANNA MARIA ORENDORFF**, born 1682 in GERMANY, PROBABLY PRUSSIA, died in GERMANY, PROBABLY PRUSSIA.
DIED YOUNG. ANNA MARIA'S NAME APPEARS AS "OHRENDORFF". Source-Parish record.

28.   f iii.   **ANNA URSULA ORENDORFF**, born 15 December 1693 in BUSCHEN, GERMANY.
3RD BORN CHILD ANNA URSULA'S NAME APPEARS AS "OHRNDORFF". SHE WAS BAPTIZED ON 12-15-1693. Source-Parish record.

29.   f iv.   **MARGARETHA ORENDORFF**, born 26 April 1691 in BUSCHEN GERMANY.
1ST BORN MARGARETHA'S NAME IS

LISTED AS "OHRNDORFF". Source-Parish record.

30.   m   v.   **PETER ORENDORFF**, born 12 March 1693 in BUSCHEN GERMANY.
PETER WAS THE 2ND CHILD BORN. Source-Parish record.

Notes for Catherina:
2nd wife. Catherina's father was Nicolaus Baumer.

Notes for Ludwig:
10th child born. Ludwig was christened on 11-02-1656 at Hof Ohrndorff Germany, probably born there also. He was married first to Elisabeth Hardt on 06-18-1679 and then to Catherina Baumer. Ludwig lived at the farm hamlet of Buschen and in a 1687 tax record is referred to as a charcoal maker for Thielmann Schmidt's ironworks. The Nassau-Siegen area had a lot of iron foundries and forges and many people in the area were involved in ironwork. Ludwigs' 1st wife was a sister to Margaretha wife of Peter Ohrndorff. No exact death date for Ludwig can be found in the Freudenburg parish register but when his widow Catherina died in July 1735 the record states that she had been a widow for twenty years. Source-Parish record.

- - - - - - - - - - -

10. GEORG[4] ORENDORFF (3.HUBERT[3], 2.HENNE[2], 1.SIMON[1]). He married **ANNA MARIA FELLOWS** 1685 in BURBACH, WESTFALLEN PRUSSIA.
They had 1 child:

31.   f   i.   **ELIZABETH CATHARINA ORENDORFF**, born 1691.
ELIZABETH CATHARINA'S NAME APPEARS AS "OHRNDORFF". Source-Parish record.

- - - - - - - - - - -

11. HENRICH[4] ORENDORFF (3.HUBERT[3], 2.HENNE[2], 1.SIMON[1]). He married **ANNA CATHARINA JUNG** 24 September 1684 in BURBACH, PRUSSIA.

They had 4 children:

32.   f   i.   **MARIA CATHARINA ORENDORFF**, born 1683 in BURBACH, WESTFALEN PRUSSIA.
MARIA CATHERINA'S NAME APPEARS AS "ORENDORFF". Source-Parish record.

33.   m   ii.   **MATHIAS ORENDORFF**, born 1685 probably in BURBACH, PRUSSIA. Source-Parish record.

34.   f   iii.   **ANNA CATHARINA ORENDORFF**, born 1689 probably in BURBACH, PRUSSIA.
ANNA CATHERINA'S NAME APPEARS AS "ORENDORFF". Source-Parish record.

35.   m   iv.   **WILHELMUS ORENDORFF**, born 25 September 1692 in BURBACH, WESTFALLEN PRUSSIA GR. Source-Parish record.

- - - - - - - - - - -

14. CHRISTIAN[4] ORENDORFF (3.HUBERT[3], 2.HENNE[2], 1.SIMON[1]) was born 27 February 1644 in HOF OHRNDORFF GERMANY. He married **ADELHEIDT SCHMIDT** 9 October 1667 in BUSCHEN GERMANY.

They had 4 children:

36.   m   i.   **JOHANNES ORENDORFF**, born 4 October 1672 probably in BUSCHEN GERMANY.
JOHANNES' NAME APPEARS AS "OHRNDORFF". Source-Parish record.

37.   m   ii.   **JACOB ORENDORFF**, born 22 January 1688 in GERMANY.
6TH CHILD BORN JACOB'S NAME APPEARS AS "OHRNDORFF". Source-

Parish record.

38. f iii. **ELISABETHA ORENDORFF**, born 14 September 1684 in GERMANY.
5TH CHILD BORN ELISABETHA'S NAME APPEARS AS "OHRNDORFF". Source-Parish record.

39. f iv. **MARGARETHA ORENDORFF**, born 13 June 1683 in GERMANY.
4TH CHILD BORN MARGARETHA'S NAME APPEARS AS "OHRNDORFF".

Notes for Christian:

2nd born. Christian's name appears as "Ohrndorff", he was baptized on 02-27-1644. They lived at the farm hamlet of Buschen. Source-Parish record.

- - - - - - - - - - -

15. GERLACH[4] ORENDORFF (3.HUBERT[3], 2.HENNE[2], 1.SIMON[1]) was born 24 May 1644 in HOF OHRNDORFF GERMANY. He married **CLARA DICKE** 13 May 1668 possibly in BUSCHEN GERMANY. CLARA died on March 1, 1683 probably in BUSCHEN.

They had 6 children:

40. f i. **GELA ORENDORFF**, born 20 January 1678 PROBABLY IN BUSCHEN GERMANY.
4TH CHILD BORN. GELA'S NAME APPEARS AS "OHRNDORFF". BAPTIZED AT FREUDENBERG GERMANY. Source-Parish record.

41. f ii. **MARGARETHA ORENDORFF**, born 8 July 1669 in GERMANY.
1ST BORN. MARGARETHA'S NAME APPEARS AS "OHRNDORFF". Source-Parish record.

42. m iii. **HEINRICH ORENDORFF**, born December

1674 in GERMANY.

3   RD BORN. HEINRICH'S NAME APPEARS AS "OHRENDORFF". Source-Parish record.

43.   m   iv. **PETER ORENDORFF**, born 10 April 1671 in GERMANY.

2ND BORN. PETER LIVED IN BOTTENBERG GERMANY, HIS NAME APPEARS AS "OHRNDORFF". Source-Parish record.

44.   f   v. **ELISABETHA ORENDORFF**, born 11 March 1685 in GERMANY.

FIRST BORN TO ANNA KRAMER. ELISABETHA'S NAME APPEARS AS "OHRNDORFF". Source-Parish record.

45.   f   vi. **ELISABETHA ORENDORFF**, born 13 February 1681 in GERMANY.

5TH BORN/DIED IN INFANCY. ELISABETHA'S NAME APPEARS AS "OHRNDORFF". Source-Parish record.

Notes for Clara:
Clara was the daughter of Peter Dicke.

Notes for Gerlach:
Gerlach was the 7th child born and married twice. Gerlach's name is listed as "Ohrndorff". His baptism is listed as 05-27-1644. He lived in Buschen and may have moved to Bottenburg after 1685. His children were baptized at Fruedenburg. He married Anna Kramer on 03-04-1684. Source-Parish record.

- - - - - - - - - - -

16. PETER[4] **ORENDORFF** (3.HUBERT[3], 2.HENNE[2], 1.SIMON[1]) was born 12 March 1649 in HOF OHRNDORFF GERMANY. PETER died 13 January 1685 AT THE AGE OF 35 AND IS BURIED AT BUSCHEN GERMANY, He married

MARGARETHA HARDT 27 April 1674 POSS. IN BUSCHEN. She was born 5 June 1653 in BUSCHEN GERMANY.

They had 2 children:

46.   m   i.   **HUBERT ORENDORFF**, born 23 March 1684 in POSS. BUSCHEN GERMANY, died in POSS. BUSCHEN GERMANY. 4TH CHILD BORN. HUBERT'S NAME APPEARS AS "OHRNDORFF".

47.   f   ii.   **CLARA ORENDORFF**, born 18 March 1677 POSS. IN BUSCHEN GERMANY. 2ND CHILD BORN. CLARA'S NAME APPEARS AS "OHRNDORFF".

Notes for Margaretha:

Margaretha Hardt was the daughter of Heinrich Hardt of Buschen. She was a sister to Elisabetha Hardt who was married to Ludwig Ohrndorff. Her children were baptized at Freudenburg Germany. Source-Parish records.

Notes for Peter:

4th child born. Peter's name is listed as "Ohrndorff' in the record. His children were baptized at Buschen Germany. Source-Parish records.

- - - - - - - - - - -

25.   HERMANN[4] **ORENDORFF**   (7.STEPHEN[3], 2.HENNE[2], 1.SIMON[1]) was born 1 January 1632 in PROBABLY HOF OHRENDORFF. HERMANN died 3 January 1676 in HALMENHOF, PRUSSIA GERMANY, at the age of 44. He married **MARGARETHA DICKE**. MARGARETHA died 6 January 1676 in HALMENHOF, PRUSSIA GERMANY.

They had 1 child:

+ 48.   m   i.   **JOHANN HEINRICH ORENDORFF**, born 15 April 1661, died 2 January 1708.

Notes for Hermann:

Herman's name appears as "Ohrndorff". Hermann lived at the farm hamlet of Halmenhof in the Buschergrund area. He and his wife died three days apart. There was probably an epidemic sweeping the area that winter since his brother Johannes and many others in the community also died during that time. Source-Parish records.

CHAPTER FIVE

GENERATION NO. 5

26. THEISS (MATHIAS)[5] ORENDORFF (9.LUDWIG[4], 3.HUBERT[3], 2.HENNE[2], I.SIMON[1]) was born 13 February 1681 in GERMANY, BUSCHEN. THEISS died in BURBACH, WESTFALLEN PRUSSIA. He married **ANNA JULIANA SAUER** 13 April 1710 in BURBACH, WESTFALLEN PRUSSIA. She was born 1688. ANNA died 12 May 1747 in BURBACH GER. OR CHESTER, CO, Pennsylvania, at the age of 59.

They had 5 children:

+ 49.   m   i.   **CONRAD ORENDORFF**, born 5 February 1719, died 1795.

+ 50.   m   ii.   **PHILIP HEINRICH ORENDORFF**, born 6 December 1716, died May 1777.

51.   f   iii.   **ANNA ELIZABETH ORENDORFF**, born 12 April 1711 in BURBACH, WESTFALLEN PRUSSIA.
IST BORN ANNA ELIZABETH'S NAME APPEARS AS "OHRNDORFF" IN THE RECORD AND SHE WAS UNMARRIED. SHE MAY HAVE BEEN CALLED "LISGEN".

52.   f   iv.   **ANNA MARGARETHA ORENDORFF**, born 11 February 1714 in BURBACH, WESTFALLEN PRUSSIA.
2ND CHILD BORN ANNA MARGARETHA'S NAME APPEARS AS "OHRNDORFF". ALSO "OHRENDORFF".

53.   m   v.   **JOHANN   CONRAD   ORENDORFF**,
                 born   5 February   1719   in   BURBACH,
                 WESTFALLEN PRUSSIA.
                 4TH CHILD BORN

Notes for Anna:

Anna Juliana's father was Gerhard Peter Sauer of Burbach and Anna Elizabeth.

Notes for Theiss:

Died in the 1700's. Theis was christened on 02-13-1681 in Freudenburg Germany, he was born in Buschen. He may have lived to about 1740. Theiss (Matthias) moved to Burbach, a village about twenty miles southeast of Freudenburg, shortly before his marriage and remained there the rest of his life. The record of his death refers to him as the "gerichts knecht" which would roughly translate as constable. It appears that only one of his children, Philip Heinrich reached adulthood and in 1753, a few years after the death of his mother, he immigrated to America with his wife and children. Source-Parish records.

- - - - - - - - - - -

48.   JOHANN   HEINRICH[5]   **ORENDORFF** (25.HERMANN[4], 7.STEPHEN[3], 2.HENNE[2], I.SIMON[1]) was born 15 April 1661 in HALMENHOF, PRUSSIA GERMANY. JOHANN died 2 January 1708 in EICHEN, PRUSSIA GERMANY, at the age of 46. He married **AGNES GIESSLER**. AGNES died in POSS. EICHEN, PRUSSIA.

They had 3 children:

+ 54.   m   i.   **CHRISTIAN   I   ORENDORFF**,   born
                 15 August 1693.
55.   m   ii. **HANS LEONHART ORENDORFF**, born
                 23 September 1685 in GERMANY.
56.   m   iii. **EBERHARDT   (EBERT)   ORENDORFF**,
                 born 23 October 1687 in GERMANY.

Notes for Agnes:

Agnes was the daughter of Johannes Giesler of Wahlbach. She remarried to Wilhelm Waschenbach of Eichen Germany in Oct of 1709. Her Ohrndorff children were all baptized at Freudenburg. Source-Parish records.

Notes for Johann:

Johann Heinrich's name appears as "Ohrndorff". Source-Parish records.

CHAPTER SIX

GENERATION NO. 6

49. CONRAD[6] **ORENDORFF** (26.THEISS[5], 9.LUDWIG[4], 3.HUBERT[3], 2.HENNE[2], I.SIMON[1]) was born 5 February 1719 in BURBACH, WESTFALLEN PRUSSIA. CONRAD died 1795 in FREDERICK MD, at the age of 75. He married **MARIA CATHERINA GROSEN** 17 June 1746 in BURBACH, WESTFALLEN PRUSSIA.

They had 2 children:

57.   f   i.   **ANNA ELIZABETH ORENDORFF**, born 17 January 1749 in BURBACH, WESTFALLEN PRUSSIA.
ANNA ELIZABETH WAS THE 1ST CHILD OF CONRAD/DIED YOUNG

58.   f   ii.   **ANNA ELIZABETH ORENDORFF**, born 21 July 1752 in BURBACH, WESTFALLEN PRUSSIA.
3RD CHILD OF CONRAD ANNA ELIZABETH'S NAME APPEARS AS "ORNDORFF".

Notes for Conrad:

Possibly had a son named Conrad in the 1750's. Name also listed as Conradt. Arrived in Philadelphia Pennsylvania on 10-02-1753 in the ship Edinburgh captained by John Lyon, from Rotterdam Holland. Conrad was 30 at this time and arrived with Johannes Peter Orendorff. Also had a second child M. Orendorff. Source-ship listing.

- - - - - - - - - - -

50. PHILIP HEINRICH[6] **ORENDORFF** (26.THEISS[5], 9.LUDWIG[4], 3.HUBERT[3], 2.HENNE[2], 1.SIMON[1]) was born 6 December 1716 in BURBACH, WESTFALLEN PRUSSIA. PHILIP died May 1777 in CHESTER CO PA, VINCENT TOWNSHIP, at the age of 60. He married **ANNA ELISABETHA LUHL** 28 January 1743 in BURBACH, WESTFALLEN PRUSSIA. She was born 10 February 1715 in MARBURG, HESSE-KASSEL, GERMANY. ANNA died in PENNSYLVANIA, AFTER 1777.

They had 6 children:

+ 59.　　m　i.　**PHILIP ORENDORFF**, born 1761, died 1838.

+ 60.　　m　ii.　**JOHN (JOHANNES PETER) ORENDORFF**, born 16 February 1744, died 11 December 1798.

61.　　f　iii.　**MARIA PHILLIPINA ORENDORFF**, born 31 January 1746 in BURBACH, WESTFALLEN, PRUSSIA.

Called Mary\2nd child born. Mary was married to a man named Heironymus Saylor or Seiler of Chester Co Pa. poss. birth date of 02-06-1746. Her name appears as "Ahrendorff" and "Orndorff", she was still living in 1777 when her father wrote his will. The register at the East Vincent Reformed Church dated January 5, 1768 states "Heironymus Seiler und frau, Maria Philippina" had a child baptized. Philip Orendorff named his daughter Mary as wife of "Cronymus Saylor" in his will in 1777.

62.　　f　iv.　**ANNA MARGARETHA ORENDORFF**, born 16 November 1748 at BURBACH, WESTFALLEN, PRUSSIA.

Called Margaret\3rd child born Anna Margaretha was married to a man named Heinrich Henkeries (Henkenius), later called Henry Hinkins. Poss. born 11-24-1748 and he died about 1777. Her name appears as "Ahrendorff" and "Ohrndorff". Their children were: Susanna Hinkins b. Sept 21, 1767, Johann Peter Hinkins b. Feb 19, 1769 and died in VA by 1798, Philipp Heinrich Hinkins b. Nov 5, 1770, Georg Hinkins b. Aug 15 1771 m. to Mary (Polly) Supinger.

63.   m   v.   **LUDWIG ERNST ORENDORFF**, born 12 March 1752 at BURBACH, WESTFALLEN PRUSSIA, died in WASHINGTON CO, VA, AFTER 1810.

Called Lewis\4th child born, Ludwig Ernst's name appears as "Ahrendorff". Also appears as "Ohrndorff" and "Orndorff". Poss. born 03-11-1752. He was married and had a family, wife unknown children-James, Mordecai, Isaac, Jeremiah, and perhaps several others. Lewis was only one year old when his family came to America and he was confirmed at the East Vincent Reformed Church in Chester Co in 1768 at the age of 16. With his mother, he was co-executor of his father's will in 1777 but by 1783 had moved to VA with other members of his family. By 1799 he was living in Washington Co VA.

64.   f   vi.   **SUSANNAH ORENDORFF**, born 1756 in PENNSYLVANIA.

STILL LIVING IN 1777/5TH BORN SUSANNAH'S NAME APPEARS AS "AHRENDORFF".

Notes for Anna:

Anna Luhl's father was George Henrich Luhl (born 04-23-1682 died 04-17-1744) who was a shoemaker and letter carrier. Her mother was named Marie Elizabeth. George's father was Johann Henrich Luhl (born 1641) and his mother was Anna Catherina Wendel, her father was Hans Wendel. The earliest known ancestors of the Luhl family are Heinrich Luhl and his wife Catherina, who lived at Ockerhausen on the outskirts of Marburg in the early 1600's. Their son, Hans Peter Luhl was baptized on October 14, 1610, married Anna Hiln daughter of Hans Hiln of Schlierbach in 1630 and lived at Ockerhausen where he died before 1674. they had seven children, among them: Johann Heinrich Luhl baptized November 7, 1641. Johann Heinrich married twice and died at Ockerhausen after 1700. by his second wife, Anna Catherine Wendel, daughter of Hans Wendel of Fronhausen, he had a son named Georg Heinrich Luhl, baptized April 23, 1682. Georg Heinrich married several times. By his first wife, Marie Elisabeth, he had six children. Marie Elisabeth died about 1730 and he married Catherina Frolich in 1733 then Elisabetha Opfer in 1735. He had no children by these wives. Georg Heinrich was a shoemaker and letter carrier at Marburg and died before 1759. His children: Johann Heinrich Luhl b. 1713 still living 1729, Anna Elisabetha Luhl b. February 10, 1715 married to Philipp Heinrich Ohrndorff, and Anna Sabina Luhl b. July 23, 1718, Anna Justina Luhl b. 06-01-1721 m. to Heinrich Berck, Anna Catherina Luhl b. 1723 living 1737, and Maria Philippina Luhl b. 12-02-1725. Johann Henrich's father was Hans Peter (Peter married in the 1600's) Luhl b. 1610 d. 1674 and his mother was Anna Hiln, her father was Hans Hiln. Hans Peter Luhl's father was Henrich Luhl who married a Catherina. John Montgomery married Anna Elizabeth to Philip Heinrich Orendorff. She had four children born in Burbach Germany and two born in America.

Notes for Philip:
Philip Heinrich was a tailor and he arrived in Philadelphia PA Tuesday 10-02-1753 on the ship Edinburgh captained by John Lion, from Rotterdam. Also arrived with Conrad and Johannes Peter Orendorff who were probably his children. Resided in Chester CO PA in 1761.

- - - - - - - - - - -

54. CHRISTIAN I[6] ORENDORFF (48.JOHANN[5], 25.HERMANN[4], 7.STEPHEN[3], 2.HENNE[2], 1.SIMON[1]) WAS BORN 15 AUGUST 1693 AT KISELBERG, FRUEDENBURG GERMANY. CHRISTIAN DIED IN PA, NEAR ELIZABETH/ SWATARA, CREEK. HE MARRIED **ELIZABETH VON MUELLER**.

THEY HAD 3 CHILDREN:

+ 65.   M   I.   **CHRISTIAN II ORENDORFF**, BORN 15 NOVEMBER 1726, DIED 10 DECEMBER 1797.

66.   F   II.   **ANNA MARG. ORENDORFF**, BORN 1724 IN GERMANY, DIED 1784 PROBABLY IN WASHINGTON, CO MD, AT THE AGE OF 60.
ANNA MARRIED JOHANN HERMAN EAKELL B.1720 GERMANY.

67.   F   III.   **ANNA BARBARA ORENDORFF**, BORN 1728 IN NASSAU, HESSEN-NASSAU, PRUSSIA.
ANNA ARRIVED IN 1741 BY SHIP WITH HER FATHER CHRISTIAN AND HER 15-YEAR-OLD BROTHER CHRISTIAN. HER NAME APPEARS AS "OHRENDORF".

Notes for Elizabeth:

A Countess or Baroness. Sources-"From Millwheel to Plowshare" book, family tradition.

Notes for Christian:

Soldier/Professional Officer Christian b. 1693 was probably a high officer in the Prussian military. The earliest land deed for Christian Orendorff states "372 acres and 73 perches on Elizabeth creek in Bethel Township" which was bought from a Peter Grove in 1749. Elizabeth creek flows into the Little Swatara River 2-miles southwest of Fredericksburg PA. This piece of land extended from

Fredericksburg to Lebanon. This region, located in the foothills of the Blue Ridge, offered a number of good mill sites, and also an abundance of springs. The tract that Christian bought in 1749 became famous for its mills, one of which functioned until the late nineteenth century. Anna Barbara's husband George Kasper Kohr received this land from his father in law Christian Sr. on April 1 1762. Whether Christian had begun the mills before this date or whether it was Kohr who began the building is unknown. The site of Kohr's mill remains the most tangible symbol of the earliest mill pioneering of the first Christian Orendorff and his son. On April 16th, 1763 Kohr entered into an agreement with Matthias Groth, the adjoining landowner on the north, for the construction of a mill race on his land. It thus appears that Kohr's mill was erected in 1763 or prior thereto. Orendorff may have built it and that was undoubtedly the first gristmill erected near to and for the convenience of the people living in the neighborhood of Fredericksburg. The deed for the property reads as follows: "this indenture, made the second day of June, in the year of our lord one thousand seven hundred and ninety six, between Casper Kohr, senior of bethel township, in the county of Dauphin and Casper Kohr, junior son and one of the heirs apparent by these presents doth grant unto the said Casper Kohr junior mills, stables, barn, orchard, gardens, and one hundred and fifteen acres of land. it being part of that certain tract of land, which by warrant of the twelfth day of march, anno domini one thousand seven hundred and thirty eight was confirmed by his bill of sale dated the twelfth day of December one thousand seven hundred and forty nine did grant, bargain, sell unto Christian Orendorf. And the said Christian Orendorf by his bill of sale dated the first day of April one thousand seven hundred and sixty two, did grant, bargain, sell unto Casper Kohr. As also all the water right to certain spring on the other land owned by the said Casper Kohr, senior, to lead the same by diches as it is now". In 1758 Christian bought two tracts of land in one day. The warrant for one of these, preserved in the Pennsylvania land office, follows: "warrant-no 4 by the proprietaries. Whereas Christian Orndorff of the county of Lancaster hath requested we should grant him to take up fifty acres of land adjoining his other land in Heidelberg Township in the said county of Lancaster for which he agrees to pay to our use at the rate of fifteen pounds ten schillings, current money of this province for one hundred acres and the yearly quit-rent of one-halfpenny sterling for every acre thereof. Given under my hand and seal of the land-office at Philadelphia, this eighteenth day of may anno domini one thousand seven hundred and fifty eight to Nicholas Scull, surveyor general." He settled in the valley of Tupelhocken creek, in Lebanon Valley Pa where he sponsored an infant named John Christian from Donntheuer on March 16, 1746. Rev. Casper Stoever, a Lutheran minister, who traveled an extensive circuit, conducted the christening at Tulpehocken church. in 1749 he became a charter member of the Hebron Moravian Church, to be followed a few weeks later by his daughter, Anna Barbara Kohr, and her young husband, and in December he bought a tract of land that became an important mill site. A Count Zinzendorf, the great Moravian scholar who reached America the same year as Christian Orendorff, had an important influence in the establishment of churches in the Lebanon valley. Originally made a bishop by Frederick William of Prussia, he won his greatest renown in the founding of the celebrated colony of Bethleham. He also pushed into the frontier of PA, establishing other Moravian churches. Christian Orendorff and his daughter were among those who caught the fire of this great spiritual revival. Hebron was built near the present city of Lebanon, about ten miles west of the Tulpehocken Reformed Church. It appears he and his son built several mills and sold out in 1762 or 1763. In June 1756 after the six Indian nations had banded together to wage war on the colonies the Indians surprised two boys and two men who were plowing in a field near little mountain and killed and scalped them. These men were neighbors of Christian Orendorff and their interments in lots 4 through 7 were among the first in Bethel Moravian cemetery, Christian's daughter was buried in lot 9. Christian himself was buried in Bethel Moravian cemetery. He is called "a great soul" in the book "From Millwheel to Plowshare". He was aged 80 years at the time of his death. Sources-"From Millwheel to Plowshare" book, land records, church records.

CHAPTER SEVEN

GENERATION NO. 7

59. PHILIP[7] **ORENDORFF** (50.PHILIP[6], 26.THEISS[5], 9.LUDWIG[4], 3.HUBERT[3], 2.HENNE[2], I.SIMON[1]) WAS BORN CIRCA 1761 IN CHESTER CO PENN. PHILIP DIED 1838 IN SHENANDOAH CO VA, AT THE AGE OF 77. HE MARRIED **ELIZABETH SEIBERT** 15 OCTOBER 1782 IN FREDERICK CO VA. SHE WAS BORN 1762 IN FREDERICK CO VA.

THEY HAD 7 CHILDREN:

+ 68.   M   I.   **JOHN WILLIAM ORENDORFF**, BORN 1794, DIED 16 DECEMBER 1878.

69. F   II.   **ELEANOR (NELLIE) ORENDORFF**, BORN 1804 IN CIRCA B. DATE, POSS. 1795. UNMARRIED/7TH CHILD BORN ELEANOR "NELLY" WAS BORN IN VIRGINIA, PROBABLY SHENANDOAH CO. SHE WAS NOT MARRIED. ALSO APPEARS AS "OHRNDORFF".

+ 70.   M   III.   **JACOB ORENDORFF**, BORN 1787, DIED 23 JULY 1859.

+ 71.   M   IV.   **PHILIP ORENDORFF**, BORN 1792, DIED 17 OCTOBER 1880.

+ 72.   M   V.   **SAMUEL ORENDORFF**, BORN 1802, DIED 17 JULY 1858.

+ 73.   M   VI.   **LEWIS ORENDORFF**, BORN 1798, DIED 1 MAY 1854.

74.   F   VII.   **ELIZABETH ORENDORFF**, BORN CIRCA 1784 IN VIRGINIA.

IST BORN ELIZABETH'S NAME IS LISTED AS "ORNDORFF" IN THE RECORD, SHE MARRIED A MAN NAMED WILLIAM WILLIAMS. SHE MAY HAVE BEEN BORN IN SHENANDOAH CO VA.

Notes for Elizabeth:

Elizabeth was a daughter of Jacob and Mary Seabert; this information came from Jacob's will dated 01-20-1801/11-30-1801. Her last name was probably spelled Seibert, it is mostly found spelled Seabert. John Montgomery married them.

Notes for Philip:

Youngest child, Philip is shown to own 50 acres, 1 horse and 2 cows in Chester Co 1767. he appears again as owning 50 acres, 2 horses, and 1 cow in Chester Co 1766. Philip also resided for a time at upper Cedar Creek Valley in Shenandoah VA. his birth date may have been 1760. His name appears as "Orndorff" and "Ohrndorff" in records. Married by John Montgomery. In his will in 1777, Philip Sr. indicated that his youngest son Philip was not yet sixteen years old, when he wrote that at sixteen Philip may apprentice for a trade. However, the date of his marriage, tax records and later census records indicate that Philip may have been at least sixteen or a bit older at the time. Philip married Elizabeth Seibert in Frederick Co VA and thus followed his brother John to VA soon after the death of his mother about 1780. He lived on the headwaters of Cedar Creek at Van Buren Furnace in Shenandoah Co VA and died without a will or estate settlement. He was listed in the 1830 census as between 70 and 80 years of age.

- - - - - - - - - - -

60. JOHN (JOHANNES PETER) [7] **ORENDORFF** (50.PHILIP[6], 26.THEISS[5], 9.LUDWIG[4], 3.HUBERT[3], 2.HENNE[2], 1.SIMON[1]) was born 16 February 1744 at BURBACH, WESTFALLEN, PRUSSIA. JOHN died 11 December 1798 in

FREDERICK CO VA, at the age of 54. He married **EVA BARBARA MENTZ** 1760 in LANCASTER CO PA. Both marriages took place there.

They had 15 children:

+ 75. m i. **JESSE ORENDORFF**, born 1780, died 1815.

+ 76. m ii. **PHILIP ORENDORFF**, born 23 March 1767, died 1818.

77. m iii. **JOSHUA ORENDORFF**, born circa 1769 possibly in LANCASTER CO, PA.
3RD BORN JOSHUA'S NAME APPEARS AS "ORNDORFF", POSS. 1774.

+ 78. m iv. **LEVI ORENDORFF**, born 1791, died 1869.

79. f v. **ELEANOR ORENDORFF**, born 1795.
BORN AFTER 1779 POSS. IN PA, OR VA ELEANOR'S NAME APPEARS AS "ORNDORFF". 16TH BORN.

80. m vi. **ISRAEL ORENDORFF**, born 1782. He married MARY WIMER 3 March 1806 in FREDERICK CO VA/SHENANDOAH, CO. ISRAEL died 1815, at the age of 33. Notes for ISRAEL:
CIRCA BIRTH DATE, IN PA OR VA

81. f vii. **REBECCA ORENDORFF**, born 1789, died 17 January 1855, at the age of 66.
BORN IN PA OR VA/13TH BORN REBECCA MARRIED FIRST JOHN RACEY (06-20-1808) BY JAMES WALLS AND MARRIED SECONDLY JOSEPH BRILL IN FREDERICK CO VA 04-04-1822 BY MINISTER JOHN B. TILDEN.

+ 82. m viii. **BENJAMIN ORENDORFF**, born 1780.

83. f ix. **ANNE "NANCY" ORENDORFF**, born 1784 in CIRCA, POSS. VA.
BORN AFTER 1779 IN PA OR VA ANNE MARRIED JOHN REID. ANNE'S NAME APPEARS AS "ORNDORFF".

84.   m   x.   **SAMUEL ORENDORFF**, born 1780 in POSSIBLY 1790'S. He married SARAH SHULL 26 December 1801 in FREDERICK CO VA.

SAMUEL died 1841, at the age of 61. Notes for SAMUEL:

BORN AFTER 1779 IN PA OR VA SAMUEL'S NAME APPEARS AS "ORNDORFF". HE WAS THE 8TH CHILD BORN.

+ 85.   m   xi.   **DAVID ORENDORFF**, born August 1787.

+ 86.   m   xii.   **PHINEAS ORENDORFF**, born 23 March 1793, died 1838.

87.   f   xiii.   **POLLY ORENDORFF**, born 1796.

BORN CIRCA 1796 IN PA OR VA POLLY DIED AT A YOUNG AGE. DIED BEFORE 1798.

+ 88.   m   xiv.   **ISAAC ORENDORFF**, born 1797.

+ 89.   m   xv.   **JOHNATHAN ORENDORFF**, born 1771, died 1859.

Notes for Eva:

Also has a circa death date of 1776. Eva Barbara Mentz was separated from her husband in 1777. Source-Pennsylvania Gazette, April 16, 1777, Philadelphia, PA.

Notes for John:

2nd wife Hannah Mcelwe married 1779, John is shown to no longer be with the militia of Dauphin Co PA between the years of 1790 and 1800. He is listed in Captain Christian Ley's company 2nd class. He lived in Elizabethtown, Lancaster Co, VA in 1763. poss. b. 02-06-1744. John was also a Sr. and he is buried in St John's Cemetery. Upon a corner of that cemetery stands St. John's Lutheran Church. This church and cemetery are located about one half mile from his home. John Orndorff was nine years old when he arrived in America with his family. He first appears on the tax lists of Vincent Township Winchester county with his father in 1766 when he was 22 years old. In 1767 he was being taxed for 70 acres of land and the following year was taxed on 200 acres. Between 1769 and 1774 he was taxed for between 100 and 200 acres, apparently having rented or leased farm land since there is no record of a land grant or purchase by John. John does not appear in the records of Vincent township after 1774 and by 1777 was living in Coventry Township. The Orndorff family had some association with the east Vincent reformed church and John and Eva Barbara had their son, Philip, baptized there in July 1769. John "Arndorf" is also named as head of a family in the records of the Brownback Reform Church in Coventry Township but no baptismal entries are recorded (records of the Reformed Congregation of East Vincent, Chester County PA, copied by William J. Hinke at the Historical Society of the Reformed Church, Franklin and Marshall College, Lancaster PA). John and Barbara obviously had marital difficulties and on April 4, 1777 he sent a notice to be published in the Pennsylvania Gazette repudiating any debts incurred by his wife, Barbara, who "doth continue in her wicked ways". He further adds " I think it proper to forwarn the public a second time, from lending or trusting the said Barbara any thing on my account, as I am determined never to pay any debts of her contracting". (Pennsylvania Gazette, April 16, 1777, Philadelphia PA). Several days later John left the county with "a girl named Hannah Muckleweb" and Barbara put a notice in the Gazette, dated April 16 and published April 23 offering a thirty pound reward to anyone who caught them and returned them to be brought to justice. In this notice John "Ornduff" was described as "a country born Dutchmen, talks good English, wore his uniform brown coat, faced with blue, a knot on his shoulder, white jacket and breeches, about 5 feet 7 or 8 inches high, fresh complexion, light brown curled hair". He and the girl, who would probably "try to pass for man and wife were last seen in Lancaster the day after they ran off, on their way over Susquehanna: they took a half silk gown from his wife, a new chintz ditto, a lawn apron and handkerchief, a white silk bonnet: he rode a young black mare, and the girl a grey mare, with a new hunting saddle with silver gilt round the edge". John and Hannah apparently went straight to Virginia and settled in the Cedar Creek area of western Frederick co about 12 miles from Winchester. There is evidence that he worked for Isaac Zane at the Marlboro ironworks on Cedar Creek. If this is the case then he may well have known his destination when he left PA because Zane had been advertising land along north mountain "about 12 miles from Winchester" in the Pennsylvania Gazette from 1775 onwards. John Orndorff drew up a will, November 17, 1798 with the help of his nephew Peter Hinkins and named all of his children, by Barbara and Hannah. To his son Joshua he gave one dollar and to Jesse one half dollar, and to the other 15 children he left one 16th of his estate and another 16th to Hannah, mother of the last named 11 children. He may have been less than generous to Joshua and Jesse because it seems they did not follow him to VA as did the other children by Barbara. The will was probated December 31 1798 (Frederick co will book "6" p. 454). Hannah appears in the 1810, 1820, and 1830 census records. In 1830 she was living in Shenandoah County and listed as between 60 and 70 years of age. A brief death notice appears in the Woodstock Sentinel of may 5 1837 and states that Mrs. Hannah Orndorff "died at her residence at the Little North Mountain on Saturday 29th, April in the 78th year of her age".

- - - - - - - - - - -

65. CHRISTIAN II[7] **ORENDORFF** (54.CHRISTIAN[6], 48.JOHANN[5], 25.HERMANN[4], 7.STEPHEN[3], 2.HENNE[2], 1.SIMON[1]) was born 15 November 1726 in PRUSSIA, GERMANY. CHRISTIAN died 10 December 1797 in SHARPSBURG MD, at the age of 71. He married **ELIZABETH ANN HOFFMAN**. She was born 1732. ELIZABETH died in HAGERSTOWN MD/ON A SUNDAY.

They had 12 children:

+ 90.   m   i.   **JESSE ORENDORFF**, born 1771, died 14 September 1846.

91.   f   ii.   **PEGGY ORENDORFF**, born 1747.

+ 92.   m   iii.   **CHRISTOPHER ORENDORFF**, born 23 November 1752, died 14 September 1823.

93. m   iv.   **CHRISTIAN JR III ORENDORFF**, born 23 November 1752. He married ANNA MARIE STILLE.

CHRISTIAN died in AT HOME, NEAR SHEPARDSTOWN VA. Notes for Christian: Revolutionary soldier/spy served in the Maryland line infantry, applied for a pension on April 16 1818 at Frederick Co MD at which time he was aged 60 years and a resident of Frederick Co MD. In November 1820 he was living in Jefferson Co VA. the arrears of pension covering the period from September 4, 1824 to October 1,1824 were paid January 22, 1845 by the treasury department to Thomas Quantrile as attorney for the children Perry Orendorff of Washington County MD and Eliza Shafer of the District of Columbia. In November he had moved to Jefferson Co VA. He died leaving children, and a son in law named Mr. Shafer. 1st Lt. MD battalion of the flying camp July 1776. Taken prisoner at Fort Washington on 16 November 1776. 1st lt. 6th MD regiment commanded by Colonel Otho Holland Williams 10th December 1776, promoted to Captain April 1 1778, transferred to 1st Maryland January 1 1781 and served to April 1783. The following is a "list of field, commissioned and staff officers of the 6th Maryland regiment dated September 18, 1779. Names 20 officers: Captain William Dent Beall, sick absent, Lieutenant Charles Beavin, Lieutenant James Bruff, Lieutenant Richard Donovan, adjundant, Captain Harry Dobison, light infantry, Lieutenant Colonel Benjamin Ford, ensign Samuel Hamilton (of Charles county Maryland) joined in August 1779, Major Henry Hardman, not commissioned but entitled to rank of Major May 22, 1779, lieutenant George Jacob, Lieutenant John Jeremiah Jacob, paymaster, ensign John Lynn, Lieutenant Edmund Moran, quartermaster, Lieutenant Jacob Norris, recruiting April 11,1779, Captain Christian Orndorff, prisoner of war November 16, 1776, surgeon Thomas Parran, Captain John Smith, sick absent, Captain Lieutenant James Somervell, Captain Alexander Trueman, furloughed August 9, 1779, Lieutenant Nathan Williams, recruiting April 11, 1779, Colonel Otho Holland Williams. Memorandum-Mr. Hamilton is recommended to the state for a commission in a former return-and has acted as ensign from the first of August. 22 sergeants (including Sergeant Major and Quartermaster Sergeant) 22 Corporals, 1 fife Major, 1 drum Major, 14 drummers and fifers, 275 privates are not listed by name. Signed Otho H. Williams Coll". Captain 1st April 1778, transferred to 1st Maryland 1st January 1781 and served to April 1783. Christian delivered a letter on June 17, 1781 from Thomas sprigg in Hagerstown to "the council" as follows "Capt. Ornorf (Christian Orndorff) delivered letters of June 9 and June 10: Henry Newcomer and Yost Pleacker have been arrested: thirty others are in jail: they expect and deserve to be hanged, Sprigg wants to know whether all laws passed at the same session are in force from the first day of the session: Captain (Abraham) Morgan will deliver this letter: fifteen or sixteen hundred Hessians and British were taken to York (pa) at (Samuel?)Hughes' works, twenty guns were proved: ten wagons have been engaged to leave for Baltimore June 18: in postscript asks that clothing be sent." He later lived in the Shenandoah Valley, Virginia. At the age of 16 he entered the Continental army as an officer in the flying camp, one of its most famous unites. On June 3, 1776 the Continental Congress, realizing the danger that threatened the colonies in the British plan of concentration at New York, made provision for a "flying camp". this unit received its name from its unexpected rapidity of movements and its unusual freedom from accoutrements. The resolution of the Continental Congress-"resolved, that a flying camp be immediately established in the middle colonies, and that it consist of 10000 men, to complete which number, resolved, that the colony of Pennsylvania be requested to furnish of their militia 6000, Maryland of their militia 3400, Delaware government of their militia 600." 12 officers were commissioned in Frederick Co MD, among these was Christian. Some of the others were Captain John Reynolds, 1st Lt. Moses Chapline, 2nd lt. Christian "Orndorff" and Ensign Nathan Williams July 18, 1776. Christian became active in enlisting other soldiers, and helped to send new companies to the front. an old colonial record- "enlisted by Lt. Christian Orndorff, July 20th. Passed by Joseph Smith, 22 men. ordered that Col. Chas. Greenbury Griffith march his battalion in detachments or companies, as they shall be armed and accoutered to the city of Philadelphia subject to the order of Congress--Christian Orendorff commissioned 2nd Lieut. July 20, 1776 of the above battalion.

Wednesday August 7, 1776. Ordered that the commissary deliver to Col. Griffith 588 knapsacks and haversacks, 110 camp kettles, 105 tents, 678 priming wires with brushes, 658 canteens--50 lb gun-powder and lead in proportion, 100 gunflints, and as many cartouch boxes with slings, bayonet belts, and gunslings, not exceeding 588 of each, as may be necessary for his corps. " Christians career was connected with several strategic battles. By forced marches, the Maryland troops were able to join Washington's army in New York at a very critical time. The British forces under the command of General Howe were well equipped and were ably supported by a naval force under his brother, Admiral Lord Howe. After the British fleet doubled Long Island and anchored within cannon shot of New York, Washington retired to the heights of Harlem. Christian served at Harlem heights and later was stationed at fort Washington, on Manhattan island, five miles north of the city, one of three thousand men under Colonel Magaw. On November 16, 1776 the British attacked Fort Washington with an overwhelming force. After a stubborn resistance, the little garrison was forced to surrender. Young Orndorff and his comrades were thrust into the prisons of New York, where they remained until they were exchanged. Christian was returned to the American forces on November 1, 1780 and joined the 6th Maryland regiment as Captain. Receiving a short leave of absence the following summer, he visited his father on the Mt pleasant plantation near Sharpsburg. Just at this time there was a group of lawless men in the Blue

Ridge Mountains who had developed a strong Tory (loyal to Britain) confederacy and Christian played a large part in breaking it up as a spy. The following quotations from documents in the archives of Maryland tell the story-June (Christ. Orendorff. information ab't the conspiracy in Washington and Fred. counties). Inform--of Christian Orendorff--about a fortnight ago henry newcomer of Washington county came to him in Sharpsburg and called him out of his father's house and asked him what he thought of these times, answered the times were very bad and precarious--he then asked if he thought the king would over-come this country answered he thought he might. I'm sure he will overcome the country and Orndorff if you can keep it a secret I lead you into a matter of great importance answered he would he said we have raised a body of men for the service of the king and we thought proper to make appl. to you to go to N. York for a fleet, asked how many men they had raised he said upwards of 6000 asked who was the commanding officer of the party, answered one Fritchy of Fred. town a Dutch man don't know his Christian name--ordered Orndorf to go to his house and he would show him the man, went to his house and rode with him to Fred. town but did not go to Fritchy's house. Newcomer informed him Fritchy would not see him in town but would meet him ten miles from town--he met him and then took him aside and said he understood Orndorff was let in to a matter that was carrying on now. Orndorff said to him I understand you are the commanding officer Fritchy said he was and told Orndorf the

name of the man in Virginia from whom he
received instructions to recruit but has forgot the
name--asked why the pitched upon him, said
because he had been in N. York so long they
thought he was the fittest person if he would
undertake--though they were not quite ready for
anything of that sort. Orndorf desired him to
get the names of all the officers which he
promised to do--before they parted Fritchy told
him not to disclose what he had communicated.
Orndorf replied he would sooner sacrifice his
life than do it-- Orndorf told him to get ready as
soon as he could and let him know it and he said
he would & as soon as he was Orndorf should be
informed of it--and than he said some of his
officers were so violent for it, that he was afraid
it would be made public--asked who they were he
said one Kelly a lawyer & an Irishman who lives
in the mountains about twelve or fourteen miles
from Fred. town--had no further conversation
with Fritchy--after Orndorf rode four or five
miles along the main road Newcomer said
Orndorf you look so dead I'm afraid you ruin
the matter, answered not at all sir--says keep it a
secret whatever you do, for we will soon give
these fellows a dam threshing--said as we were
not ready I must send my boy up the south
mountain and let them know. We are not ready
yet. Our boys are so violent we can hardly keep
them in, said he sent an express last week to
Lancaster to hush them a little while longer--he
slapt Orndorf on the shoulder and said I am so
glad as if I had 10000 pounds we have got you
Orndorf for they could not get one so proper for
the expedition as you are--said we have consulted

one another a good while and were afraid to mention the matter on your fathers account as we know him to be a violent rebel and then they parted and Newcomer went towards Hagerstown. Newcomer lives within five or six miles of Hager's town. Two or three days after Orndorf got home, Bleacher one of the Captains came to him and called him out aside and said I understand you are let into a secret that is going on now--answered he was and said I suppose you are one of the officers. Bleacher said he was, Orndorf asked him what rank he was--he answered a Captain--Orndorf asked how many men he had recruited he said he had fifty men, Orndorf asked him to let him look at his warr he said he had it not about him and made it a rule not to carry it about him. Orndorf asked him to put it in his pocket and bring it to his house and show it to him, he said he would--and then Orndorf asked him how he managed to make known his doings to those he wanted to join him he said he had applied to twenty that had refused him and asked Orndorf how he thought he must have felt after being refused--said to Orndorf you are acquainted with our secrets and if you expose them you must abide by the consequences Orndorf asked him how he thought they would do if he went & brought the fleet to George town for you have no arms Bleacher said they would mount on horses and ride down there and receive their arms for the troops...and further said he could take the magazine in Fred. town with their man--and then they parted. Orndorf was at one Tinkles (who lives nigh to Kelly) who told him Jacob Young was informed of the matter, made answer and said why is Jacob Young informed of the matter--he said he was--Orndorf said why Jacob Young will certainly expose the matter for he is a magistrate, he said he would not. Council circular of Frederick and Washington county. Enclosed you have warrants to apprehend Henry Newcomer of Washington county, Fritchy of Frederick town, Kelly of Frederick county, Bleachy of Washington and Tinkles near Kelly, whose going at large we have the strongest reason to believe from the information of Capt. Orndorff is dangerous and may be detrimental to the state. The Capt. intends to have another interview with them and conversefully on the subject. He thinks they repose the utmost confidence in him and will disclose all their views and will mention the names of principal persons concerned in the plot...we wish you would see Capt. Orndorff and talk with him. June 10--council circular. Lieut. of Fred. and Washington county. Late last night and after our dispatches of yesterday were closed a law for the trial of spies, and such as may join the enemy, was enacted by the legislature, a copy whereof you have enclosed. Such a law has been for a long time necessary, and it has now hastened from the information of Orndorff. June 17--red book #27 letter 95--(Thomas Sprigg, co'ty lt. Hagers town to the council) (for'd by Capt--Morgan) I rec'd your hon. favor by Capt. Orndorf of the 9th and 10th before his return the conspiracy was discovered and several persons apprehended among them the two persons mentioned in yours of the 9th Henry Newcomer and Yost Pleaker. I've been busy exam. evidences for several days and find a great no are concerned in this Co. many in Virg. some in Fred. Co. there is about 30 in goal and expect the guards every moment that are detach'd for 50 or 60 more....they confess very freely. They say they expect and desire to be hang'd and I pray god they may not be disappointed. "Notes on the above-seven men were convicted of high treason and sentenced to be hung, including Yost Plecker and Casper Frietchie. Four were pardoned and three executed, one of these being "Fritchy" the leader in Frederick county MD who had been promised the rank of Colonel in the British army. He was the father of John Casper Frietchie, the husband of Barbara Frietchie who became the heroine of Whittier's poem. She was a Pennsylvania German born in Lancaster, Pennsylvania, in December 1766, a daughter of Michael and Catherine Hauer. These German names are spelled differently, according to whether the one spelling it spelled it by sound or not, omitting letters when one saw fit. The revolutionary records for 1780-81 also reveal the following: "arrangements of Maryland line in five regts: January 1st, 1781. 1st regiment Capt. Christian Orendorff. That the commissary of stores deliver to Capt. Christian Orndorff cloth and trimming for a suit of cloathe and linen for four shirts due him for the year 1780. Thursday 11th July 1782 that said treasuer pay to Christian Orendorff thirty pounds agreeable to a resolution of this board on the 22nd day of July 1781--sixty pounds in lieu of the two suits of cloaths and eight shirts for the last and present years and twenty pounds, fourteen shillings of the same emission for stores to the first instant on account." The following is a summary of his war service-commissioned July 18, 1776 and served in Captain Reynolds's company in the flying camp. He was in the battles of Harlem heights (October 1776) and White Plains. At the surrender of Fort Washington he was taken prisoner, and so continued until November 1, 1780 when he was exchanged and joined the 6th Maryland regiment as Captain April 1, 1778. He was at the surrender of Cornwallis, serving until the end of the war. Christian also fought in the Indian wars in 1791 enlisting in a company as a Major poss. that June. He fought in the Miami Valley across the Ohio River. He evidently returned to Maryland with the conviction that the well established Orendorff mills in Washington county had markets not to be surpassed in the wilderness of the west and northwest, for years to come. On April 2, 1785 Christopher had purchased from Francis Reynolds "three parcels of land...part Anderson's delight, part of john's chance and abstones forest for 1186 pounds, five shillings, which the said John Reynolds Sr., deceased by will dated march 22,1784 willed to his son Francis...one half of his real estate lands." In about 1800 Christian and his two brothers Christopher and Henry moved across the state line into western VA, now West VA. Soon after his return from the battle of Yorktown he invested in confiscated Tory land, the following being from a land record: "deed from Vlement Hollyday and Nathaniel Ramsey, commissioners appointed to preserve confiscated British property by an act of the general assembly of

Maryland...to Christian Orndorff JR and George Adams of Washington and Frederick counties lot no. 12 being part of monacocy manor, containing 248 acres of land, consideration-2535 pounds. Deed dated February 7, 1783." Before the year was out however, Christian had sold his interest to Adams. In the spring of 1786 Christian bought a plantation in Berkeley County VA. Here he conducted mills and farmed as his father had. In the 1790 census his residence still seems to have been in MD, but by 1795 Berbeley County was his legal residence. In that year he sold the Virginia plantation with its mills to his brother Christopher for 1100 pounds Pennsylvania currency. In January 1797 Christian acquired two lots in Shepardstown Va. he had 5 children, Perry, Eliza, William, and Christian, also a daughter whose name is unknown. In a book about Shepardstown VA there is a note that says Christian distinguished himself at the battles of Bennington and Skeenesborough.

94. f v. **ELIZABETH ORENDORFF**, born 1754 in CIRCA, POSS. MD.
BORN BETWEEN 1752 AND 1768 ELIZABETH MARRIED PETER STILLE B. 1748 D. OCT. 2, 1803.

95. f vi. **CATHARINE ORENDORFF**, born 1763. CATHERINE MARRIED JOHN ROHRER B. 1764 D. 1855. THERE WAS ALSO A CATHARINE WHO MARRIED JACOB SAUM BUT THIS IS NOT HER.

96. f vii. **MARY MAGDALINE ORENDORFF**, born 20 October 1769 in SHARPSBURG, WASH CO MD OR 1767, died 8 June 1845, at the age of 75.

Married twice Mary Magdaline, name also listed as Mary Madaline Orendorf, was present at an entertainment given a number of patriot officers in Baltimore during the revolutionary war (she was 17) and General Horatio Gates proposed but she refused because he was old enough to be her father. She afterwards married a son of Jonathan Hager on 11-17-1783, founder of historical old Hagerstown. Her husband died in a few years, leaving her with one child and a large estate; she rejected a proposal of marriage from famous Maryland lawyer Luther Martin and subsequently married a Col. Lawrence of Virginia. Poss. married in Hagerstown, Wash Co VA. Jonathan Hager b. 1755 d. 1798, they had a child named Elizabeth who married Upton Lawrence. Mary Magdaline may have been born in 1767. Johnathon may have stopped by Mt Pleasant (Mary father's plantation) on his way home and got a glimpse of Mary when she was young. Jonathan and his sister Rosanna had often visited the plantation. In July Mary greeted him by a spring as he was going off to the front to fight and was knitting a pair of socks for her brother Christian who was also leaving at the same time. Jonathan Hager JR enlisted at age 19, fought in the battle of Long Island, was captured in August by the British and sent to Halifax, Nova Scotia. Here he remained for a long time in a Canadian prison. His career was strangely unlucky, for his active service lasted only a month, and there after he remained in dark dungeon or as a prisoner of war under naval guard. After a year of close confinement in Nova Scotia, his brother in law General Daniel Heister visited him in August 1777, for the purpose of securing a "love gift" of 1400 acres of the Hagar estate to his sister, Rosanna, with a life interest to the general. The general achieved his purpose. But the irony of fate was not complete. Young Hager promised a guard five hundred pounds to secure his release, only to find that he was playing into the hands of a British spy. Immediately a special guard was placed over him and he found himself cruising around the Atlantic in a British war ship. He was not returned to Halifax until a month before the proclamation of peace. On his return to Washington Co MD he was acclaimed a hero and promptly feted with huge bonfires appropriate for the homecoming of the "proprietor" of Hagerstown. The following day he wed the beautiful Mary Orndorff, and they took up their residence in the stone house at the northeast corner of the square, formerly occupied by his father. An old record says- "his marriage to Mary Magdalene, the daughter of Major Christian and Elizabeth Ann (Hoffman) Ohrendorff of Pleasant Valley, MD occurred November 17, 1783. Their daughter Elizabeth "proprietess" of Hagerstown married upton Lawrence, whose daughter married Robert James Brent. Captain Hager died of disease Dec. 18, 1798 contracted in a dungeon in Nova Scotia." The famous lawyer, Luther Martin, and the defender of Aaron Burr courted Mary Orndorff Hager as a widow. But she rejected him on account of his intemperate habits and married Colonel Henry Lewis. Another record adds-Hagerstown was the center of an exceptionally refined and highly cultivated society.

In addition to the intelligent German families, who had settled in the vicinity or in the town itself, it had received valuable accessions from the wealthiest and most aristocratic of the leading southern Maryland and eastern shore families. The period was one of fine dress and courtly equippage...on one occasion Mrs. Johnathon Hager wore plum colored satin trimmed with fine black lace, cord, and tassels. Her wardrobe also included a bewildering assortment of silk and satin costumes, the colors comprising old gold, black, bronze, sage, and other hues which the English renaissance had made fashionable once more; light blue satin scarfs with trimming of lace and ribbons, capes trimmed with down, a green camel's hair shawl, with green bonnet to match, brocades of light blue and deep pink, embroidered with bunches of flowers, etc. among the leading citizens of Washington county...and one of the most conspicuous figures in the social, legal and political circles of Hagerstown was Upton Lawrence, a gentleman of exceptional talents and of a high standard of moral and intellectual attainments. Upton Lawrence married Elizabeth, daughter of Col. Jonathan Hager...Mrs. Lawrence, like her mother, the gifted Mary Orndorff, was lovely in person and character, and was one of the belles of Hagerstown. The daughters of Upton S. Lawrence and Elizabeth were Mary Ann Hoffman, Elizabeth Ann Lawrence and Martha West Lawrence. They retained the original plat of Hagerstown, the gold watch of Jonathan Hager, Sr. and many articles of clothing worn by Jonathan Hager, Jr., including some massive engraved silver shoe buckles, a gold ring set with a ruby and diamonds, a handsome silver stock-buckle set with brilliants and attached to a stock of black lace and blue satin, a brooch of brilliants for the shirt...a full dress suit of lace and ruffles. This costume consisted of two vests--one of white satin embroidered with spangles and colored silks, and the other of apple-green. She was married to Captain Henry Lewis on May 26, 1802. Her middle name may have been Magdalena.

97.   m   viii.   **JACOB ORENDORFF**, born 3 February 1770 in POSS. MD. He married SUSANNAH MILLER 9 February 1794 in ON A SUNDAY/ MD. She was born 1771. SUSANNAH died 19 September 1832, at the age of 61. Notes for SUSANNAH:

Susannah Miller was married to Jacob Orendorff. They had a child, Johannes Orendorff b. 01-14-1796 in Hagerstown, Washington Co MD. After her husbands' death she went with her son John to Baltimore and did not sell the property until later. "April 1826-indenture between Susannah Orndorff of Baltimore city of one part and Samuel Newman the other part for the sum of 1500 pounds for all that portion of ground in Hagerstown no. 86 fronting on W. Franklin St. with house buildings."

JACOB died 6 November 1803 in MD, at the age of 33. Notes for Jacob:

Soldier Jacob's name appears as "Orndorff", he left a widow, Susannah and several small children at the time of his death. In 1805 after selling her dower rights in the plantation this Susannah moved to Hagerstown with Jacobs mother Elizabeth after his death and later moved to Baltimore. The newspaper Washington spy of Sept 3, 1794 says "member, Captain Zeller's company of Col. Thomas Sprigg's regiment reorganization militia account whisky rebellion, Jacob Orendorff." Washington spy of Feb. 14, 1794 says, "married on Sunday last, Mr. Jacob Orendorff at Hagerstown, MD, by Rev. Jonathan Rawhauser, minister of the German reformed church, to the amiable and agreeable Miss Susan miller, daughter of Mr. Jacob Miller of Franklin County, Penna." Jacob was the only son of Major Christian Orendorff who remained in Maryland, and one of his sons became a leading Baltimore merchant. Jacob inherited the tract of land called Anderson's delight and john chance from his father, subject to the dower rights of his mother, and cash payments to his sisters. He died at the age of thirty-three, leaving four children. His wife Susanna sold her dower right to Jacob Mumma, removing first to Hagerstown and later to Baltimore. The following notice appeared in the Hagerstown weekly advertiser- "march 10, 1813-to be sold or rented-that large and convenient two story brick house in Franklin Street, Hagerstown near the public spring, now occupied by the subscriber. Possession will be given on the first day of April next. For terms apply Susanna Orndorff." Jacob is listed in his mothers bible as having died "in god" at age 33 years 10 months and 3 days and that he left a wife and 4 children.

98.   m   ix.   **JOHN ORENDORFF**, born 16 April 1775. He married SUSAN WOHLGEMUTH 12 August 1795 in READING PA. She was born 1771. Notes for SUSAN:

Susan Wohlgemuth died at the home of Colonel David Schnebley, which was probably in KY.
JOHN died 21 June 1807 in RUSSELVILLE KY, at the age of 32. Notes for JOHN:
Marriage information for John was taken from the Goshenhoppen register. John did not go to KY with the rest of his family in 1805, he showed up later. He was a "sort of Rip Van Winkle" whose chief accomplishments were hunting and playing the flute. John is listed in his mother's bible as dying at age 32 years 3 months and 25 days and that he left a wife and 3 children and as being buried in Russelville, KY.

99.   f   x.   **BARBARA ORENDORFF**, born 21 August 1759, died 23 June 1841 in AT HOME, HAGERSTOWN MD, at the age of 81.

Possibly born between 1775 and 1780. Barbara bought two lots in Hagerstown MD. On them there were houses and buildings paying an annual rent to the town of five shillings 6 pence sterling for each lot over and beside the taxes that may grow due to the government. They were bought from Jonathan Hager for 16 pounds in May of 1798 or 1797. She married at age 40 to a leading citizen of Hagerstown MD. the following is an old newspaper clipping: "Sept. 26, 1799. By Rev. Mr. Bower, John Ragan---inkeeper to Barbara Orendorff both of Hagerstown." another: "Washington spy-Wednesday, may 5, 1802. A stage and horses for the accommodation of passengers may be had at any time by applying to John Ragan sign of the Indian king Hagerstown." another: "the Maryland herald and Elizabeth-town weekly advertiser-June 23, 1841 (Wednesday)--died--at her residence in this place on Sunday past, Mrs. Barbara Ragan in the 82nd year of her age consort of the late John Ragan senior. The deceased was one of the oldest and most respectable inhabitants of Hagerstown, Hagerstown herald of freedom."

100.　　f　xi.　**ROSE ORENDORFF**, born 30 January 1780, died 30 March 1821 in LEXINGTON KY/ POSS. LOGAN, CO, at the age of 41.

Known as St. Rozo Vitozo, Rose appears in the book "of Washington County, Maryland" page 93 as follows: "on her way to Bath visited St. Rozo Vitozo, the most celebrated person in this part of the country and now residing near Sharpsburg. For several weeks the reader is left entirely in ignorance of who St. Rozo Vitozo is, but then the following partial explanation is given: fifty or sixty persons pass through Shepardstown daily to visit miss Rosa Orndorff near Sharpsburg, some through curiosity, others conscientiously affected by the surprising situation and appearance presented by this young woman, many coming two hundred miles. Rosa Orndorff here spoken of was a daughter of Major Christian Orndorff, a distinguished citizen of the county, and a man of wealth and great hospitality. Many officers of the revolutionary army in traveling between the north and south crossed the Potomac at the Shepardstown ford and many spent of them spent the night at Major Orndorff's. Among these was General Horatio Gates, who during one of these stoppages became desperately enamored of Miss Mary Orndorff, the sister of Rosa, who was at that time but fifteen years of age, and distinguished for her great beauty. She rejected General Gates and married young Jonathan Hager. Rosa Orndorff was subject to attacks of the singular disease known as catalepsy probably a majority of reported cases of this disease are impostures but this seems to have been a genuine one. No copy of the published description of her case is known to exist but the descendants of the family say that in her trances, she seemed to be entirely insensible to any pain, so that pins could be stuck into her flesh without producing any effect upon her, and that hundreds of visitors were anxious to experiment upon her, and a strict watch had to be maintained over her to save her from being converted into a pin cushion. It appears that she was a spiritualist, and whilst entirely unconscious of all her surroundings would converse with spirits and messages from the spirit world to those who wished to communicate with their departed friends. It is not surprising, therefore, that in that credulous age persons came from long distances to see so remarkable a personage. It must have been an intolerable nuisance to have several hundred visitors each week although they did bring their own provisions with them. Later, the Orndorffs moved to Kentucky and there Rosa died, having first obtained a promise from her father that her body should be buried on the old homestead near Sharpsburg. This promise was faithfully performed although it must have been at a heavy cost. She married Jacob Rohrer.

101.   m   xii.   **HENRY ORENDORFF**, born in POSS. MD CIRCA 1764. He married MARGARET ALBERTS. Notes for HENRY:
Soldier/officer Capt. Henry is listed as the head of a family in Washington Co MD 1790

as follows-"2 free white males of 16 years and upward including head of family, 1 free white male under 16 years of age, 3 free white females, and 2 slaves". The name is spelled "Orendorff" in that record. Henry was the third son born, and served in the revolutionary war. But since he did not enlist until the close of the war, few records have been preserved of his service. On Friday, January 12, 1781 Henry is listed as Captain in Col. Peter Adam's regiment. On August 20, 1791 a land deed was done giving Henry a tract of his fathers plantation called Mt pleasant, costing 1400 pounds, and described as follows: "being parte of a tract of land called the resurvey of Smith's Hills...running with outline of the whole tract...south...to intersect the given line of a tract of land called vultons grove...to the bank of antietam creek and then down to the east bank of said creek s 38 degrees w 20 perches...then across the creek n 58 degrees...then by a division line between the said Henry and Christopher Orndorff, 200 acres...let the said run called Sharpsburg Run 3 days in week forever from the first day of April, until the last of October hereafter through his the said Henry Orndorffs ditches...made for the use of watering the meadow...a full passage into a ditch made for the use of watering Christopher Orndorffs meadow." This land was the last of his father's plantation. At about 1800 henry moved with his brothers Christian III and Christopher across the state line into western VA, now west VA. They all sold out their interests in MD and bought plantations near Shepardstown VA keeping close to the Potomac river. In the fall of 1793 Henry had purchased 343 acres along the south side of the Potomac River, but he did not remove to VA permanently until he sold his portion of smith's hills and bought another plantation near Shepherdstown containing 322 acres for 3097 pounds. An old slave record: "certificate-Berkeley. I do hereby certify that Henry Orndorff personally appeared before me Abraham Shepard a justice of the peace for said county and took the oath prescribed by law for the removal of slaves into this state and has given their names and age as follows to wit-James about forty six years of age-Mercury about forty five years of age. Given under my hand and seal this sixteenth day of may 1796. Abraham Shepard."

Notes for Elizabeth:

97 years old when she died Elizabeth Ann was "formerly of Washington Co MD" and the widow of Major Christian Orndorff. A newspaper article from the torchlight and public advertiser (Hagerstown) says, "It is supposed that not less than 500 of her children's children are now living. Two of her children, one 60, the other 70 years of age, witnessed her internment. Up to the 6th generation followed her to the tomb." She died at her granddaughter's house on the Sunday night before 07-16-1829. In 1805 Elizabeth sold her dower rights to the plantation to Jacob Mumma whose son John latter married a granddaughter of Margaret Orndorff Hess and moved with his daughter in law Susanah to Hagerstown. She lived for a time in the stone house on the square, built by Jonathan Hager, SR. but at the time of her death she was living in the now famous Rochester House. This house was purchased by Upton Lawrence, a talented and eloquent lawyer of his day, in 1803 after his marriage to Elizabeth who was the only daughter of Jonathan Hager Jr. Lawrence built an addition to the east end of the house, which faced prospect

street, the lot having a frontage of three hundred feet. There were two large living rooms with open fireplaces. On the front door was a large brass locking six by twelve inches, made in rochesterlock factory. After Lawrence's death in 1831 the property was sold. His wife later bought the Reynolds property next door. In the records of the descendants of Jonathan Hager JR is the following item: "Christian Orndorff's wife, Elizabeth Ann Hoffman, was a lady of small stature and delicate health, her last residence for a number of years was with her daughter and granddaughter at #122 Washington St. Hagerstown, MD. At her death she was 99 years of age said her great granddaughter Martha W. Lawrence." in the Hagerstown mail of Friday July 24, 1829 is published the following obituary: "died at her granddaughter's on Sunday night last in the 97th year of her age, Elizabeth Ann Orndorff, widow of Major Christian Orndorff, formerly of this county. Thus, full of years and with an unshaken confidence in the merits of her redeemer has this venerable lady paid her debt to nature. It is supposed that not less than one hundred of her children's children are now living. Two of her children are 60 (Mary Hager Lewis) the other 70 years of age (Barbara Ragan) witnessed the solemn ceremony of internment. Several of her grandchildren from forty to sixty years of age and great grandchildren from twenty to forty years of age and son on to the sixth generation followed her to the tomb. How inscrutable, yet how just are the ways of an ever-ruling god...his goodness is most graciously displayed--the lisping infant is taken pure as the new born rose from the bosom of its parent, into the blessedness of heaven, and if there is a pang left behind there is also an accompanying concolation, virtuous age sinks under the weight of infirmities at peace with that world and with the promise of immortality. The lamented husband of the subject of this notice was well known in this county as a high toned Whig of former times--Mrs. Orndorff devoted much of her time to the persual of the holy bible; this source of all light and wisdom seemed to yield her pure delight in the evening of her days and made easy and placid the moment of her mortal exit."

CHAPTER EIGHT

GENERATION NO. 8

68. JOHN WILLIAM[8] ORENDORFF (59.PHILIP[7], 50.PHILIP[6], 26.THEISS[5], 9.LUDWIG[4], 3.HUBERT[3], 2.HENNE[2], 1.SIMON[1]) was born 1794 in BORN 1789-1797 FREDERICK, CO VA. JOHN died 16 December 1878 in FREDERICK VA, PINE HILLS, at the age of 85. He married **ELIZABETH PEER** 7 March 1814 in PROBABLY VA. She was born 1799. ELIZABETH died 1870, at the age of 71.

They had 9 children:

+ 102.   m   i.   **JAMES HAMPTON ORENDORFF**, born 29 December 1822.

103.   f   ii.   **LOUISA C. ORENDORFF**, born 1822 in CIRCA BIRTH DATE/FREDERICK, VA, died in MARTINSBURG WEST VIRGINIA. LOUISA'S NAME IS LISTED AS "ORNDORFF" IN THE RECORDS, SHE MARRIED EDMUND H. RIDINGS. THE MINISTER WAS JOHN ALLEMONG.

104.   m   iii.   **WILLIAM H. ORENDORFF**, born 1827 in CIRCA B. DATE/FREDERICK, CO VA. He married SARA JOHNSON GARDNER 5 June 1872 in FREDERICK CO VIRGINIA. Notes for SARA: SARA WAS A WIDOW WILLIAM died in FREDERICK CO VA. Notes for WILLIAM: WILLIAM H. WAS BURIED IN SALEM

BRETHREN CHURCH CEMETERY, STEPHENS CITY VIRGINIA.

105.   f   iv.   **HARRIET ANN ORENDORFF**, born 1829 in CIRCA B. DATE/FREDERICK, CO VA. HARRIET'S NAMES IS LISTED AS "ORNDORFF" IN THE RECORD, SHE MARRIED A MAN NAMED WILLIAM MUMMA.

106.   f   v.   **JANE M. ORENDORFF**, born 1842 in CIRCA B. DATE/FREDERICK, CO VA. JANE M.'S NAME WAS LISTED AS "ORNDORFF" IN THE RECORD, SHE MARRIED BENJAMIN F. STEELE.

+ 107.   m   vi.   **JOHN ALFRED ORENDORFF**, born 1843, died 20 December 1922.

+ 108.   m   vii.   **LEWIS ORENDORFF**, born 18 March 1822, died 16 June 1905.

109.   m   viii.   **WESLEY ORENDORFF**, born 1835. MARRIED MARY ANN BORN 1825

+ 110.   m   ix.   **HAMILTON ORENDORFF**, born 1833.

Notes for Elizabeth:
Elizabeth Peer's mother was Elizabeth Peer Swaney 1772-1850 and granddaughter of Philip Peer 1735-1799.

Notes for John:
John Williams's name is listed as "Orendorff" and "Orndorff" in the records. John was a farmer and was married to a woman named Elizabeth. His father may have been a John Orendorff married to a woman named Ellen.

- - - - - - - - - - -

70. JACOB[8] **ORENDORFF** (59.PHILIP[7], 50.PHILIP[6], 26.THEISS[5], 9.LUDWIG[4], 3.HUBERT[3], 2.HENNE[2], 1.SIMON[1]) was born 1787 in VIRGINIA, PROBABLY SHENANDOAH.

JACOB died 23 July 1859, at the age of 72. He married **MARGARET FINLEY**. She was born 1794. MARGARET died 1856, at the age of 62.

They had 5 children:

+ 111. m i.   **ANDREW ADDISON ORENDORFF**, born 1817, died 1894.

+ 112. m ii.   **JACOB J. JR ORENDORFF**, born 24 December 1831, died 3 March 1919.

113. m iii. **ARCHIE ORENDORFF**.
DIED AT AGE 11 ARCHIE'S NAME APPEARS AS "ORNDORFF", HE WAS KILLED BY A SHEEP.

+ 114. f iv.   **MARY ELIZA ORENDORFF**, born 8 January 1832, died 30 September 1905.

115.   f v.   **JANE ORENDORFF**, born 1836 in CIRCA, died in CIRCA, POSS. VA.
UNMARRIED JANE DIED AT ABOUT AGE 30 DURING THE CIVIL WAR, HER NAME APPEARS AS "ORNDORFF".

Notes for Margaret:

Margaret Finley's father was Archibald Finley 1757-1839 married to Margaret. Archibald's father was Henry Finley 1726-1805 married to Elizabeth Walker who died in 1816. Henry's father was Archibald Finley 1686-1750 married to Margaret Kelso who came to America in 1734 and settled in Bucks County PA.

Notes for Jacob:

2nd child born Jacob's name appears as "Orndorff". Also as "Ohrndorff", possibly died 07-22-1859.

- - - - - - - - - - -

71. PHILIP[8] **ORENDORFF** (59.PHILIP[7], 50.PHILIP[6], 26.THEISS[5], 9.LUDWIG[4], 3.HUBERT[3], 2.HENNE[2], 1.SIMON[1]) was born 1792 in VIRGINIA, PROBABLY SHENANDOAH.

PHILIP died 17 October 1880, at the age of 88. He married **CHRISTINA PEER** 30 June 1823 in SHENANDOAH VIRGINIA. She was born 1802 in POSS. 1803. CHRISTINA died 21 August 1890, at the age of 88.

They had 3 children:

+ 116.   m   i.   **HEZEKIAH ORENDORFF**, born 27 October 1845.

+ 117.   m   ii.   **PERRY W. ORENDORFF**, born 24 February 1841.

118.   f   iii.   **DELILAH ORENDORFF**, born 1840. POSSIBLY BORN 1834 OR 1835 DELILAH'S NAME APPEARS AS "ORNDORFF", SHE APPARENTLY LIVED TO BE 81. SHE NEVER MARRIED.

Notes for Philip:
4th child born Philip's name is listed as "Orndorff" in the record. Also "Ohrndorff".

- - - - - - - - - - -

72. SAMUEL[8] **ORENDORFF** (59.PHILIP[7], 50.PHILIP[6], 26.THEISS[5], 9.LUDWIG[4], 3.HUBERT[3], 2.HENNE[2], 1.SIMON[1]) was born 1802 in VIRGINIA, PROBABLY SHENANDOAH. SAMUEL died 17 July 1858, at the age of 56. He married **COMFORT JANE PEER** 14 February 1826 in PROBABLY FREDERICK CO, VA. She was born 15 May 1805, maybe in 1808.

They had 7 children:

119. f   i.   **FRANCIS ORENDORFF**, born 1828 in VA. CIRCA BIRTH DATE

+ 120.   m   ii.   **LEMUEL ORENDORFF**, born 1833, died 1914.

+ 121.   m   iii.   **MEGUS (SIMON) ORENDORFF**, born 25 April 1834, died 26 July 1908.

+ 122.   m   iv.   **LEWIS ORENDORFF**, born 5 April 1847, died 17 August 1893.

123.   m   v.   **SIMON M. ORENDORFF**, born 1836 in VA.
                    SIMON M.'S NAME APPEARS AS "ORNDORFF".

+ 124.   m   vi.   **GEORGE WASHINGTON ORENDORFF**, born 15 October 1838, died 27 September 1918.

125.   m   vii.   **LOUIS ORENDORFF**, born 1846 in VA.
                    LOUIS' NAME APPEARS AS "ORNDORFF".

Notes for Comfort:
Comfort Jane also had a daughter named Mary C. b. 1844 VA.

Notes for Samuel:
6th child born Samuel also had a son named Samuel b. 1833 VA. His name appears as "Orndorff".

- - - - - - - - - - -

73. LEWIS[8] **ORENDORFF** (59.PHILIP[7], 50.PHILIP[6], 26.THEISS[5], 9.LUDWIG[4], 3.HUBERT[3], 2.HENNE[2], I.SIMON[1]) was born 1798 in CIRCA B. DATE, VA, SHENANDOAH. LEWIS died 1 May 1854, at the age of 56. He married **ISABELLA COPELAND** 12 September 1829 in PROBABLY SHENANDOAH, CO VA. She was born 24 April 1833 in POSS. BORN 1809.

They had 4 children:

126.   f   i.   **SARAH ELIZABETH ORENDORFF**, born 6 October 1832 in VAN BUREN FURNACE, VA, died 8 February 1904 in VAN BUREN FURNACE/VA, SHENANDOAH, at the age of 71.
                    Possibly born in 1833 Sarah Elizabeth married Snowden Whitaker who was born in 1829. There was a Sarah Elizabeth who married Peter Townsend b. 08-19-1831.

127.　f　ii.　**MARY CATHERINE (KATE) ORENDORFF**, born 1840, died in TOLEDO?

　　　　　　Mary Catherine's name is listed as "Orndorff" in the record. She is buried in or near Hampshire Co VA and her name appears as "Orendorff".

+ 128.　m　iii.　**BENJAMIN ORENDORFF**, born 1826.

+ 129.　m　iv.　**JAMES HARRISON ORENDORFF**, born 6 February 1830, died 29 January 1917.

Notes for Isabella:
2nd wife. Maybe born 1834.

Notes for Lewis:
Married twice. Williams Lewis was the 5th child born, his name appears as "Orndorff" in the record. He married Rebecca Williams on 04-18-1825 in Shenandoah Co VA.

- - - - - - - - - - -

75.　JESSE[8] **ORENDORFF** (60.JOHN[7], 50.PHILIP[6], 26.THEISS[5], 9.LUDWIG[4], 3.HUBERT[3], 2.HENNE[2], 1.SIMON[1]) was born 1780 in POSS. 1777. JESSE died 1815 in GREENE CO PENNSYLVANIA, at the age of 35. He married **CATHERINE STROSNIDER** 2 August 1799 in FREDERICK CO/ BOTETOURT, VA.

They had 2 children:

130.　f　i.　**RHODA ORENDORFF**, born in PROBABLY VA.

　　　　　　RHODA'S NAME APPEARS AS "ORNDORFF". RHODA MARRIED JAMES WELLS.

131.　f　ii.　**NANCY ORENDORFF**, born 1805 in CIRCA B. DATE/BEFORE, 1816 VA.

　　　　　　NANCY'S NAME APPEARS AS "ORNDORFF", SHE MARRIED JACOB GROVES.

Notes for Jesse:

Soldier married to Catherine Strosnider. Jesse served in the war of 1812. He died in about 1815 and left a family. Jesse enlisted August 9, 1814 to serve in the war of 1812. At the time of his discharge 06-12-1815 he was recorded as being about 35 years of age. His honorable discharge papers are on file in the national archives in Washington DC. Also among those records in are affidavits signed by Jacob Bailey, and William Orendorff, son of Jesse of Greene County PA, June 11, 1833 which affirm the fact Jesse died during the winter of 1815. Possibly married 1803.

- - - - - - - - - - -

76. PHILIP[8] **ORENDORFF** (60.JOHN[7], 50.PHILIP[6], 26.THEISS[5], 9.LUDWIG[4], 3.HUBERT[3], 2.HENNE[2], 1.SIMON[1]) was born 23 March 1767 in CHESTER CO PA. PHILIP died 1818 in FREDERICK CO VA, at the age of 50. He married **ELEANOR WILLIAMS** 29 September 1795 in FREDERICK CO VA.

They had 6 children:

+ 132.   m   i.   **HARRISON ORENDORFF**, born 31 May 1815, died 23 November 1890.

133.   f   ii.   **ANN "ANNIE" ORENDORFF**, born 1799. ANNIE'S NAME APPEARS AS "ORNDORFF". SHE MARRIED A MR. JACOB WILLIAMS.

134.   f   iii.   **BETSY ORENDORFF.** BETSY'S NAME APPEARS AS "ORNDORFF", SHE MARRIED A MR. COOPER.

+ 135.   m   iv.   **HAMPTON ORENDORFF,** born 15 October 1818, died 7 May 1886.

136.   m   v.   **JAMES ORENDORFF**, born 1813 in CIRCA B DATE/VA, died in POSSIBLY WOODSTOCK VA/OR, BIRTH. JAMES'S NAME APPEARS AS "ORNDORFF".

137. f vi. **LIZA ORENDORFF**, born in AROUND 1814/VA.
LIZA'S NAME APPEARS AS "ORNDORFF", SHE MARRIED SAMUEL BOND AND EITHER LIVED IN KNOX CO IN OR DIED THERE.

Notes for Philip:
Poss. b. date 1769/2nd born. Christian Streit married Philip. Philip died in Cedar Creek Valley in Shenandoah Co VA.

- - - - - - - - - - -

78. LEVI[8] **ORENDORFF** (60.JOHN[7], 50.PHILIP[6], 26.THEISS[5], 9.LUDWIG[4], 3.HUBERT[3], 2.HENNE[2], 1.SIMON[1]) was born 1791. LEVI died 1869, at the age of 78. He married **ELEANOR YOUNG** 7 June 1813 in FREDERICK CO VA/ SHENANDOAH, CO. She was born 1791.
They had 10 children:

+ 138. m i. **WESTFALL ORENDORFF**, born 1828.
139. f ii. **SALINA ORENDORFF**.
PROBABLY 8TH CHILD BORN SALINA'S NAME APPEARS AS "ORNDORFF".
140. m iii. **SETH ORENDORFF**.
PROB. BORN IN CAPON SPRINGS WV. SETH'S NAME APPEARS AS "ORNDORFF". APPEARS TO BE THE 9TH CHILD BORN.
+ 141. m iv. **AMOS ORENDORFF**, born 1847.
142. f v. **SALOME ORENDORFF**, born 1853.
13TH CHILD BORN SALOME'S NAME APPEARS AS "ORNDORFF".
+ 143. m vi. **PHILIP SETZER ORENDORFF**, born 16 February 1833.
144. f vii. **REBECCA ORENDORFF**, born 1814 or BORN AFTER 1813 in VA or IL.

REBECCA'S NAME APPEARS AS "ORNDORFF", SHE APPARENTLY MARRIED A COUSIN.

+ 145. m viii. **PHINEAS ORENDORFF**, born 1834.

146. m ix. **LEVI ORENDORFF**, born 1841 in POSS. VA.

LEVI'S NAME APPEARS AS "ORNDORFF".

147. f x. **SARAH ORENDORFF**, born 1815 in POSS. FREDERICK CO VA.

Sarah is listed in the 1850 census for Frederick Co VA dist. 16 as living with her parents? Levi age 60 and Ellen age 59, name appears as "Orndorff".

Notes for Eleanor:

Also called Ellen. Eleanor appears in the 1850 census for Frederick Co VA.

Notes for Levi:

Born in PA or VA/farmer. Levi's name appears as "Orndorff". He appears in the 1850 census for Frederick Co VA. 14th born.

- - - - - - - - - - -

82. BENJAMIN[8] **ORENDORFF** (60.JOHN[7], 50.PHILIP[6], 26.THEISS[5], 9.LUDWIG[4], 3.HUBERT[3], 2.HENNE[2], 1.SIMON[1]) was born 1780 in CIRCA, VA. BENJAMIN died in POSS. VA. He married **CATHERINE HARBAUGH**. She was born 1785.

They had 1 child:

148. m i. **WILLIAM ORENDORFF**, born 1821 in PROBABLY VA.

WILLIAM'S NAME APPEARS AS "ORNDORFF".

Notes for Catherine:

Catherine appears in the 1850 census for Frederick Co VA district 16 along with her husband and 6 younger members of the Racey family. Her age is listed as 65.

Notes for Benjamin:

b. After 1779 PA or VA/farmer Benjamin's name appears as "Orndorff". He appears in the 1850 census for Frederick Co VA district 16, age listed is 71, real estate $1,000.00. Also listed living with him are the following: John Racey age 29 farmer, Mary A. Racey age 29, George L. Racey age 7, Eliza C. Racey age 3, Benjamin Racey age 2, and George G. Racey age 9 months. He was the 9th born.

- - - - - - - - - - -

85. DAVID[8] **ORENDORFF** (60.JOHN[7], 50.PHILIP[6], 26.THEISS[5], 9.LUDWIG[4], 3.HUBERT[3], 2.HENNE[2], 1.SIMON[1]) was born August 1787. He married **ISABELLA RACEY**.

They had 6 children:

+ 149.   f   i.   **MAHALA ORENDORFF**, born 1810, died 1848.

+ 150.   m   ii.   **HARRISON ORENDORFF**, born 17 August 1813.

151.   m   iii.   **PARMENES ORENDORFF**, born 1850. CIRCA B. DATE PARMENES MARRIED A LANDACRE, HIS NAME APPEARS AS "ORNDORFF".

152.   f   iv.   **ROSANA ORENDORFF**, born 1877. ROSANA'S NAME APPEARS AS "ORNDORFF", SHE MARRIED FRANKLIN BROOKS.

153.   m   v.   **BENAIR ORENDORFF**. DIED IN EARLY CHILDHOOD BENAIR'S NAME APPEARS AS "ORNDORFF", HE WAS BORN IN THE 1800'S.

+ 154.   m   vi.   **ISAIAH ORENDORFF**, born 1824.

Notes for Isabella:
1st wife of David.

Notes for David:
2nd wife was Eliza Strosnider. David's name appears as "Orndorff". He was married three times. 12th born.

- - - - - - - - - - -

86. PHINEAS[8] **ORENDORFF** (60.JOHN[7], 50.PHILIP[6], 26.THEISS[5], 9.LUDWIG[4], 3.HUBERT[3], 2.HENNE[2], 1.SIMON[1]) was born 23 March 1793. PHINEAS died 1838 in POSS. 1836, at the age of 44. He married **ELEANOR BORDEN** 20 August 1823 in FREDERICK CO VA/POSS., 08301823. She was born 1794.

They had 1 child:

+ 155.   m   i.   **MASON D. ORENDORFF**, born 1832, died 1879.

Notes for Eleanor:
Eleanor was called Ellen.

Notes for Phineas:
Born in PA or VA/15th born Phineas' name appears as "Orndorff". He was possibly married in Shenandoah Co VA.

- - - - - - - - - - -

88. ISAAC[8] **ORENDORFF** (60.JOHN[7], 50.PHILIP[6], 26.THEISS[5], 9.LUDWIG[4], 3.HUBERT[3], 2.HENNE[2], 1.SIMON[1]) was born 1797. He married **REBECCA H. LOWERY**.

They had 6 children:

156.   f   i.   **MARGARET   ANN   ORENDORFF**, born 1818 in VIRGINIA, died 1894 in MARYLAND, at the age of 76.
Margaret Ann married Jacob Saum; they were either married in Hagerstown Maryland or lived there. They had the following children: Rebecca

J. Saum b.1843, Elisha Saum b. 1845, Mary E. Saum, and Isiah Saum.

157.   f   ii.   **MARY ANN ORENDORFF,** born 11 March 1831 in PENDELTON CO VA.
MARRIED JOHN W. SLATER MARY ANN'S NAME APPEARS AS "ORNDORFF".

158.   f   iii.   **SUSAN ELLEN ORENDORFF,** born 15 September 1834 in PENDELTON CO VA, NOW IN WEST VA.
Susan Ellen married Charles W. Hicks, her name appears as "Orndorff". They had one girl Maggie Hicks who married a Mr. Carr. Mr. Hicks was either born in Centenial WY or the family lived there at some time.

159.   m   iv.   **BENJAMIN FRANKLIN ORENDORFF,** born 8 January 1836 in PENDELTON CO VA.
PENDELTON CO IS NOW PART OF West Virginia NEXT TO HARDY CO WHERE THERE WAS OTHER ORENDORFFS.

160.   f   v.   **HANNAH KATHERINE ORENDORFF,** born 1838 in PENDELTON CO VA.
Hannah Katherine married a Mr. Grogg, apparently in West VA. Her name appears as "Orndorff". They had the following children: a Miss Grogg, and David Grogg apparently at Plattsmouth NE.

161.   f   vi.   **RACHEL ORENDORFF,** born 11 March 1821, died 9 January 1897, at the age of 75.
RACHEL MARRIED ELIAS PEER B. 04-06-1817 D. 03-06-1899.

Notes for Rebecca:
2nd wife of Isaac Orendorff.

Notes for Isaac:

Married twice. Isaac married his 1st wife Hannah Strosnider 03-16-1819 in Shenandoah Co VA.

- - - - - - - - - - -

89. JOHNATHAN[8] **ORENDORFF** (60.JOHN[7], 50.PHILIP[6], 26.THEISS[5], 9.LUDWIG[4], 3.HUBERT[3], 2.HENNE[2], 1.SIMON[1]) was born 1771 in MD. JOHNATHAN died 1859, at the age of 88. He married **PRISCILLA FRY** 29 April 1799 in FREDERICK CO VA/SHENANDOAH, CO.

They had 4 children:

162.	f	i.	**SALLIE ORENDORFF.** BORN CIRCA 1801
163.	f	ii.	**PRISCILLA ORENDORFF.** BORN CIRCA 1820 PRISCILLA'S NAME APPEARS AS "ORNDORFF", SHE MARRIED JOHN LINEBURG. MARRIED BY MINISTER LEWIS EICHELBURGER.
164.	f	iii.	**CATHERINE ORENDORFF.** BORN CIRCA 1812 CATHERINE'S NAME APPEARS AS "ORNDORFF", SHE MARRIED A MR. BRILL.
+ 165.	m	iv.	**JOSEPH ORENDORFF**, born 1799, died 1877.

Notes for Johnathan:

2nd wife Mary Lantz/4th born Jonathan's Last name appears as "Orndorff", he married secondly Mary Lantz (Lants) on 11-20-1816 or 05-28-1817 Frederick Co VA. He appears on the 1850 census for Frederick Co VA living with his son Joseph. Age listed as 80 in 1850.

- - - - - - - - - - -

90. JESSE[8] **ORENDORFF** (65.CHRISTIAN[7], 54.CHRISTIAN[6], 48.JOHANN[5], 25.HERMANN[4], 7.STEPHEN[3], 2.HENNE[2], 1.SIMON[1]) was born 1771 in FREDERICK CO

VA NEAR, WINCHESTER. JESSE died 14 September 1846 in BRECKINRIDGE CO KY, at the age of 75. He married **MARY ELIZABETH (BETSY) CASHMAN** 29 December 1803 in BOTETORT CO VA. She was born 1772 in LANCASTER CO PA. MARY died 1 February 1847 in BRECKINRIDGE CO KY, at the age of 75.

They had 6 children:

+ 166.   m   i.   **WILLIAM HENRY ORENDORFF**, born 18 April 1807, died 25 April 1892.

+ 167.   m   ii.   **MEXICO ORENDORFF**, born 18 May 1812, died 5 February 1854.

+ 168.   m   iii.   **ALEXANDER ORENDORFF**, born 11 February 1815.

169.   f   iv.   **ELIZA JANE ORENDORFF** died in PROBABLY KY.

Breckinridge County Kentucky records vol. 1. Records the marriage of Eliza Jane Orendorff to Peyton Henderson Jr. on December 17, 1839, with consent of father, Jesse Orendoff. Peyton Henderson Jr. was born in Adair County on January 18, 1816, and came to Breckinridge Co about 1830 and was a prominent member of that county. He married 2 more times after Eliza's death. They had 6 children, one of which was T.B. Henderson born September 4,1848 in Breckinridge Co KY. May have been married October 1840. Spelling of her name in marriage record is "Orendoff". Marriage date Breckinridge Co. Ky. records (vol. 1)

170.   f   v.   **NANCY ORENDORFF**.

NANCY WAS PROBABLY THE FIRST CHILD OF JESSE. HER NAME IS SHOWN AS "ORENDORFF". NANCY MARRIED A MR. GARRETT.

171.   m   vi.   **JOHN ORENDORFF**, born 3 October

1804 in PROBABLY VA, died in PROBABLY BRECKINRIDGE, CO KY.

John was probably the 2nd child of Jesse. He is buried in Breckinridge Co KY, his name appears as "Orenduff".

Notes for Mary:

Mary E. Cashman was probably married in the town of Fincastle, which is in Botetourt County, VA. May also have been Bedford Co VA. She died at age 70 and is buried in Breckinridge Co.

Notes for Jesse:

Soldier/farmer. Jesse was possibly born in Farquier Co VA. According to KY biographies by Perrin he was born in Frederick Co VA near Winchester and later moved to Fincastle VA/this could mean either the town in VA which is near Winchester or Fincastle Co which made up all of what is now KY. Jesse was of a very prominent family both in VA and MD and was born near the Maryland/Virginia state line. They may have been married or met in Bedford Co VA. Jesse and his wife Mary E. (Betsy) Cashman lived in Bedford Co Virginia when their child Mexico was born in 1812. They also lived in Lynchburg Co VA in 04-18-1807 when their child William Henry was born. Jesse's wife also died in Breckinridge Co Ky. in 1830 he immigrated to Kentucky and settled in Breckinridge Co on a farm later owned by a John M. Fisher. Jesse died on that farm when he was 75. Buried in Breckinridge Co KY, the name on his stone is "Orendufff".

Source: Visit to KY 2001

- - - - - - - - - - -

92. CHRISTOPHER[8] **ORENDORFF** (65.CHRISTIAN[7], 54.CHRISTIAN[6], 48.JOHANN[5], 25.HERMANN[4], 7.STEPHEN[3], 2.HENNE[2], 1.SIMON[1]) was born 23 November 1752. CHRISTOPHER died 14 September 1823 in ADAIRVILLE KY POSS. THE, 24TH, at the age of 70. He married **MARY THOMAS**. She was born 1755 in CIRCA, PROBABLY GERMANY. MARY died 4 October 1823 in POSS. KY AT AGE 68, at the age of 68.

They had 5 children:

+ 172.   m   i.   **AARON ORENDORFF.**

+ 173.   m   ii.   **ENOCH T. ORENDORFF**, born 1799.

+ 174.   m   iii.   **ESAU ORENDORFF**, born 1789.

175.   m   iv.   **ELI ORENDORFF**, born 1803 in VIRGINIA. He married MARY PAISLEY 13 January 1826 in RUSSELLVILLE KY. She was born 1805 in TENNESSEE. MARY died in PROBABLY KY. Notes for MARY:

Mary is listed in the 1850 census for Logan Co KY. She is shown to be 45 years old and to have been born in Tennessee. She and Eli possibly had 5 children.

Eli died in probably Ky. Notes for Eli:

Farmer Eli is listed with his 6 other family members in the August 6th 1850 Kentucky census, district #2 Logan co page 76. Eli is shown to be 47, a farmer, born in VA, and to own 12,000.00 worth of real estate.

176. m   v.   **JOHN ORENDORFF**, born 1782 in MD OR VA, died in POSS. KY.

John's name appears as "Orndorff", in 1803 he received an 81- acre tract of land from his father and he was 21 at that time. John was later a large landowner in KY. He also received land, mills, houses, untincles, from his father in his will dated 1823. He kept a diary of the Orendorff migration to KY; he built a flourmill and a sawmill on the Red River, which he improved from time to time. He was of a mechanical turn of mind and found much time to experiment with various types of machinery. As a mechanical enthusiast, John is an embodiment of the manufacturing spirit of the first half of the 19th century. He rarely carried his experiments to perfection. He applied for a patent for a "spinning wheel" on March 10, 1829. Through his letters to his brother Esau in Illinois his particular hobbies are revealed. They are extant from the later part of his life 1838-1848. on January 6, 1838 John wrote-Mr. price came up at Christmas to carry on the farm I hired old Mr. Hellums to carry on my factory I am to give him $9 per month I expect him here on Monday I have not yet got a patent for my press I received a letter from Underwood a few weeks past that my papers are not yet properly prepared I wrote to him to send them all back and I will make another trial I believe I got my press to stand at last tho the last trial we broke one of the weels but that I do not regard my racks and pinions stood the wheels are easily strengthened I have a double rack and redused all my wheels to two feet I have only calculated this press for common bailing I do not believe I shall be able to make it strong enough for compressing that will injure the sale of it considerable Mcclanehas also gone on with his press and it is an exolent press he is able to compress with his, but genuary has threatent to bring soot against him and I have no doubt but he will as Mcclane makes use of his principle I consider mcclares press superior to genuarys I was informed a few days past that mcclane had sold Jackson county in the Mississipy for $5000 and there was two of genuarr's presses in the county this appears they are prefferable to jenuarys I have tested the principle of my improvemnt on the sawmill with a double flutterwheel on elys mill it has proven superior to my expectation ely thinks it gives the saw fully one third more power he says he would not have the improvement taken from his mill for $500 he cut thru a log 12 feet longand 20 inches deep in 2 minutes and 50 seconds by close attention he can cut 2500 feet per day, I tryed it first with a 30 inch wheel that is the lowerwheel with a 2 feet cogwheel but it did not do well I had some 4 feet wheelssurplis from my press I applyed one of them and a 5 feet waterwheel it then went right ahead the wheel cleared itself well, but the first wheel was so low it was wallowed in the water. This invention is a valuable one I shall have a model made immediately and prepare the drawings and specifycation and send for a patent old Mr. Hardy has been here several times he wishes to go onto Washington City and attend to my business. I expect to send him on and take him in as an agent and let him attend to the whole business (I shall reserve some few states) and give him one half he makes, I will let him have the sawmill and press and ventilator he thinks he can do an exolent business with the ventilator in the seaport towns to take the stagnated are out of the sellers to avoid sickness. Jacob Miller died a few weeks past I was at his house when he died the rest of the connection are all well flour at nashv is worht three dollars, our bridge was completed yesterday the men boarded at my house upwards of 2 months I calculate going down the river this spring and probable take a few set of press irons with me Delilah and myself remember our best wishes to you all write when convienant John Orndorff."

Notes for Mary:

Mary Thomas was a German girl. She grew up and had a similar background as her husband and when the family lived in MD they spoke only German in the family circle. Later after moving to VA they, as her son Aaron said "in an English settlement, where the family learned and ever after spoke the English language." Yet even after they had moved on to KY, Mary still sang the old German songs to her grandchildren gathered about her knee.Source:Book From Millwheel to Plowshare

Notes for Christopher:

Soldier/farmer buried in the Orendorff-Morgan cemetery NE of Adairville Ky. patriotic service for the state of MD during the revolution as I Lt. Christopher received a grant for 200 acres in 11-23-1807 in Logan County Kentucky along the Little Whipporwill watercourse this was south of the Green River. Christopher was the oldest son, and early assumed responsibilities which made him an efficient assistant to his father. Later, as a pioneer into southern Kentucky he was to follow similar methods in selling the products of his mills in Nashville, Tennessee. While still in his teens, Christopher had charge of the wagon trains in hauling flour and tobacco from the gristmill and plantation to Baltimore. He had inherited his father's business ability and also the genial, straightforward integrity, which made him successful in his early business contacts. His skillful management of the men who were in the long line of drivers is said to have been proverbial. Probably the oldest son. On October 3, 1789 Christopher bought "Negro Nell and her issue for sixty pounds current money". In his will probated in KY he only lists one slave and makes provisions for her freedom. On April 20, 1776 Christopher is mentioned as an officer of the Maryland militia being a 2nd lieutenant. He was experienced in handling men and efficient in organization. As the war continued and calls were made for large amounts of grain and supplies, he no doubt felt that his services were needed in helping supply the needy continental army. On Monday June 22, 1778 Christopher appears as a 1st lieutenant and serving in the Washington

Co militia. During this time he also ran his fathers mills, and the following are quotes from records: "Thursday September 20, 1781 ordered that the (western shore) treasurer pay to Capt. Christopher Orendorff fifteen pounds of the bills under the act for the emission of bills of credit and of the money appropriated for the present campaign for the stores account. Sept. 20, 1781 that the said treasurer pay to Capt. Christ. Orendorff six gallons of rum and twenty-four pounds of sugar." During the revolutionary war Christopher married a German girl named Mary Thomas who lived on an adjoining plantation. He purchased land near his father and assisted him in the selling of the large quantities of flour which the Antietam mills produced. In 1782-1783 Christopher built new mills near the Mt Pleasant homestead. When the last of these mills were razed in 1904 cornerstones were discovered which gave information concerning their construction. The first stone bears the date Sept. 2, 1782 and the initial sc. o. and m. o. another stone (this cornerstone as of 1930 was in the yard of Mt pleasant on the present Lohman farm. it rests on a stone ledge 30 feet from the front gate and 20 feet from the side of the house that is shown in the illustration in millwheel and plowshare book) was set up six feet distant with this data: "June 20, 1783. chr. Orendorff" and a verse in German. The Hagerstown globe thus refers to the Ondorff mill: "an old landmark torn down." The old stone and weather boarded gristmill, which for 122 years stood along the historic Antietam at the bridge between keedysville and Sharpsburg, was recently torn down. The old mill was built in 1782 by Christopher Orndorff. In the southwest gable, 20 feet above the ground was a large stone on which was carved the following: 1782, Sept. 2 C.O. M.O. this was supposed to mean Christopher Orndorff and Mary Orndorff. Six feet distant from the stone on a coating of plaster of paris set in a recess in the wall-two feet long, one foot wide and three inches deep was the following well preserved inscription German script: June 20, 1783. Chr. Orndorff. all ein auf gott sets deinvertrauen, wanen thust eine muhle bauen, auf euschen hilf, verlase dichnicht, sonst euschen hilf darf du nicht trauen. This is translated as follows: in god alone put your trust, when you do build a mill, do not rely on outside help, for on outside help you dare not trust. These mills traded mostly with the coast; probably a little of their flour went west to be used by wilderness men who could not grow any grain for themselves due to Indian trouble. Large amounts of flour left the mills almost every week east in long wagon trains going to the coast 80 miles away. The wagon trains were made up of large Conestoga wagons. On October 3, 1789 Christopher bought "Negro Nell and her issue for sixty pounds current money." In his will probated many years later in KY Christopher lists only one slave and makes provisions for her freedom. Thomas Hogg, a scotch neighbor, owned a plantation called Parkhall. Before his death in 1791 Hogg made Christopher his administrator. Numerous bequests were made to young people in the neighborhood, with the three oldest sons of Christopher receiving the rest of the estate. Hogg made specific provisions for the care of his old slaves and the freeing of the able bodied Negroes. Christopher and his father were closely associated in business at this time and lived near each other. Their households seem to have been given together under Christopher's name. Christian III owned land in VA at this time, but must have removed there later as he is not listed in the VA census for 1790. Christopher's children as well as those of his brothers were all under 16 at this time, so the males over 16-listed must have included the white artisans living on their plantations. Christopher had two younger brothers, Jacob and John, living at home at this time and two sisters, Barbara and Rose. The following information is from the 1790 census from Washington Co MD-Jonathan Hager-1 male, 4 free white females, no slaves. Christopher Orendorff-4 males over 16, 6 under 16, 4 females, 7 slaves. Christian Orendorff-2 free white males over 16, 1 under 16, 2 females, 4 slaves. Henry Orendorff-2 free white males over 16, 1 under 16, 3 females, 2 slaves. John Rohrer-2 free white males of 16 years or over, 1 male under 16, 2 free white females, 1 slave. Jacob rohrer-1 free white male, 5 white males under 16, 6 free white females. Jacob Rohrer-3 males over 16, 3 under 16, 4 females, 3 slaves. Thomas Sprigg-44 slaves. In 1791 he received a portion of his fathers plantation called Mt Pleasant-303 acres of smith's hills tract, and the eleven-acre tract adjoining. The deed was made on May 2 and specifies 500 pounds as the price that he paid. The land is described-"the first tract of land being parte of the resurvey on Smith's hills and beginning forsaid parte at bounded white oake it being the original beginning of Henry Orndorff's part of Smith's hills...to the beginning of Henry Orndorff's part of smith's hills as was surveyed to him by James Smith and with the outline of said deed north 46 degrees...west 36 perches and containing 303 acres. Second tract of land called Porto Sancto lying and adjoining Potomac river...to piles delight containing 11 acres of land except one hundred feet square of a burying ground on the west side of Antietam creek." The mills were on this land and so his father, in this transaction, turned over to him the business, which the two had carried on for many years together. On the same day Christopher sold his father a smaller plantation, the one he had bought from Reynolds a few years earlier. At the same time, Christopher was increasing his holdings from outside the family as well as from within; becoming it's most landed member. In June 1791, he secured a special warrant to resurvey vulton's grove, containing 100 acres, and added 72 acres and three quarters of an acre of vacant land. He paid the treasurer of the western shore thirteen pounds, twelve shillings and ten pence current money caution, also eleven pounds fifteen shillings 'for some improvements thereon. On august 20 Christopher bought Valtimo Grove, 100 acres, 410 pounds. In October he sold to Henry Botler the tract of land called Poplar Spring for 1500 pounds. This was a part of a tract of land called park hall "that I have a right by the last will and testament of Thomas Hogg deceased to sell...only two acres exempted and laid off to build a church and school house." in 1795 Christopher bought land from his brother Christian near Shepardstown with mills already in operation. A year later he sold his part of Mt Pleasant and the mills, which he and his father had made famous to Jacob Mumma. The following is from the land deed: "deed dated may 6, 1796 Christopher Orndorff to Jacob Mumma consideration 5500 pounds. All the following tracts of land, lying and being in the county and state aforesaid: part of the resurvey on Smith's hills. Part of the resurvey on hills, dales and the vineyard. Part of tract "sancto" lying on the east bank of the Antietam creek. No. I-containing 303 acres. No.

2-containing 10 1/4 acres. No. 3-lying and adjoining the Potomac River and containing 11 acres. To hold the three tracts of land and every part thereof no erected on the part of the resurvey on smiths hills to be forever excepted from the said Jacob Mumma, his heirs and assigns forever and free passage through said land to said two burying grounds whenever required and wanted." About 1800 Christopher moved with his brothers Christian III, and Henry across the state line into western VA, now West VA. They all sold out their interests in Maryland and bought plantations near Shepardtown VA keeping close to the Potomac River. He bought and sold various tracts of land near Shepardstown, including a farm from Nicholas Young, land from his brother in law, John Rohrer, and a 120-acre tract from the estate of one John Wilson. The same day on which he bought the Wilson tract, a Thomas Turner gave bond to assure Christopher the advantage of a mill race located on turner's land: "know all men by these presents that I Thomas Turner of Berkeley county & state of Virginia am held and firmly bound to Christopher Orndorff of the county and state afore said in the sum of 2000 pounds Virginia currency for the due payment of which to be made to said Christopher Orndorff his heirs or assigns I bind myself my heirs executors and administrators...witness my hand and seal the 25th of November, 1796. The condition of the above obligation is such that whereas the said Thomas Turner and Christopher Orndorff have this day purchased the lands lots of John Wilson deceased and-whereas upon a division of the said land a part of the said Christopher's tail race was included in the said Thomas turners part ofsaid land...his heirs, executors or administrators shall not molest or hinder the said Christopher Orndorff his heirs and assigns from occupying the said race for the intended purpose and also from making the necessary improvements on the said race. Provided that it is not extended any further into the said Thomas Turner in fencing across the said race or from leading the water out of said race on his own land so as he does not injure the said Orndorff's mill-then the above obligation to be void otherwise to remain in full force and virture...Thomas Turner." In 1803 Christopher transferred 81 acres of land to his son John who was 21 years old. He also paid taxes on 140 acres near

Shepardstown until 1805. In 1796 Christopher's residence was in Berkeley county VA but he did not live there for long. Not long after here turned to Maryland: "I the subscriber late of Jefferson county (Jefferson county was formed from Berkeley county in 1801) in the state of Virginia but now in Frederick county in the state of Maryland with a bonifida intention of settling there declare that I bought with me from the county of Jefferson and state of Virginia the following slave for my use, Peggy aged about thirty years who is a native of the united states. Witness my hand the 29th of march, 1802 Christopher Orndorff." Evidently his intention held at least a year, for the deed made out to the Presbyterian trustees in may of 1803 gives Frederick County as his residence. Yet soon a greater change was to be undertaken, the trek to Ky. He inherited the old German bible, of the Martin Luther translation published in Basel Switzerland in 1753 and he carried it into KY with him. He also had a large mirror that the 1st Christian brought over from Germany with him, this may have been the same mirror that Horatio Gates saw the lovely Mary admiring herself in, also packed away in a big chest were the silver knee buckles that Christopher had worn during the revolution. The migration to KY was made in covered wagons. The day of the month they left for KY was probably April 22, 1805. They followed the old trail down the Shenandoah Valley through Winchester, Staunton, and Salem. Crossing New River at Ingles ferry, they passed southwest through Pulaski, Wyethville, and Abingdon (Washington courthouse). There was ample game in this area at that time and the men no doubt did some hunting. His will is as follows: "In the name of God amen, I Christopher Orndorff, of Logan county and state of Kentucky, being very sick and weak in body but sound in mind and memory thanks be given to god and knowing that it is appointed unto all men to die do make this my last will and testament, that is to say principally and first of all I recommend my sole to god who gave it and my body to the earth to be buried in a decent Christian burial at the discretion of my friends. And touchingly my wordly estate witnesseth, it hath pleased god to help me in this life, I give, devise and dispose of it in the following manner and form. Item-I will and bequeth unto my beloved wife Mary Orndorff during her natural life, one third part of all my real estate also...my Negro Warner Aucky during her natural life, and after her death to my daughter Delilah Orndorff as long as she remains single but if she married Aucky is then free. item-I will and bequeth unto my sons John Orndorff and Aaron Orndorff, all the land that was laid off including mills, houses, and unticles to them their heirs and assigns forever. Item-whereas I have given my son Christian Orndorff the full amount of his legacy heretofore, I will that he shall enjoy the benefits resulting therefrom. Item-I will and bequeth to my son Esau Orndorff two hundred acres of land where he now lives to him and his heirs and assigns forever. Item-I will and bequeth unto my son Enoch Orndorff adjoining John and Aaron Orndorff's land, also my wagon, horses, gears and all unticels belonging to my farm and my clock to him and his heirs and assigns forever. Item-I will and bequeth unto my daughter Leah Morgan two hundred acres of land including a moity, I will hereafter name and including the place where William Morgan now lives and running with the Nashville road and adjoining john and Aaron Orndorff's land to her and her heirs and assigns forever. Item-I will and bequeth unto my daughter Delilah orndorff two hundred acres of land adjoining Leah Morgan including a moity of timber, I will hereafter name running with the Nashville road to chick's line. I hereby bequeth unto her a full legacy of household goods stock and &, as the rest of my daughters that are married, to her and her heirs and assigns forever. Item-I will and bequeth unto my daughter Elizabeth Miller all the balance of my barrorer on the East Side of the Nashville road to her heirs and assigns forever. Item-as there will be a balance of timber, I will and bequeth it to my three daughters jointly, Elizabeth, Leah, and Delilah Orndorff to be divided by my executors to them or their assigns forever. Item-all the before named lands are to be laid off by my executors hereinafter as they will think proper; and lastly I appoint my sons john and Aaron orndorff and William Morgan executors of this my last will and testament... in witness whereof I have hereunto set my hand and seal this 6th day of September in the year of our lord one thousand eight hundred and twenty three. Christopher Orndorff (seal)." The home plantation of Christopher Orndorff, containing the Orndorff-Morgan cemetery, was a large wedge of land extending down the Red River to the brick house of Capt. John. John's 1,300-acre plot, beginning there, connected with the 1,000-acre tract. At the request of Jacob Mumma the following power of attorney was recorded the 8th of January 1811: "state of Maryland Washington county. Know all men by these presents to whom it may concern that I Christopher Orndorff of the state of Kentucky do...appoint my trusty friend Jacob Mumma of Washington county my whole and sole attorney to act in my stead for all my part of a tract of land called vultons rest that lyes to the south of the great road leading from Sharpsburg to Fredericktown & to sell & dispose of the same and do...empowere the said Mumma to make a deed of conveyance of the afsd tract of Vultons Rest...the said Christopher Orendorff hath here unto set his hand and affixed his seal the tenth day of August eighteen hundred and ten. Christopher orndorff (seal)." On June 231794 Christopher sold 153 1/2 acres of a resurvey on vulton's rest to the great wagon road to Gabriel Thomas for 918 pounds. On may 3 1794 christopher sold five acres of vultons grove to peter Thomas together with houses, barns, buildings, and improvements for 35 pounds. In these land deeds Mary was taken aside to see that she agreed to the transactions.

CHAPTER NINE

GENERATION NO. 9

102. JAMES HAMPTON[9] ORENDORFF (68.JOHN[8], 59.PHILIP[7], 50.PHILIP[6], 26.THEISS[5], 9.LUDWIG[4], 3.HUBERT[3], 2.HENNE[2], 1.SIMON[1]) was born 29 December 1822 in FREDERICK CO VIRGINIA. JAMES died in CHERRY GROVE FREDERICK, CO VA. He married **NANCY ANN BAKER**.

They had 5 children:

177.	f	i.	**FLORENCE E. ORENDORFF**, born 2 December 1875 in PINE HILLS FREDERICK, CO VA. HAD 4 CHILDREN FLORENCE E. MARRIED WM. A. GRANDELL.
178.	f	ii.	**HARRIET V. ORENDORFF**, born 12 January 1871 in FREDERICK CO VA. HARRIET V. MARRIED JOHN WILLIS.
179.	f	iii.	**EDITH ORENDORFF**, born 2 December 1875 in PINE HILLS FREDERICK, CO VA. Had one daughter. Edith's name is listed as "Orndorff" in the record, she married a man named S. Jackson Miller. Edith was a twin.
180.	f	iv.	**MARY REBECCA ORENDORFF**, born in WARREN VIRGINIA. Had a daughter named Mary Rebecca. Married Chas Henry Rinker, her name is listed as "Orndorff" in the record.
181.	m	v.	**JOSEPH D. ORENDORFF**, born 7 September 1886 in CHERRY GROVE VIRGINIA.

Notes for James:

Farmer, James Hampton was christened at St James Lutheran church in Frederick Co VA on 12-29-1822.

- - - - - - - - - - -

107. JOHN ALFRED[9] **ORENDORFF** (68.JOHN[8], 59.PHILIP[7], 50.PHILIP[6], 26.THEISS[5], 9.LUDWIG[4], 3.HUBERT[3], 2.HENNE[2], I.SIMON[1]) was born 1843 in FREDERICK CO VA. JOHN died 20 December 1922 in STEPHENS CITY, FREDERICK CO VA, at the age of 80. He married **REBECCA SUSANNAH BRINDLE** 13 January 1870 in STEPHANS CITY, FREDERICK CO, VA. She was born 1 August 1852 in STEPHENS CITY, FREDERICK CO, VA. REBECCA died in STEPHENS CITY, FREDERICK CO, VA.

They had 3 children:

182. m i. **JOHN DANIEL ORENDORFF**, born 1 June 1871 in STEPHANS CITY, FREDERICK CO, VA. He married LINA GSCHWENDTNER 20 September 1906 in ST MARY'S, PONTIAC, ILL.

JOHN died 22 November 1946 in PONTIAC, LIVINGSTON, ILL, at the age of 75. Notes for JOHN:

John Daniel's name appears as "Orndorff", he was buried at St. Mary's Catholic Cemetery, Pontiac, Ill.

183. m ii. **JESSIE B. ORENDORFF**, born 2 August 1875 in STEPHANS CITY, FREDERICK CO, VA. Died in STEPHANS CITY, FREDERICK CO, VA.

Jessie B.'s name appears as "Orndorff", he was buried in Salem Brethren Cemetery Frederick VA.

184. f iii. **MARY ELIZABETH ORENDORFF**, born 8 January 1880 in STEPHANS

CITY, FREDERICK CO VA, died 1960 in STEPHANS CITY, FREDERICK CO VA, at the age of 79.

Mary Elizabeth's name appears as "Orndorff", she was buried in Salem Brethren Cemetery, Stephans City VA. She married William J. Cline.

Notes for Rebecca:

Church affiliation: Dunkard. Rebecca Susannah was buried at Salem Brethren Cemetery in Stephans City VA. Her parents were Daniel Brindle and Mary M. Wise.

Notes for John:

Farmer, John Alfred's name was listed as "Orndorff" in the record, he was buried in the Salem Brethren Cemetery in Stephens City VA. His church affiliation was Dunkard.

- - - - - - - - - - -

108. LEWIS[9] **ORENDORFF** (68.JOHN[8], 59.PHILIP[7], 50.PHILIP[6], 26.THEISS[5], 9.LUDWIG[4], 3.HUBERT[3], 2.HENNE[2], 1.SIMON[1]) was born 18 March 1822. LEWIS died 16 June 1905, at the age of 83. He married **LEVINA RUDOLPH**. She was born 18 July 1823. LEVINA died 22 August 1916, at the age of 93.

They had 2 children:

+ 185.   m   i.   **EMMANUEL LUTHER ORENDORFF**, born 1863, died 1943.

+ 186.   m   ii.   **JOHN RANDOLPH ORENDORFF**, born 1855, died 25 February 1938.

Notes for Levina:

Maybe spelled Lavina. Levina's father was John R. Rudolph 1794-1854, her mother was Mary (Polly) Secrest born 1800. She was granddaughter of George Rudolph JR born 1764 and Mary Hotsinpillar 1770-1868, also Frederick Secrest and Catherine.

Notes for Lewis:
Lewis'name appears as "Orndorff".

- - - - - - - - - - -

110. HAMILTON[9] **ORENDORFF** (68.JOHN[8], 59.PHILIP[7], 50.PHILIP[6], 26.THEISS[5], 9.LUDWIG[4], 3.HUBERT[3], 2.HENNE[2], 1.SIMON[1]) was born 1833 probably in VA. His spouse has not been identified.

They had 3 children:

187.	m	i.	**ALAN ORENDORFF**, born in POSS. VA AFTER 1850. ALAN'S NAME APPEARS AS "ORNDORFF".
188.	f	ii.	**MYRTLE ORENDORFF**, born in POSS. VA AFTER 1857. MYRTLE'S NAME APPEARS AS "ORNDORFF".
189.	f	iii.	**FLORENCE ORENDORFF**, born in POSS. VA. FLORENCE'S NAME APPEARS AS "ORNDORFF".

Notes for Hamilton:
Hamilton's name appears as "Orndorff".

- - - - - - - - - - -

111. ANDREW ADDISON[9] **ORENDORFF** (70.JACOB[8], 59.PHILIP[7], 50.PHILIP[6], 26.THEISS[5], 9.LUDWIG[4], 3.HUBERT[3], 2.HENNE[2], 1.SIMON[1]) was born 1817. ANDREW died 1894, at the age of 77. He married **RACHEL ANN CRETSINGER** 26 November 1846 in FREDERICK CO VA. She was born 1823. RACHEL died 16 March 1909 in OR NEAR HAMPSHIRE, CO W. VA, at the age of 86.

They had 7 children:

+ 190. f   i.   **HARRIET ELLEN ORENDORFF**, born

March 1868, died 22 March 1932.

191.   f   ii.   **MARGARET J. ORENDORFF**, born 5 December 1847, died 4 March 1937, at the age of 89.

Margaret J.'s name appears as "Orndorff'", she married Adam Bollinger born 1832 died 06-03-1884. their children were 1) Edward Bollinger who married Elsi, 2) Olive (Olie) Bollinger, 3) Rachel Bollinger married to Mr. Shumaker, 4) Andrew Bollinger, 5) Lee Bollinger.

192.   f   iii.   **MARTHA VIRGINIA ORENDORFF**, born 24 November 1848 in ZEPP, SHENANDOAH CO VA, died 25 March 1923, at the age of 74.

Martha Virginia's name appears as "Orndorff", she married John Asbury (Henry Murchison Asbury 12-02-1850 died 02-11-1915). They had one child, Henry Asbury who married Emily Middleton Bradshaw.

+ 193.   m   iv.   **ASHBY MARION ORENDORFF**, born 1864.

+ 194.   m   v.   **ADAM DECALB ORENDORFF**, born 9 December 1866.

195. f   vi.   **LYDIA FRANCIS (FANNY) ORENDORFF**, born 28 July 1852 probably in VA, died 30 December 1936, at the age of 84.

Lydia Francis's name appears as "Orndorff", she married William Nathan Peer b. 02-13-1847 d. 03-18-1915. Their first child was Fitzhugh Cleveland Peer born 10-08-1886 died 06-27-1963 who married Eula Eather Brill born 01-12-1886 died 10-29-1952. Their children were: a) Fitzhugh Cleveland Peer JR b. 04-08-1915 died 01-22-1926, b) Vincent Peer, Thurston Peer who married Joyce Racey who had Randy Peer and Wayne Peer who married Joyce Racey, c) Barbara Peer who married a Mr. Fredericks who had David Fredricks, Susan Fredricks, Royce (rl) Fredricks, and Debra Fredricks, e) Alexander (Dave) Peer b. 10-23-1919 d. 02-27-1981, f) Nancy Peer, g) James Peer 02-19-1925 d. 11-03-1980 who married Kitty Miller who had Lana Peer married to a Mr. Himmelright, Connie Peer married to a Mr. Rudolph, and Tranda (Tandy) Peer married to a Mr. Pepperman. second child of William Nathan Peer and Lydia Francis Orndorff: Viola Peer b. 1877, 3)Huie E. Peer 10-28-1888 d. 05-11-1975 who married Anna Jane Lundsford. 10-08-1900 d. 04-16-1962 who had Anne Peer b. 07-28-1932 married to Stewart Keller, 4)Quie Eli Peer b. 10-28-1888 (twins?) died 12-20-1963, 5)Malon Peer b. 07-27-1882 d. 03-14-1898, 6)Ola Peer married to Will Orndorff, and 7)Helen Peer married to a Mr. Strosnider.

+ 196.   m   vii.   **WALTER N. ORENDORFF**, born 1872.

Notes for Rachel:

Maybe born 1826 Rachel Ann's parents were Joe and Dorothy Cretsinger. Her last name may have been spelled Cretzinger. She is buried in or near Hampshire Co W. Va.

Notes for Andrew:

Maybe born 1816.

- - - - - - - - - - -

112. JACOB J. JR [9] **ORENDORFF** (70.JACOB[8], 59.PHILIP[7], 50.PHILIP[6], 26.THEISS[5], 9.LUDWIG[4], 3.HUBERT[3], 2.HENNE[2], 1.SIMON[1]) was born 24 December 1831 probably in VA. JACOB died 3 March 1919 probably in VA, at the age of 87. He married **RACHEL REGINA WILLIAMS** 13 September 1844 probably in VA. She was born 15 June 1836. She probably died in VA.

They had 7 children:

+ 197.   m   i.   **PHILIP P. ORENDORFF**, born 1856, died 11 November 1926.

+ 198.   m   ii.   **EARLY LEE ORENDORFF**, born 1867.

199.   f   iii.   **LAURA B. ORENDORFF**, born 1860 in POSSIBLY 1853/VA.
Laura B.'s name appears as "Orndorff", she married Moses E. Himmelright born in 1859.

200.   f   iv.   **CATHERINE ORENDORFF**, born 1858 in CIRCA B. DATE/PROBABLY, VA.
MARRIED SILAS LITTLE. CATHERINE'S NAME APPEARS AS "ORNDORFF".

+ 201.   m   v.   **JOSEPH WILLIAM ORENDORFF**, born 1862, died 1908.

202.   m   vi.   **LUCAS J. ORENDORFF**, born 1878 in PROBABLY VA.
LUCAS J.'S NAME APPEARS AS "ORNDORFF", HE WAS UNMARRIED.

203. f   vii.   **CHARLOTTE (LOTTIE) ORENDORFF**, born 19 September 1870 in POSS. VA.
CHARLOTTE'S NAME APPEARS AS "ORNDORFF", SHE MARRIED SAMUEL P. BAUSERMAN.

- - - - - - - - - - -

114.   MARY   ELIZA[9]   ORENDORFF   (70.JACOB[8], 59.PHILIP[7], 50.PHILIP[6], 26.THEISS[5], 9.LUDWIG[4], 3.HUBERT[3], 2.HENNE[2], 1.SIMON[1]) was born 8 January 1832 in PROBABLY VA/GUESS ON, 1832. MARY died 30 September 1905, at the age of 73. She married **PURNELL B. BRILL** 6 November 1850 probably in VA. He was born 1 December 1826. PURNELL died 8 June 1888, at the age of 61.

They had 2 children:

+ 204. f i. **CEATTA BRILL**, died April 1913.
+ 205. f ii. **OCTAVIA BRILL**, born 6 February 1854, died 19 October 1930.

Notes for Purnell:

Purnell B.'s daughter apparently married a cousin of her mothers.

Notes for Mary:

Mary Eliza's name appears as "Orndorff". 2 of her daughters apparently married cousins of their mothers as well as 1 of her sons. Mary Eliza's other children were: Adolph Brill, Kalen Brill, and Emily Brill who married a Mr. Stine.

- - - - - - - - - - -

116. HEZEKIAH[9] **ORENDORFF** (71.PHILIP[8], 59.PHILIP[7], 50.PHILIP[6], 26.THEISS[5], 9.LUDWIG[4], 3.HUBERT[3], 2.HENNE[2], 1.SIMON[1]) was born 27 October 1845 in POSS. VA. HEZEKIAH died in WEST VA. He married **AMANDA KACKLEY**. She was born 12 January 1851 in POSS. VA. AMANDA probably died in WEST VA.

They had 2 children:

206. m i. **SYDNOR M. ORENDORFF**, born 13 May 1872 probably in WEST VA, probably died in WEST VA.

      SYDNOR M. IS BURIED WITH HIS FAMILY IN WEST VA, HIS NAME APPEARS AS "ORNDORFF". Source- Tombstone inscription.

+ 207. m ii. **BARZELLA B. ORENDORFF**, born 3 September 1884.

Notes for Amanda:

Buried in West VA with family.

Notes for Hezekiah:
Hezikiah is buried in West VA, his name appears as "Orndorff".

- - - - - - - - - - -

117. PERRY W.[9] **ORENDORFF** (71.PHILIP[8], 59.PHILIP[7], 50.PHILIP[6], 26.THEISS[5], 9.LUDWIG[4], 3.HUBERT[3], 2.HENNE[2], 1.SIMON[1]) was born 24 February 1841. He married **MARY A. RUDOLPH**. She was born 1848.

They had 5 children:

208.	f	i.	**PHASIE ORENDORFF.**
			PHASIE'S NAME APPEARS AS "ORNDORFF".
209.	m	ii.	**HILEY S. ORENDORFF**, born 1882.
			HILEY'S NAME APPEARS AS "ORNDORFF".
210.	m	iii.	**GUS ORENDORFF.**
			GUS' NAME APPEARS AS "ORNDORFF".
211.	m	iv.	**HARRY EDWARD ORENDORFF**, born 1887. He married MARY CATHERINE RUDOLPH.
			HARRY died in circa 1965.
212.	f	v.	**ELSIE M. ORENDORFF**, born 1890.
			ELSIE M.'S NAME APPEARS AS "ORNDORFF", SHE MARRIED A MR. BOLINGER.

Notes for Perry:
1st wife Elizabeth C. Racey. Perry W.'s name appears as "Orndorff", he was married twice.

- - - - - - - - - - -

120. LEMUEL[9] **ORENDORFF** (72.SAMUEL[8], 59.PHILIP[7], 50.PHILIP[6], 26.THEISS[5], 9.LUDWIG[4], 3.HUBERT[3], 2.HENNE[2], 1.SIMON[1]) was born 1833. LEMUEL died 1914, at the age of 81. He married **MARY FRANCES VIRTS (BERTS)**. She was born 1840. MARY died 1918, at the age of 78.

They had 4 children:

+ 213.   f   i.   **MINERVA ORENDORFF**, born November 1868.

214.   f   ii.   **VERNA (VERNIER) ORENDORFF**, born 1875.

215.   m   iii.   **CLARENCE ORENDORFF**, born 12 February 1880. He married VESTA M. SHAFFER. VESTA died 5 January 1960. CLARENCE died 24 July 1961, at the age of 81. Notes for CLARENCE: CLARENCE'S NAME APPEARS AS "ORNDORFF".

216.   m   iv.   **RILEY M. ORENDORFF**, born 1882 in MARRIED LUCY. RILEY M.'S NAME APPEARS AS "ORNDORFF".

Notes for Lemuel:
Lemuel's name was listed as "Orndorff".

- - - - - - - - - - -

121. MEGUS (SIMON)[9] ORENDORFF (72.SAMUEL[8], 59.PHILIP[7], 50.PHILIP[6], 26.THEISS[5], 9.LUDWIG[4], 3.HUBERT[3], 2.HENNE[2], I.SIMON[1]) was born 25 April 1834 in POSS. VA. MEGUS died 26 July 1908 in PROB. W. VA., at the age of 74. He married **CATHERINE DELANO WYMER**. She was born 1844.

They had 3 children:

+ 217.   m   i.   **RHESA ALLEN ORENDORFF**, born 8 April 1866.

+ 218.   m   ii.   **REUBEN LOSTON ORENDORFF**, born 1869.

219.   m   iii.   **BRITT ORENDORFF**, born 1875. He married CATHERINE SWAYNE. She was born 24 May 1852. Notes for BRITT: BRITT'S NAME APPEARS AS "ORNDORFF".

Notes for Megus:

Megus's last name appears as "Orndorff". Megas is buried in or near Hampshire Co W. VA, his name also appears as Magus.

- - - - - - - - - - -

122. LEWIS[9] **ORENDORFF** (72.SAMUEL[8], 59.PHILIP[7], 50.PHILIP[6], 26.THEISS[5], 9.LUDWIG[4], 3.HUBERT[3], 2.HENNE[2], 1.SIMON[1]) was born 5 April 1847 probably in VA. LEWIS died 17 August 1893 in or near HAMPSHIRE CO W. VA, at the age of 46. He married **MARTHA MAHALA ORENDORFF (See number 227)** 15 October 1874 in POSS. VA. She was born 1855. She was the daughter of BENJAMIN ORENDORFF and MARIA EVANS.

They had 4 children:

+ 220.   m   i.   **SIDNEY CLINTON ORENDORFF**, born December 1876, died May 1964.

+ 221.   m   ii.   **LUTHER S. ORENDORFF**, born 5 September 1880.

+ 222.   m   iii.   **HUGH CALVIN ORENDORFF**, born 12 August 1888, died 13 August 1961.

223.   m   iv.   **EDWARD L. ORENDORFF**, born 12 April 1884.

         EDWARD L.'S NAME APPEARS AS "ORNDORFF". HE MARRIED A WOMAN NAMED CLARA A. BORN JUNE 1889 AND DIED 11-08-1960.

Notes for Martha:

Martha Mahala's name appears as "Orndorff", she apparently married a cousin.

Notes for Lewis:

Lewis's name appears as "Orndorff", he apparently married a cousin. He is buried in or near Hampshire Co W. VA.

- - - - - - - - - - -

124.   GEORGE   WASHINGTON[9]   **ORENDORFF** (72.SAMUEL[8],   59.PHILIP[7],   50.PHILIP[6],   26.THEISS[5], 9.LUDWIG[4], 3.HUBERT[3], 2.HENNE[2], 1.SIMON[1]) was born 15 October 1838 in POSS. VA. GEORGE died 27 September 1918 in OR NEAR HAMPSHIRE, CO W. VA, at the age of 79. He married **REBECCA ELLEN ORENDORFF (See number 232)** 20 June 1872 in PROBABLY VA. She was born 18 December 1852 in PROBABLY VA. She was the daughter of BENJAMIN ORENDORFF and MARIA EVANS. REBECCA died 25 December 1908 in POSS. VA, at the age of 56.

They had 3 children:

224.   m   i.   **BUSH W. ORENDORFF**, born 17 October 1886 in PROBABLY VA. He married MYRTLE A. HERBAUGH 29 August 1889 in PROBABLY VA. She was born 29 August 1889 in POSS. W. VA. MYRTLE died in or near HAMPSHIRE CO W. VA. Notes for MYRTLE:
BURIED W/HUSBAND IN W. VA HAMPSHIRE CO
BUSH died 17 February 1956 in NEAR HAMPSHIRE CO W., VA, at the age of 69. Notes for BUSH:
Married twice Bush W.'s name appears as "Orndorff", he married secondly Nora Stewart date unknown. He is buried in or near Hampshire Co W. VA.

225.   m   ii.   **ARTHUR ORENDORFF**, born in POSS. VA.

226.   f   iii.   **FRANCES ORENDORFF**, born 15 June 1880 in PROBABLY W. VA, died in OR NEAR HAMPSHIRE, CO W. VA.
Frances is buried in or near Hampshire Co W. VA with her parents, her name appears as "Orndorff".

Notes for REBECCA:
Rebecca E.'s name appears as "Orndorff".

Notes for GEORGE:
George Washington is buried in or near Hampshire Co West VA his name appears as "Orndorff", he is buried with family. Poss. died 08-27-1918.

- - - - - - - - - - -

128. BENJAMIN[9] **ORENDORFF** (73.LEWIS[8], 59.PHILIP[7], 50.PHILIP[6], 26.THEISS[5], 9.LUDWIG[4], 3.HUBERT[3], 2.HENNE[2], I.SIMON[1]) was born 1826. He married **MARIA EVANS**. She was born 1832.

They had 6 children:

+ 227. f i. **MARTHA MAHALA ORENDORFF**, born 1855.

228. f ii. **ISABELLE ORENDORFF**.
ISABELLE'S NAME APPEARS AS "ORNDORFF".

229. f iii. **CORDELIA (ELLA LEE) ORENDORFF**, born 1867.
CORDELIA'S NAME APPEARS AS "ORNDORFF".

+ 230. m iv. **CHARLES MONROE ORENDORFF**, born 28 December 1856, died 23 January 1927.

231. f v. **MARGARET LANE ORENDORFF**, born 1860 in PROBABLY VA.
MARGARET LANE'S NAME APPEARS AS "ORNDORFF".

+ 232. f vi. **REBECCA ELLEN ORENDORFF**, born 18 December 1852, died 25 December 1908.

Notes for Benjamin:
Benjamin's name appears as "Orndorff".

- - - - - - - - - - -

129. JAMES HARRISON[9] **ORENDORFF** (73.LEWIS[8], 59.PHILIP[7], 50.PHILIP[6], 26.THEISS[5], 9.LUDWIG[4], 3.HUBERT[3], 2.HENNE[2], I.SIMON[1]) was born 6 February 1830 probably in VA. JAMES died 29 January 1917, at the age of 86. He married **ISABELLA SIBERT** 10 August 1854 probably in VA. She was born 1834.

They had 5 children:

233.　　f　i.　　**LARA V. ORENDORFF**, born 1859 in PROBABLY VA.
LARA V.'S NAME APPEARS AS "ORNDORFF", SHE MARRIED A MR. STROMSTER.

234.　　f　ii.　　**Lula (LEULAH) ORENDORFF**, born 1863 in PROBABLY VA.
POSS. 06-24-1855 TO 06-12-1922 LULA'S NAME APPEARS AS "ORNDORFF", SHE MARRIED A MR. PERRY J. BRILL BORN 11-18-1848 DIED 05-09-1927. THEY HAD THE FOLLOWING CHILDREN-CARRIE NOMA BRILL. 05-04-1886 DIED 02-19-1887. ADA BELLE BRILL B. 05-28-1892 D.02-26-1893. HARRY O. BRILL B. 10-28-1876 D. 01-14-1898. GORDON P. BRILL B. 04-20-1910 D.12-06-1911.

235.　　f　iii.　　**LOLA B. ORENDORFF**, born 1863 in PROBABLY VA.
LOLA B.'S NAME APPEARS AS "ORNDORFF", SHE MARRIED A MR. URIAH BRILL.

236.　　m　iv.　　**RALPH A. ORENDORFF**, born 17 October 1860 probably in VA, died in POSS. VA.
RALPH A.'S NAME APPEARS AS "ORNDORFF".

237.　　m　v.　　**MOSES ORENDORFF**, born 27 August 1855.
MOSES' NAME APPEARS AS "ORNDORFF".

Notes for James:
James Harrison's name is spelled "Orndorff".

- - - - - - - - - - -

132. HARRISON[9] **ORENDORFF** (76.PHILIP[8], 60.JOHN[7], 50.PHILIP[6], 26.THEISS[5], 9.LUDWIG[4], 3.HUBERT[3], 2.HENNE[2], I.SIMON[1]) was born 31 May 1815 in SHENANDOAH CO VIRGINIA. HARRISON died 23 November 1890 in MISSOURI, HALFROCK MERCER CO, at the age of 75. He married **HANNAH HARBOUGH** 9 June 1834 in SHENANDOAH CO VIRGINIA. She was born 8 November 1818 in SHENANDOAH CO VA. HANNAH died 25 December 1877 in HALFROCK, MERCER CO, MO, at the age of 59.

They had 12 children:

+ 238.   m   i.   **WILLIAM ALLEN ORENDORFF**, born 28 May 1840, died 5 September 1914.

+ 239.   m   ii.   **LORENZO DOW ORENDORFF**, born 2 April 1839, died 1 March 1923.

240. f   iii.   **MARY MAHALA ORENDORFF**, born 14 October 1834 in SHENANDOAH CO VA.
MARRIED JOHN H. WILLIAMS

241.   m   iv.   **HENRY HAMPTON ORENDORFF**, born 27 September 1845 in OHIO.
DIED DURING CIVIL WAR. HENRY HAMPTON WAS POSS. A CONFEDERATE SOLDIER, HIS NAME APPEARS AS "ORNDORFF".

242.   f   v.   **HARRIET J. ORENDORFF**, born 12 March 1849 in OHIO, died 1941, at the age of 91.
MARRIED TO JOHN MCCLOUD HARRIET J.'S NAME APPEARS AS "ORNDORFF". MOTHER COULD BE HANNAH GARRET.

243.   f   vi.   **IDA KATE ORENDORFF**, born 20 May

1856 in STEADY RUN, KEOKUK CO IA, died 7 May 1926, at the age of 70.

MARRIED DANIEL EGO. IDA KATE WAS CALLED "SELA", HER NAME APPEARS AS "ORNDORFF".

244.   f   vii. **IONA ORENDORFF**, born 6 July 1859 in KEOKUK CO IA.

MARRIED JAMES BARKER BARNES. IONA'S NAME APPEARS AS "ORNDORFF".

+ 245.   m   viii. **DANIEL M. ORENDORFF**, born 16 May 1854.

246. f   ix. **MAHALA ORENDORFF**, born 1835 in POSS. VA.

MAHALA'S NAME APPEARS AS "ORNDORFF".

247. f   x. **JENORETT ORENDORFF**, born 1847 in POSS. VA.

JENORETT'S NAME APPEARS AS "ORNDORFF".

248. m   xi. **HAMPTON ORENDORFF**, born 1845 in POSS. VA.

HAMPTON'S NAME APPEARS AS "ORNDORFF".

249. f   xii. **ELLEN JENNETTE ORENDORFF**, born 16 March 1847 in OHIO.

ELLEN JENNETTE WAS MARRIED TO JAMES CLIPPER, HER NAME APPEARS AS "ORNDORFF".

Notes for Hannah:

Hannah Harbough's father was Isaac Harbough born in the 1700's. Isaac's father was Peter Harbough also born in the 1700's. Peter and his family resided in Shenandoah Co VA in 1810 as did Isaac and his family. She had a brother named Jacob married 03-21-1827 in Shenandoah Co VA to Rachel Strosnider, Lawrence married 03-21-1825 to Ruth Conneg, a sister named Susannah, a sister named Catherine who married 11-05-1832 in Shenandoah Co VA to Henry Lutz.

Notes for Harrison:
2nd wife Kitty Susan. Lewis Harrison is listed in an Iowa genealogical surname index as Harrison/Holder Orndorff and as being married to Hannah Herbrough. Married to Hannah Garret 03-15-1841 born 1818 circa, was she a third wife?. Harrison was possibly born in 03-31-1815.

- - - - - - - - - -

135. HAMPTON[9] **ORENDORFF** (76.PHILIP[8], 60.JOHN[7], 50.PHILIP[6], 26.THEISS[5], 9.LUDWIG[4], 3.HUBERT[3], 2.HENNE[2], 1.SIMON[1]) was born 15 October 1818 in PROBABLY VA. HAMPTON died 7 May 1886, at the age of 67. He married **LYDIA O'HAVER** 16 April 1853 probably in VA. She was born 1828.

They had 4 children:

250.	m	i.	**WALLACE ORENDORFF**, born 1858 in POSS. IN.
			WALLACE'S NAME APPEARS AS "ORNDORFF".
251.	f	ii.	**KATIE W. ORENDORFF**, born 1870.
			KATIE W.'S NAME APPEARS AS "ORNDORFF".
252.	m	iii.	**LEANDER ORENDORFF**, born 1853.
			LEANDER'S NAME APPEARS AS "ORNDORFF".
253.	f	iv.	**HARRIET JANE ORENDORFF**, born 1849 in POSS. VA.
			HARRIET JANE'S Name appears as "Orndorff". Her mother was Hampton's first wife Catherrine, apparently the only child by that marriage.

Notes for Hampton:
First wife was named Catherine. Hampton's name appears as "Orndorff", he was married twice. He either lived in Knox Co at some point, died there, or his wife was from there.

- - - - - - - - - - -

138. WESTFALL[9] **ORENDORFF** (78.LEVI[8], 60.JOHN[7], 50.PHILIP[6], 26.THEISS[5], 9.LUDWIG[4], 3.HUBERT[3], 2.HENNE[2], 1.SIMON[1]) was born 1828. His spouse has not been identified.
They had 1 child:

254.   f   i.   **REBECCA ORENDORFF**, born 1851.
REBECCA'S NAME APPEARS AS "ORNDORFF". HER MOTHER WAS NAMED ELENOR J. BORN 1829.

Notes for Westfall:
Westfall's name appears as "Orndorff". He married a woman named Elenor J. born 1829.

- - - - - - - - - - -

141. AMOS[9] **ORENDORFF** (78.LEVI[8], 60.JOHN[7], 50.PHILIP[6], 26.THEISS[5], 9.LUDWIG[4], 3.HUBERT[3], 2.HENNE[2], 1.SIMON[1]) was born 1847. His spouse has not been identified.
They had 5 children:

255.   f   i.   **DAISY H. ORENDORFF**, born 1880 in CIRCA, POSS. VA.
DAISY H.'S NAME APPEARS AS "ORNDORFF". HER MOTHER WAS NAMED MARGARET E.

256.   f   ii.   **BESSIE V. ORENDORFF**, born 1871 in POSS. VA, CIRCA.
BESSIE V.'S NAME APPEARS AS "ORNDORFF". HER MOTHERS WAS MARGARET E.

257.   f   iii.   **ADA B. ORENDORFF**, born 1869 in CIRCA, POSS. VA.

ADA B.'S NAME APPEARS AS "ORNDORFF". HER MOTHER WAS A MARGARET E.

258.   m   iv.   **ISSAC M. ORENDORFF**, born 1868 in CIRCA, POSS. VA.
ISSAC M.'S NAME APPEARS AS "ORNDORFF".

259.   f   v.   **SARAH L. ORENDORFF**, born 1872 in CIRCA, POSS. VA.
SARAH L.'S NAME APPEARS AS "ORNDORFF".

Notes for Amos:

12th child born Amos' name appears as "Orndorff", he married a Margaret E. born 1842 or 1844.

- - - - - - - - - - -

143. PHILIP SETZER[9] ORENDORFF (78.LEVI[8], 60.JOHN[7], 50.PHILIP[6], 26.THEISS[5], 9.LUDWIG[4], 3.HUBERT[3], 2.HENNE[2], I.SIMON[1]) was born 16 February 1833 in PROB. W. VA, POSS. 1838. PHILIP died probably in WEST VA. He married **MARY J. TEVALT.** She was born 18 November 1833 in WEST VA, POSS. 1835. MARY died in WEST VA, POSS. 04-05-1923.

They had 9 children:

+ 260.   m   i.   **LUTHER EDGAR ORENDORFF**, born 17 August 1860.

261.   f   ii.   **MINERVA ORENDORFF**, born 1864.
POSSIBLY BORN 1865 MINERVA'S NAME APPEARS AS "ORNDORFF".

262.   m   iii.   **ADAM ORENDORFF**, born 1869.
8TH CHILD BORN ADAM'S NAME APPEARS AS "ORNDORFF".

263.   m   iv.   **THOMAS JACKSON ORENDORFF**, born 1862 in VA/POSSIBLY 1863. He married JENNIE CLINE. Notes for THOMAS:

THOMAS JACKSON'S NAME APPEARS AS "ORNDORFF".

+ 264. m v. **BRUCE MORGAN ORENDORFF**, born 1870.

265. m vi. **GEORGE F. ORENDORFF**, born 23 October 1857 in CAPON SPRINGS, HAMPSHIRE CO VA, died in PROBABLY WEST VA.
GEORGE F. IS BURIED WITH HIS PARENTS IN WEST VA, HIS NAME APPEARS AS "ORNDORFF".

266. m vii. **ARTHUR S. ORENDORFF**, born 1877 in POSS. VA.
ARTHUR S.' NAME APPEARS AS "ORNDORFF".

267. m viii. **HARVEY M. ORENDORFF**, born 1879 in POSS. VA.
HARVEY M.'S NAME APPEARS AS "ORNDORFF".

268. f ix. **IDA ORENDORFF**, born 1865 in POSS. VA/ SOMETIME IN, 1860'S.
IDA MARRIED WILL MILLER, HER NAME APPEARS AS "ORNDORFF".

Notes for Mary:
Buried in West VA with family.

Notes for Philip:
Prob. 5th child born, Doctor Philip Setzer's name appears as "Orndorff". Appears in the 1850 census for Frederick Co VA.

- - - - - - - - - - -

145. PHINEAS[9] **ORENDORFF** (78.LEVI[8], 60.JOHN[7], 50.PHILIP[6], 26.THEISS[5], 9.LUDWIG[4], 3.HUBERT[3], 2.HENNE[2], I.SIMON[1]) was born 1834 in VA or CLARK CO IL. His spouse has not been identified.

They had 5 children:

269. f i. **SARAH P. ORENDORFF**, born 1865 in POSS. IL.
SARAH P.'S NAME APPEARS AS "ORNDORFF".

270. m ii. **WILLIAM F. ORENDORFF**, born 1868 in POSS. IL.
WILLIAM F.'S NAME APPEARS AS "ORNDORFF".

271. m iii. **EDWARD L. ORENDORFF**, born 1872 in POSS. IL.
EDWARD L.'S NAME APPEARS AS "ORNDORFF".

272. m iv. **CLARENCE B. ORENDORFF**, born 1877 in POSS. IL.
CLARENCE B.'S NAME APPEARS AS "ORNDORFF".

273. f v. **MINNIE E. ORENDORFF**, born 1880 in POSS. IL.
MINNIE E.'S NAME APPEARS AS "ORNDORFF".

Notes for Phineas:

Married to Mary J. Phineas's name appears as "Orndorff". The last name of his wife is unknown. Appears in the 1850 census for 1850 Frederick Co VA.

- - - - - - - - - - -

149. MAHALA[9] ORENDORFF (85.DAVID[8], 60.JOHN[7], 50.PHILIP[6], 26.THEISS[5], 9.LUDWIG[4], 3.HUBERT[3], 2.HENNE[2], 1.SIMON[1]) was born 1810. MAHALA died 1848, at the age of 38. She married **JAMES WADE ORENDORFF** 26 January 1830 in PROB. VA. He was born 23 April 1807. He was the son of WILLIAM ORENDORFF and ELIZABETH COOPER. JAMES died 17 September 1888 in OR NEAR HAMPSHIRE, CO W. VA, at the age of 81.

They had 6 children:

274.   m   i.   **WILLIAM HARRISON ORENDORFF**, born 1838.
NEVER MARRIED/CIRCA BIRTH DATE WILLIAM HARRISON'S NAME APPEARS AS "ORNDORFF", HE DIED DURING THE CIVIL WAR.

275.   m   ii.   **MORGAN H. ORENDORFF**, born 1840.
NEVER MARRIED MORGAN H.'S NAME APPEARS AS "ORNDORFF", HE DIED DURING THE CIVIL WAR.

276.   f   iii.   **FRANCES (FANNIE) ORENDORFF**, born 21 July 1843 in POSS. VA, died in OR NEAR HAMPSHIRE, CO W. VA.
NEVER MARRIED FRANCES (FANNIE)'S NAME APPEARS AS "ORNDORFF". SHE IS BURIED WITH HER FATHER IN OR NEAR HAMPSHIRE CO W. VA.

+ 277.   f   iv.   **MAHALA ORENDORFF**, born 1848, died 1919.

278.   f   v.   **JEMIMA E. ORENDORFF**, born 1833.
MARRIED TWICE JEMIMA E.'S NAME APPEARS AS "ORNDORFF", SHE MARRIED FIRST SAMUEL VIERETS AND SECONDLY MR. SINE.

279.   f   vi.   **ISABEL C. ORENDORFF**, born 1835 in POSS. VA.
ISABEL C.'S NAME APPEARS AS "ORNDORFF", SHE MARRIED JOHN W. SAYLOR.

Notes for James:

James Wade's name appears as "Orndorff', apparently his wife was a cousin. Buried in Hardy Co W. VA with his daughter.

Notes for Mahala:

Mahala's name appears as "Orndorff", her husband was apparently a cousin. Married by minister Robert F. Ferguson.

- - - - - - - - - - -

150. HARRISON[9] **ORENDORFF** (85.DAVID[8], 60.JOHN[7], 50.PHILIP[6], 26.THEISS[5], 9.LUDWIG[4], 3.HUBERT[3], 2.HENNE[2], I.SIMON[1]) was born 17 August 1813. HARRISON died in PROBABLY HARDY CO W., VA. He married **MARY HEISHMAN**. She was born 21 May 1821. MARY probably died in W. VA.

They had 5 children:

280.	f	i.	**EVELINE ORENDORFF**, born 1841.
+ 281.	m	ii.	**BAKER C. ORENDORFF**, born 1860.
282.	f	iii.	**HANNAH ORENDORFF**, born 1863.
+ 283.	m	iv.	**HARRISON RILEY ORENDORFF**, born 20 March 1854.
+ 284.	f	v.	**AMANDA M. ORENDORFF**, born 1849.

Notes for Mary:

Also spelled Hashman. Mary Heishman is buried in Hardy Co W. VA.

Notes for Harrison:

Harrison's name appears as "Orndorff". He is buried in Hardy Co W. VA.

- - - - - - - - - - -

154. ISAIAH[9] **ORENDORFF** (85.DAVID[8], 60.JOHN[7], 50.PHILIP[6], 26.THEISS[5], 9.LUDWIG[4], 3.HUBERT[3], 2.HENNE[2], I.SIMON[1]) was born 1824. He married **SARAH WEBSTER**. She was born 1832.

They had 1 child:

| 285. | f | i. | **ALICE ORENDORFF**, born 1850. |
| | | | ALICE'S NAME APPEARS AS "ORNDORFF". |

Notes for Isaiah:

Circa birth date, Isaiah's name appears as "Orndorff".

- - - - - - - - - - -

155. MASON D.[9] **ORENDORFF** (86.PHINEAS[8], 60.JOHN[7], 50.PHILIP[6], 26.THEISS[5], 9.LUDWIG[4], 3.HUBERT[3], 2.HENNE[2], 1.SIMON[1]) was born 1832 in POSS. VA. MASON died 1879, at the age of 47. He married **MARY C. ORENDORFF** 4 October 1866 in POSS. VA. She was born 1850 possibly in VA.

They had 2 children:

286. m i. **HOMER L. ORENDORFF**, born 1869 in PROBABLY VA OR W. VA, died in OR NEAR HAMPSHIRE, CO W. VA.

HOMER L. IS BURIED IN OR NEAR HAMPSHIRE CO W. VA, HIS NAME APPEARS AS "ORENDORFF".

287. m ii. **MARSHALL N. ORENDORFF**, born 1867 in POSS. VA.

MARSHALL N.'S NAME APPEARS AS "ORNDORFF".

Notes for Mary:

Mary C.'s name appears as "Orndorff", she was apparently a cousin of her husbands.

Notes for Mason:

Mason D.'s name appears as "Orndorff". Married to a cousin named Mary C. Orendorff.

- - - - - - - - - - -

165.   JOSEPH[9]   **ORENDORFF**   (89.JOHNATHAN[8], 60.JOHN[7], 50.PHILIP[6], 26.THEISS[5], 9.LUDWIG[4], 3.HUBERT[3], 2.HENNE[2], 1.SIMON[1]) was born 1799. JOSEPH died 1877 in PROBABLY VA, at the age of 78. He married **ELIZABETH BRILL** 20 September 1820 probably in VA. She was born 1795.

They had 5 children:

+ 288.   m   i.   **ROBERT FRANCIS ORENDORFF**, born 1832.

289.   f   ii.   **HARRIET STICKLEY ORENDORFF**, born 1825 in PROBABLY VA.
HARRIET STICKLEY'S NAME APPEARS AS "ORNDORFF", SHE MARRIED A MR. JOSEPH SAUNDERS.

290.   f   iii.   **CATHERINE ANN ORENDORFF**, born 1820 in PROBABLY VA.
CATHERINE ANN'S NAME APPEARS AS "ORNDORFF", SHE MARRIED A JOHN H. MCILWEE.

291.   m   iv.   **ELISHA FRYE ORENDORFF**, born 1823 in POSS. VA. He married MARGARET MCILWEE 1849 in POSS. VA. Notes for ELISHA:
ELISHA FRYE'S NAME APPEARS AS "ORNDORFF".

+ 292.   m   v.   **WILLIAM B. ORENDORFF**, born 1834.

Notes for Elizabeth:
Elizabeth appears in the 1850 census for Frederick Co VA, the towns of Newton and Stephensburg; her age is listed as 54.

Notes for Joseph:
Farmer. Joseph appears in the 1850 census for Frederick Co VA, the towns of Newton and Stephensburg. His name appears as "Orndorff" and his real estate is valued at $4460.00.

- - - - - - - - - - -

166. WILLIAM HENRY[9] ORENDORFF (90.JESSE[8], 65.CHRISTIAN[7], 54.CHRISTIAN[6], 48.JOHANN[5], 25.HERMANN[4], 7.STEPHEN[3], 2.HENNE[2], 1.SIMON[1]) was born 18 April 1807 in LYNCHBURG, VA. WILLIAM died 25 April

1892 in MELISSA, TX, at the age of 85. He married **MARY ELIZABETH HAYES**. She was born 23 May 1808 in or near NORFOLK VIRGINIA. MARY died 18 August 1859 in COLLIN CO, TX, at the age of 51.

They had 4 children:

+ 293.   m   i.   **ROBERT HOUSTON ORENDORFF**, born 1847.

294.   f   ii.   **CORA H. ORENDORFF**, born 1839 in BRECKINRIDGE CO KY, died 1925 in FORT WORTH, TARRANT CO TEXAS, at the age of 86.

Cora married Edward L. Morris, her children were Kay Morris, Willie Morris, Ruby Morris, Otis Morris who never returned from Mexico, and Jesse a daughter. Cora died in Fort Worth Texas at the age of 86.

+ 295.   m   iii.   **JESSE WILLIAM ORENDORFF**, born 19 March 1843, died 17 July 1928.

+ 296.   m   iv.   **JOHN HAYES ORENDORFF**, born 4 July 1837, died 6 June 1913.

Notes for Mary:

Mary Elizabeth Hayes was born near Norfolk VA. She was the daughter of William Hayes c. 1770-1861 and Elisabeth Foster b. 04-01-1777 d. 06-17-1842 and who married circa 1794. Her grandmother was Mary Degge and her grandfather was Joel Foster d. 1821 who married 03-17-1767. Mary had 6 brothers and sisters which are as follows: Joel Hayes b. 12-15-1798 d. 12-27-1865 m. 02-24-1820 to Margaret Billups, m. 2nd Elizabeth Billups 09-30-1840, m. 3rd Susan Stubblefield 01-19-1843; Anna Hayes; William Hayes 1806-1864 m. Sarah Jane Hogg on 01-03-1827, m. 2nd Rebecca Partridge on 01-28-1836; Jesse Henry Hayes b. 08-11-1812 d. 1853 married Sarah E. Cooke 10-23-1834; Martha Ann Hayes b.03-20-1816 d. 11-28-1893 m. Peter W. Johnston on 08-25-1837: and James B. S. Hayes. (Source-Kingston Virginia Parish Register) As a young lady she traveled to Breckinridge County KY with her father and met William Henry Orenduff. A mortality schedule for Collin county taxes listing persons who died during the year ending 1st. June 1860 lists a Mary E. Orenduff-age 51-f. -married- b. VA. month of death-Aug.-cause of death- typhoid fever-number of days ill- 2 months. Mary is buried in the old Orenduff cemetery near McKinney TX. Sources obtained from tombstone, probate papers, Collin Co courthouse records, and book "Hays of Virginia".

Notes for William:
Religion: Methodist.
Orenduff spelling. Farmer/planter. William Henry Orenduff was born in Virginia on April 18,1807. His parents Jesse and Mary Elizabeth Cashman moved to Breckinridge Co. KY in the winter of 1830-1831. A member of royal arch mason chapter 20. He joined on August 25 year unknown at Hardinsburg, Breckinridge Co KY. They moved to Collin Co Texas in 1855. His plantation and ranch was located where McKinney Texas now stands. He had two brothers, Mac who lived in KY and Jesse from VA. William Henry bought a lot of land in Texas and began building his home with lumber from Jefferson in 1855. It consisted of two 18-ft rooms with a 16-ft open hall in between. Porches extended the length of the house with square colonial columns. The Negroes cooked out in the yard, bringing the food in the house at mealtime. The children learned beautiful penmanship, correct spelling, and mathematics from a private school at Mantuo taught by Professor Greer. According to his granddaughter Lena, William always kept a little brown jug in the closet and made a toddy every morning and would call the children up on his lap. William is showed to have owned 202 acres surveyed by John Hart, 234 acres surveyed by S.M. Pulliam, 235 acres surveyed by P.A. Boone, and 18 acres surveyed by Thomas plus 30 horses, 27 cattle with $280.00 in personal property for a total of $3,730.00, this was approx. 1860. William also had 2 slave cabins on his property. His land was very beautiful, with lots of trees, green fields and streams running through out. William is listed as a registered voter for Collin County Texas September 21, 1871 and as

voting "v". A picture of William Henry was given to Stephen Bradley Orendorff during a visit with Ross Orenduff in Melissa Texas 1995. He is buried with his wife and family in the Orenduff family cemetery outside of Melissa TX. His tombstone is an obelisk type. Sources: Collin Co. census records, tombstone, book "Hays of Virginia".

- - - - - - - - - - -

167. MEXICO[9] **ORENDORFF** (90.JESSE[8], 65.CHRISTIAN[7], 54.CHRISTIAN[6], 48.JOHANN[5], 25.HERMANN[4], 7.STEPHEN[3], 2.HENNE[2], 1.SIMON[1]) was born 18 May 1812 in BEDFORD COUNTY VIRGINIA. MEXICO died 5 February 1854 in BRECKINRIDGE CO KY, at the age of 41. He married **MARY A. E. CAIN.** She was born 1818 in SALEM VIRGINIA. MARY died sometime after 1896.

They had 8 children:

297.　　m　i.　　**HENRY ORENDORFF,** born 6 October 1841 in BRECKINRIDGE CO KENTUCKY. Doctor of medicine "Henry Orendorff grew to manhood in his native county, receiving his education in private schools, and in Franklin Indiana college which he attended for two years and completed his college course at the Ocilian College in Hardin County. He then attended the Kentucky school of medicine in Louisville. After which he was graduated in 1871. He then was employed as an intern in the city hospital for eighteen months after which he entered the office of doctor J.M. Holloway in Louisville and was associated with him for four years being in the meantime visiting physician at the city hospital. In 1876 he went to Savannah Georgia as acting surgeon U.S.A. at that post. He remained three months and on account of yellow fever was transferred to Charleston in the same capacity.

He returned to Louisville in 1877, since which time he has been engaged in the practice of his profession in that city. In 1879 he was elected the chair of materia medica and therapeutic in the Kentucky school of medicine, a position which he still occupies. He is also clinical lecturer on genital-urinary and diseases of the skin in the same institution. Dr. Orendorff has been a member of all the medical societies as they have come and gone, at the present holds his membership in the principal national, state and city medical societies and associations. He was united in marriage May 12, 1876 to Mattie Ormsby, youngest daughter of the late Colonel Stephen Ormsby of Louisville, who commanded the famous Louisville legion in the Mexican war. She is the granddaughter of Judge Stephen Ormsby, who was the first federal judge of Kentucky. Doctor and Mrs. Orendorff have two daughters and one son; Louisa Ormsby, Marie Ormsby and Stephen Ormsby Orendorff."
Source: the Biographical Encyclopedia of Kentucky published in 1896.

298.   m   ii.   **CHRISTOPHER C. ORENDORFF**, born 1843 in KENTUCKY, PROBABLY BRECKINRIDGE CO.
Lived in KANSAS CITY MO. Christopher C. was probably the 2nd child of Mexico. His name is listed as "Orendorff"

299.   f   iii.   **FRANCES EDMONIA ORENDORFF**, born 1845 in KENTUCKY, PROBABLY BRECKINRIDGE CO.
Frances had a son named Taylor Orendorff Perrin who was a Presbyterian minister who had churches in Birmingham Alabama and Greenville

Texas, also possibly other places. She is listed in the 1850 census for Breckinridge co KY; the spelling of her name is "Francis Orendorff".

300.   f   iv.   **EDMONIA B. ORENDORFF**, born 1846 in PROBABLY KENTUCKY. She married WILLIAM HENRY PERRIN 1868. He was born 27 March 1834 in BRECKINRIDGE CO. Notes for WILLIAM:
Religion: INCLINED   TO   THE PROTESTANT EPISCOPAL CHURCH

Notes for Edmonia:

Nicknamed "Eddie" Edmonia married Mr. Henry Perrin a prominent Kentuckian when she was 22 and he was 33. His father was born in Virginia and his mother was born in Kentucky. The marriage record says Henry Perrin was a secretary living in Louisville KY and that "Edie B. Orenduff" was given consent for marriage by her mother Mary A.E. Orendorff at her home. The bond was filed 02-26-1868; the bondsman was Amos Skillman. Perrin was a teacher, store clerk for 2 years at Webster KY. In the fall of 1864 he went to Louisville KY to escape military persecution and worked in the office of the Louisville journal. As secretary of the journal company he remained with the paper until its consolidation with the courier in the fall of 1868. He then in connection with John E. Hatter, took charge of the Louisville daily democrat under the firm name of Hatter and Perrin. In 1875 he went to Illinois, remaining there a few years. In 1881 he moved back to Louisville. His best literary effort was a history of Kentucky of which he was the editor in chief and also an author. Perrin and Edmonia had 5 children: William Guy Perrin, Mary De Perrin, Taylor Orendorff Perrin and Ben Hardin Perrin who were twins, and Edmonia Ormsby Perrin. Mr. Perrin was also a member of the Masonic order and was the master of two lodges; one in Illinois and one in KY. He was first elected master at age of 24. He also served one year as grand marshal of the grand lodge of KY. In his religious views he was liberal, inclining to the Protestant Episcopal Church and neutral in politics.

Sources: Breckinridge County Kentucky marriage records 1800's (page 145). "February 26, 1868-w. Henry Perrin, 33, secretary, resident Louisville, Kentucky, (father b. Virginia, mother b. Kentucky), to Edie B. Orenduff, 22(father and mother b. Virginia); Amos Skillman< bondsman: consent of Mary A.E. Orenduff for daughter "Eddie"; to be married February 27, 1868 at residence of Mary A.E. Orenduff."

SOURCE: DESCRIPTIVE AND PERSONAL BRECKINRIDGE COUNTY (PAGES 150&151)

301.	m	v.	**TAYLOR T. ORENDORFF,** born in PROBABLY KY. PHYSICIAN TAYLOR WAS A WEALTHY CITIZEN OF MISSISSIPPI IN THE MID TO LATE 1800'S. HIS NAME IS LISTED AS "ORENDORFF".
302.	m	vi.	**WILLIAM A. ORENDORFF.** He married SARILDY DOOLEY 3 July 1860 in TEXAS/ MAY NOT BE SAME, PERSON. Notes for WILLIAM: Born after 1840. His name is listed as being spelled "Orendorff".
303.	m	vii.	**THOMAS J. ORENDORFF,** born in PROBABLY KY. Born after 1840 Thomas J. was probably the 6th child of Mexico. Thomas would have been born before 1854, his name is listed as being spelled "Orendorff". He was a wealthy planter in Mississippi.
304.	f	viii.	**LENA ORENDORFF,** born in PROBABLY KY. LENA WAS BORN AFTER 1840.

Notes for Mary:
Possibly spelled Kane her father was Thomas E. Cain (Kane) who came to Breckinridge Co KY around 1836 from VA, the family was from England. and he died there of cholera in 1849. Mary's

mother was Ona (Meador) Kane who was a daughter of Benjamin and Mary H. (Morris) Meador. Thomas Cain was a son of Micajah and Elizabeth (Wilkerson) Cain. Mary had 7 children with Mexico. After the death of her husband, Mary made her home in Louisville KY. She was a member of the Methodist Episcopal Church South as were most of her children.

Notes for Mexico:

Farmer/livestock trader. Mexico is listed in the 1850 census for Breckinridge Co KY as being 37 year sold, the head of the household, and owning $2,200.00 worth of real estate. It also says he was a farmer born in VA. He is also shown to have living in his household Sarah E. Cain age 21 and Robert Garrett age 16. Mexico is listed in the "Kentucky genealogy and biography" by Perrin and it states the following about him- "Mr. Orendorff was a plain and unpretending farmer, with no aspirations for office or political aggrandizement. Prosperous and successful he was fast attaining wealth, and but for his sudden death, which occurred in the prime of his life, he would doubtless have become one of the wealthiest farmers of the county." It also says he "was brought up on the farm and received such educational advantages as were afforded by neighborhood schools." He is buried in Breckinridge Co KY and his name on his stone is "Orendorf". Died at age 41 years, 8 months and 18 days.

- - - - - - - - - - -

168.   ALEXANDER[9]   **ORENDORFF**   (90.JESSE[8], 65.CHRISTIAN[7],   54.CHRISTIAN[6],   48.JOHANN[5], 25.HERMANN[4], 7.STEPHEN[3], 2.HENNE[2], 1.SIMON[1]) was born 11 February 1815. ALEXANDER died in BRECKINRIDGE CO KY. He married **MARY BRUINGTON**. She was born 1 May 1819. MARY probably died in KY.

They had 1 child:

305.   f   i.   **LETITIA ORENDORFF.**

Letitia was shown to be living in Tazewell Co Illinois in the 1820 census. Tazewell Co is near the town of Bloomington IL. Letitia married Thomas H. Payne fourth child of Robert and Nancy (Scott) Payne, born in Breckinridge Co August 2, 1843. he was raised on a farm and remained with his parents until his 18th year receiving a fair education in the country schools and later attending one term the Hardinsburg high school one session. At the outbreak of war he joined company b 27th Kentucky federal infantry with which he served for 2 years before being discharged due to disability. Immediately after being discharged he returned home and remained there for 2 years. He then spent 2 years in Illinois and Missouri engaged in farming, then two years later he purchased a place within 1 mile of Hardinsburg and resided there for 9 years. At the end of that time he purchased his present farm of 243 acres in Bewleyville village. He and Letitia had 5 children: Alfred H. Payne, Victoria Payne, Olive Payne, Junius Payne, and Mary A. Payne. Thomas took considerable interest in politics and voted with the republican party. He was also a member of the Masonic lodge. He and Latitia both belonged to the Baptist church and he held the office of moderator in the Bewleyville congregation.

Notes for Mary:
Mary Bruington is buried in Breckinridge Co KY, her name appears as "Orendorff".

Notes for Alexander:
Alexander was probably the 3rd child of Jesse. His name appears as "Orendorff". Buried in Breckinridge Co KY.

- - - - - - - - - - -

172. AARON[9] **ORENDORFF** (92.CHRISTOPHER[8], 65.CHRISTIAN[7], 54.CHRISTIAN[6], 48.JOHANN[5], 25.HERMANN[4], 7.STEPHEN[3], 2.HENNE[2], 1.SIMON[1]) was born in WASHINGTON CO MARYLAND. AARON died in EARLY SPRING, ILL. He married **MARTHA MCDOWELL**.

They had 5 children:

306.   m   i.   **THOMAS HOGG ORENDORFF**, born 1814 in KENTUCKY. He married LETICIA C. MITCHELL 1843 in ILLINOIS. LETICIA died November 1863 in ILLINOIS. Notes for LETICIA:

1ST WIFE

THOMAS died in ILLINOIS. Notes for THOMAS:

Farmer / married twice. Thomas H. moved to Tazewell Co Illinois in 1827 at the age of 13 with his parents, moved there from Kentucky. The following is from a history of Tazewell Co- "almost before the magic hand of civilization had waved its scepter over the native wildness of the prairie state. More than half a century has rolled its ponderous wheels through the trackless starless course of time since Thomas Orendorff set his foot on the unplowed soil of Tazewell Co. Even at that early age his keen foresight and shrewdness led him to see that this section must take rank among the best localities in the northwest. He received his education by private tuition before the advent of our free school system. When about age 23, while engaged in farming in Swayler Co Ill, he met and loved Miss Leticia C. Mitchell, whom he married and brought to Hopedale on his return, about 1843. From this union four children were born, only one of whom, G.P. Orendorff, now sitting in the general assembly of Illinois, is living. Mr. O. did much to advance the interests of this county, and a few years before his death, which was in Dec 1878, he laid out the village of Hopedale, and by his influence established a post office there. Nov 1863 occurred the death of his wife, and during the year 1866 he was married to Miss S. Maggin of Blooming Grove, Mclean Co who survived him and lived in Hopedale". Resided in Tazewell Co Illinois, which is near Bloomington in the 1830 census. still living there in the 1840 census. Thomas was the oldest son.

307.   m   ii.   **DARIUS WHITE ORENDORFF**, born in ILLINOIS, died in prior to December 21, 1921.

4th son Darius' name appears as "Orendorff", he traveled extensively across the United States and he intensified the interest in the early history of the family. He inspired the first Orendorff reunion, which was held in Bloomington Ill October 12-14 1886. Darius was the son of Aaron. He built a sawmill with his brother Thomas who was the eldest in Hopedale Ill. They built the mill during the winter of 1849-1850. Thomas owned the land where Hopedale now stands. In 1853 he laid out the lots for the new town and also served as the postmaster. Darius built the first store and shortly afterwards Thomas formed a partnership with T.A. Smith for the second store. Darius also had apart in building a Presbyterian church and a number of the first houses. He later withdrew from the sawmill and Thomas added steam power and a flourmill. Darius sold his store and traveled extensively, planning to find a new location. He invested in Kansas's lands. During his visits to KY he had become interested in the woolen mills of his cousin Eli Orendorff and he decided that a woolen mill might be profitable in Illinois. For years he had raised sheep on the prairies but he now decided to buy imported stock. He invested in five hundred Spanish sheep and in 1865 bought new machinery at a cost of 15000 dollars. He established a large woolen mill and built a number of houses for his employees. He also started a school and secured Mrs. Jasper Mount, previously principal of the Hopedale schools, as the first teacher. The following paragraph is quoted from the Tazewell county atlas- "Jasper Mount is one of the young and enterprising farmers of Hopedale Township. He is the oldest son of Mathias Mount, esq. so well and favorably known throughout Tazewell county, and Abigail Orendorff Mount. Jasper received his first education in the common schools of Tazewell County, and completed his education in Notre Dame College Indiana, where he received a degree in 1866. After this he returned to his home and labored for his father until 1867 when he was joined in marriage to Mrs. Angeline Waldon who was born in Elm Grove Township in 1846. She was recognized as one of the popular teachers of the county for several years. Immediately after their marriage, Mr. Mount moved to Orendorff's woolen mills, where he was bookkeeper and general foreman. He later settled on a farm on section 22 of Hopedale township; he is a collector at Hopedale at present. He is held in high esteem for his moral worth, integrity, and promptness, and we know of no young man who has more warm friends than Jasper Mount. "Darius also opened a lumber yard, established a furniture store, and he built a public hall in Hopedale. In January 1876 he sold out his interests and took a prospecting tour through Texas, Arkansas, and Missouri to look for a new site for a woolen mill. In January 1878 he moved his mill to Judsonia Arkansas and during four summers he operated mills at that place. One of his daughters accompanied him to Arkansas but the rest of the family remained on the home farm near Hopedale. In his dealings with the public his motto was "manufacture and deal in the best and guarantee satisfaction." Darius also spent much time on family history. He once remarked that he had seen the picture of senator Benton's wife, who before her marriage was Elizabeth McDowell, and "she was the very image of my mother, Martha McDowell Orendorff." He was also the first white child born in the township and one of the first born in the county. He was 13 years old when he moved to Ill with his father. He wrote his own obituary prior to his death, it was published in the Bloomington Pantagraph in Bloomington Ill Dec. 21, 1921. Darius wrote a booklet entitled "American Orendorff Families".

308.   m   iii.   **SOLON ORENDORFF**, born 1832. He married LYDIA E. TEFFET 22 April 1858 in TAZEWELL CO IL.

SOLON died 1930, at the age of 98. Notes for SOLON:

Solon's name appear as "Orndorff". He was the youngest son and during the 1870's owned a ranch and greenhouse near Pueblo Colorado. He completed a life of nearly a century in Los Angeles, CA. In a letter dated July 26, 1928 he said-"father must have fixed a place and planted an orchard about the first thing he did for my early recollection we had apples and peaches and I remember the turkeys would come through the orchard gathering their feed. In the early days they had no scarcity of wild meat, turkeys, deer and prairie chickens." In another he wrote-"the orchard was mostly of the seedling variety only six grafted trees in orchard of over a hundred trees. Many of them had local names. The graft was of the lady finger variety. Our local names were various, such as kitchen corner, which was the earliest, getting ripe about the middle of August. Never get ripe was a sweet apple but never got mellow, but always hard and tough, dumpling was only fit for dumpling. Tazewell sweet was an early winter and was an excellent variety...I must not leave out old choke as we called it. When it was fully mellow they were as hard to eat as a green persimmon".

| 309. | f | iv. | **DELILAH JANE ORENDORFF.** MARRIED SAMUEL MCCLURE DELILAH'S NAME APPEARS AS "ORENDORF". SHE WAS THE OLDEST DAUGHTER. |
| 310. | f | v. | **MINERVA ORENDORFF.** MINERVA MARRIED ALFRED REED, HER NAME APPEARS AS "ORENDORFF". SHE WAS THE FOURTH DAUGHTER. |

Notes for Martha:

Martha McDowell received a farm in northern Tenn. from her father Joseph McDowell.

Notes for Aaron:

Married to Martha Aaron is shown to live in Illinois in 1830 in Tazewell County, which is near the town of Bloomington. If this Aaron is Enoch's brother he had the other grandfather clock that was brought oversees from Germany. He was always enthusiastic over family heirlooms and he carried several with him to Illinois, including a desk and the grandfather clock. An owner of that clock (1930's) who married into the family, determined to make it function again, so he worked at odd moments for several weeks until he finally got the clock to strike at fairly regular intervals. Then a member of the family heard it strike seventeen times at midnight. The others, hearing the old clock make its usual single strokes the next day, doubted the story, until, during the evening meal, it burst out with fifty-three strokes. The clock still possessed its former functioning ability and was soon on its way to regular service again. Aaron built his first house on as high an elevation as possible on the level prairie in Ill. He also built the first brick house in the county by experimenting with the clay on his farm. He found that it made bricks successfully. This was about 1830. This house was still standing about 1930 and could be seen from either the highway or the railroad about one and a half miles from the town of Hopedale in Ill. another reason he built it of brick was for additional warmth in the winters. This house had 2 rooms downstairs and two rooms upstairs and the influence of southern architecture was shown by the two large fireplaces with their walnut mantels. There were also two well-built staircases, one leading up from the northwest corner of the living room, and the other from the southeast corner of the kitchen. On examining the two large rooms above one finds a pile of lathes on the floor, hand split from hardwood trees on the farm. Later a larger house was built nearby to provide more rooms but the old brick house must have filled a vital need when the days were cold and a heavy snowstorm raged outside. The Orendorff brothers including Aaron became the largest landowners in Tazewell County Ill. Between October 27 1829 and November 20 of the same year Aaron bought 1,380 acres from the Springfield land office. Within a few years he owned 6000 acres of fertile prairies interspersed with virgin forests. Aaron started off for the northern grass region in the fall of 1827, after the crops had been harvested. The trip was made in "a wooden spindle, linch pin wagon" drawn by a yoke of oxen. His daughter Mary aged seven later told how she and her four year old sister Abigail sat in the chairs held in by the big chest, the grandfather clock, and their father's desk. The great clock, a valuable possession in the family, was as highly treasured as the books that her father as a young man had brought from the east. Aaron disliked slavery, although he was sympathetic toward those who held slaves and believed that they should be guaranteed their right to property. He did hope however that his sons would not own Negroes. His son Darius later said-"politically Aaron Orendorff was a supporter of Jacksonian principles and the African Colonization Society. The dislike of slavery was one of his reasons for leaving the south. Having a thorough knowledge of the low moral condition of the African race, he was conscientiously opposed to their freedom in America." He moved from Maryland to Shepardstown VA, later to KY and TN, and carried with him the family tradition of service and business sagacity. During his childhood he was inspired by the stories of Major Christian Orendorff regarding his role in the revolutionary war. He was also raised on stories of his grandfather's wartime exploits. He never forgot the part played by his father and grandfather in the revolutionary war or their strict integrity in business associations. Aaron lived on a farm in northern TN after marrying his wife, she received that farm from her father Joseph McDowell. This was prior to 1825. His attention was temporarily centered in the new tracts of land he had purchased on the Red River on the KY border. But by 1825 a movement began which swept pioneers northward. Travelers passing through told of the great parries in central Ill, inhabited by only a few wandering Indians and great herds of wild deer. Aaron, who had previously held a surveying commission for the Illinois territory, became interested and decided to investigate. By 1822 only four hundred Indians remained in Ill, but for years they tarried along the creeks, loathe to leave their old homes. When Aaron returned from school in the east in 1808 he had a commission from the government to survey the "Illinois county", but Indian uprisings were reported and his father urged him to give it up and remain in Logan Co. Since his father and his brother John had very good business prospects in the growing town of Nashville he felt that his assistance was needed until the grist and saw mills were completed and the flower industry was well established. Aaron then became the principal teamster and sold the products of the Orendorff mills in Tennessee. He also assisted his brother in the management of mills. Russelville KY is within 2 miles of the Orendorff homestead.

- - - - - - - - - - -

173. ENOCH T.[9] ORENDORFF (92.CHRISTOPHER[8], 65.CHRISTIAN[7], 54.CHRISTIAN[6], 48.JOHANN[5], 25.HERMANN[4], 7.STEPHEN[3], 2.HENNE[2], 1.SIMON[1]) was born 1799 in VA. ENOCH died in PROBABLY ILL. His spouse has not been identified.

They had 4 children:

311.   m   i.   **QUINTUS ORENDORFF**, born 1829 in IL, POSS. TAZEWELL CO. He married EMMA E. KELLY 24 September 1854 in TAZEWELL CO IL. Notes for QUINTUS: FARMER QUINTUS'S NAME APPEARS AS "ORENDORFF". HE ATTENDED THE FIRST ORENDORFF REUNION HELD IN BLOOMINGTON ILL OCT 1886 AND APPARENTLY LIVED IN DELAVAN ILL.

312.   m   ii.   **CHARLES ORENDORFF**, born 1833 in IL, POSS. TAZEWELL CO. FARMER CHARLES' NAME APPEARS AS "ORENDORFF", HE IS SHOWN ON THE 1850 CENSUS FOR TAZEWELL CO ILL.

313.   f   iii.   **ELIZA ORENDORFF**, born 1838 in ILL, POSS. TAZEWELL CO. ELIZA'S NAME APPEARS AS "ORENDORFF", SHE IS LISTED IN THE 1850 CENSUS FOR TAZEWELL CO ILL.

314.   m   iv.   **JOHN L. ORENDORFF**, born 15 September

1835 in HOPEDALE TOWNSHIP, TAZE.
CO IL. He married MARY E. ARNOLD
21 July 1858 in DEVELAN, TAZEWELL CO
ILL. Notes for MARY:

Mary E. Arnold had at least 3 children. Notes
for John:

Jeweler/farmer. In his early years John L.'s name
appears as "Orendorff", he received a common
school education in Hopedale township in
Tazewell Co Ill, moved to Develan where he was
engaged in the jewelry business in which he was
successful. His middle initial might have been T.
He appears as "Orendorff" in the 1850 federal
census for Tazewell Co Ill as being 15 years old
and living with Enoch T.

Notes for Enoch:

Married to Romania b. 1808 SC Enoch is shown to have lived
in Tazewell Co Illinois, which is near the town of Bloomington, in
the 1830 census. Also still living there in 1840 census. Also appears
in the 1850 census Tazewell Co Ill. He is shown to be 51, a farmer
b. in VA. He was one of the earliest pioneers of this Tazewell Co Ill,
having gone there in 1826. He lived in Hopedale Township, Tazewell
Co Ill in 1835. If this is the Enoch who was the brother of Aaron he
owned one of two grandfather clocks that were said to have come from
Germany. Enoch went to Illinois as a bachelor and left his cumbersome
inheritance with Christian. The descendants in Logan Co KY who
retained the clock only remembered that a great uncle had given it to
the family. His father gave him land adjoining his brother's John and
Aaron's land in his will. He also left him a wagon, horses, gears and all
utensils belonging to his farm.

- - - - - - - - - - -

174. ESAU[9] ORENDORFF (92.CHRISTOPHER[8],
65.CHRISTIAN[7], 54.CHRISTIAN[6], 48.JOHANN[5],

25.HERMANN[4], 7.STEPHEN[3], 2.HENNE[2], 1.SIMON[1]) was born 1789 in MARYLAND. His spouse has not been identified.

They had 7 children:

315.　　m　i.　**ENOCH S. ORENDORFF**, born 1836 in KY. ENOCH S. APPEARS IN THE 1850 CENSUS FOR TAZEWELL CO ILL LIVING WITH HIS PARENTS, HIS NAME APPEARS AS "ORENDORFF".

316.　　m　ii.　**NOAH ORENDORFF**, born 1831 in KY. NOAH IS LISTED IN THE 1850 CENSUS FOR TAZEWELL CO ILL LIVING WITH HIS PARENTS, HIS NAME APPEARS AS "ORENDORFF".

317.　　m　iii.　**VAN ORENDORFF**, born 1838 in ILL, POSS. TAZEWELL CO. VAN IS LISTED IN THE 1850 CENSUS FOR TAZEWELL CO ILL LIVING WITH HIS PARENTS, HIS NAME APPEARS AS "ORENDORFF".

318.　　f　iv.　**BARBARA L. ORENDORFF**, born 1829 in KY. BARBARA L. APPEARS IN THE 1850 CENSUS FOR TAZEWELL CO ILL LIVING WITH HIS PARENTS, HIS NAME APPEARS AS "ORENDORFF".

319.　　f　v.　**SUSANNAH ORENDORFF**, born 1834 in KY. SUSANNAH APPEARS IN THE 1850 CENSUS FOR TAZEWELL CO ILL LIVING WITH HER PARENTS, HER NAME APPEARS AS "ORENDORFF".

320.　　f　vi.　**FRANCIS M. ORENDORFF**, born 1827 in KENTUCKY, POSS. LOGAN CO. FRANCIS M. APPEARS AS "ORENDORFF" IN THE 1850 FEDERAL CENSUS FOR

TAZEWELL CO ILL AS LIVING WITH HER FAMILY AND BEING AGE 23.

321.   f   vii.   **MARY ANN M. ORENDORFF**, born 1825 in KY, POSS. LOGAN CO.
MARY ANN M. IS LISTED IN THE 1850 FEDERAL CENSUS FOR TAZEWELL CO ILL AS "ORENDORFF", BEING AGE 25 AND LIVING WITH HER FAMILY.

Notes for Esau:

Farmer Esau was shown to live in Tazewell Co Illinois, which is near the town of Bloomington, in 1840. His name appears as "Orendorff", in the 1850 census for Tazewell Co IL he is shown to have owned 10000.00 worth of property. Married to a woman named Mary born in N. Carolina 1807. Esau migrated to Illinois; he had a plantation willed to him by Christopher Orendorff. He then sold it to Wash Hummer who had married into the family. Leah Orendorff's descendants later inherited this land which was still in Orendorff hands as of the 1930's. All these farms lay near the Tennessee line and were watered by the Red River. This land was 200 acres.

CHAPTER TEN

GENERATION NO. 10

185. EMMANUEL LUTHER[10] **ORENDORFF** (108.LEWIS[9], 68.JOHN[8], 59.PHILIP[7], 50.PHILIP[6], 26.THEISS[5], 9.LUDWIG[4], 3.HUBERT[3], 2.HENNE[2], I.SIMON[1]) was born 1863. EMMANUEL died 1943, at the age of 80. He married **HARRIET ELLEN ORENDORFF (See number 190)**. She was born March 1868. She was the daughter of ANDREW ADDISON ORENDORFF and RACHEL ANN CRETSINGER. HARRIET died 22 March 1932, at the age of 64.

They had 9 children:

322.	f	i.	**TACY FRANCES (TERESA, TESSIE) ORENDORFF**, born 23 March 1890. TACY MARRIED A MR. WILLIAM TYRRELL, HER NAME APPEARS AS "ORNDORFF".
323.	m	ii.	**ROGER RIGO ORENDORFF**, born October 1892. He married FANNY GRIMES. Notes for ROGER: NO CHILDREN ROGER RIGO'S NAME APPEARS AS "ORNDORFF".
324.	f	iii.	**RADY LARUE (RITA) ORENDORFF**, born 20 October 1894, died February 1967, at the age of 72. RADY LARUE'S NAME APPEARS AS "ORNDORFF", SHE MARRIED HAROLD HUTCHINSON FLINT BORN 02-05-18999 DIED FEBRUARY OF 1980.

325. f iv. **ADIGAIL ANN ORENDORFF**, born 7 July 1896.
        MARRIED TWICE ADIGAIL ANN'S NAME APPEARS AS "ORNDORFF", SHE MARRIED FIRST GROVER A. FAULK SR. BORN 04-29-1895 DIED 11-07-1933, AND SECONDLY JESSE WILLIAM BRIAN .

326. m v. **LOYAL ADDISON ORENDORFF**, born April 1898. He married ETHEL KEELER. Notes for LOYAL:
        LOYAL ADDISON'S NAME APPEARS AS "ORNDORFF".

327. m vi. **CARL LEWIS ORENDORFF**, born May 1900.
        CARL LEWIS' NAME APPEARS AS "ORNDORFF"

328. f vii. **FLOSSIE ROSELLA (FLORENCE) ORENDORFF**, born 19 January 1902.
        FLOSSIE ROSELLA'S NAME APPEARS AS "ORNDORFF", SHE MARRIED A MR. HARRY (JIMMY) CHRIST GARMAN BORN 11-12-1904, DIED 08-22-1976.

329. m viii. **ERNEST ALPHONSO ORENDORFF**, born 1905. He married GRACE HALL. Notes for ERNEST:
        Ernest Alphonso's name appears as "Orndorff".

330. f ix. **ALMA JUSTINE ORENDORFF**, born 1908.
        Married twice. Alma Justine's name appears as "Orndorff", she married first Curtis Philips, and secondly George Jones.

Notes for Harriet:
Maybe born 1865 Harriet Ellen's name appears as "Orndorff", she was apparently a first cousin of her husband Emmanuel Luther "Orndorff".

Notes for Emmanuel:

Maybe born 1862 Emmanuel Luther's last name appears as "Orndorff", he was apparently a first cousin of his wife Harriet Ellen.

- - - - - - - - - - -

186. JOHN RANDOLPH[10] **ORENDORFF** (108.LEWIS[9], 68.JOHN[8], 59.PHILIP[7], 50.PHILIP[6], 26.THEISS[5], 9.LUDWIG[4], 3.HUBERT[3], 2.HENNE[2], 1.SIMON[1]) was born 1855 in POSS. 1855/VA. JOHN died 25 February 1938, at the age of 83. He married **MARTHA E. RACEY** 28 March 1877 possibly in VA. She was born 1856. MARTHA died 1929, at the age of 73.

They had 4 children:

+ 331.   m   i.   **LUTHER MILTON ORENDORFF**, born 14 June 1882.

332.   f   ii.   **SAVILLA ORENDORFF**, born 1878 in CIRCA/POSS. VA.

Married 3 times Savilla's name appears as "Orndorff", she married 3 times first to David Mcilwee, secondly to Charles Oliver Mcilwee, and thirdly to a Mr. Brill. Her children are as follows: a) Clyde McIlwee who married Edna Orndorff who had Clyde McIlwee JR married to Minnie Fishel, b) Forrest McIlwee married to Mamie Colvin, c) Curtis (buck) McIlwee married to miss Reynolds who had Norma McIlwee, Neva McIlwee married to Courtney Strosnider, Anna Jane McIlwee, Ronnie McIlwee, d) Wayne (Pete) McIlwee who had Wayne McIlwee JR, Kenny McIlwee, Vernon McIlwee, Eloise McIlwee, and Ronnie McIlwee who may have died in 1969, e) Elmer McIlwee married to Willie Himmelright (no children).

+ 333.   m   iii.   **WILLIAM THEODORE ORENDORFF**, born 1879.

334.   m   iv.   **ROMANTUS ORENDORFF**, born 1888 in

POSS. VA. He married MABLE CLEM. Notes for MABLE:

No children

Romantus died in VA or W. VA. Notes for Romantus:

Romantus never had children, his name appears as "Orndorff". Married to a woman named Maud. Name also appears as Romanus.

Notes for John:

John Randolphs name appears as "Orndorff".

- - - - - - - - - - - -

190. HARRIET ELLEN[10] **ORENDORFF** (111.ANDREW[9], 70.JACOB[8], 59.PHILIP[7], 50.PHILIP[6], 26.THEISS[5], 9.LUDWIG[4], 3.HUBERT[3], 2.HENNE[2], 1.SIMON[1]) was born March 1868. HARRIET died 22 March 1932, at the age of 64. She married **EMMANUEL LUTHER ORENDORFF (See number 185)**. He was born 1863. He was the son of LEWIS ORENDORFF and LEVINA RUDOLPH. **See number 185** listed above.

- - - - - - - - - - - -

193. ASHBY MARION[10] **ORENDORFF** (111.ANDREW[9], 70.JACOB[8], 59.PHILIP[7], 50.PHILIP[6], 26.THEISS[5], 9.LUDWIG[4], 3.HUBERT[3], 2.HENNE[2], 1.SIMON[1]) was born 1864. He married **MINERVA ORENDORFF (See number 213)**. She was born November 1868. She is the daughter of LEMUEL ORENDORFF and MARY FRANCES VIRTS (BERTS).

They had 5 children:

335.   m   i.   **ORESTUS W. (ODE) ORENDORFF**, born 1889. He married NELLIE WITTINGTON.

336.   m   ii.   **PERKINS ORENDORFF.**
                       MARRIED A NURSE

337.   m   iii.   **ADA ORENDORFF**, born 1892. He married PAT RACEY.

338.   m   iv.   **WALFORD P. ORENDORFF**, born 1893.

339.   f   v.   **MARIE ORENDORFF.**

MARIE'S NAME APPEARS AS "ORNDORFF", SHE MARRIED A MR. HALL.

Notes for Ashby:
Ashby Marion's name appears as "Orndorff", he was apparently a cousin of his wife.

- - - - - - - - - - - -

194. ADAM DECALB[10] **ORENDORFF** (111.ANDREW[9], 70.JACOB[8], 59.PHILIP[7], 50.PHILIP[6], 26.THEISS[5], 9.LUDWIG[4], 3.HUBERT[3], 2.HENNE[2], 1.SIMON[1]) was born 9 December 1866. He married **EMMA F. PEER.** She was born 7 February 1870.

They had 2 children:

+ 340.　m　i.　**MELVIN ADDISON ORENDORFF**, born 1897.

+ 341.　f　ii.　**DELLA M. ORENDORFF**, born 1891.

Notes for Adam:
Adam's name appears as "Orndorff".

- - - - - - - - - - - -

196. WALTER N.[10] **ORENDORFF** (111.ANDREW[9], 70.JACOB[8], 59.PHILIP[7], 50.PHILIP[6], 26.THEISS[5], 9.LUDWIG[4], 3.HUBERT[3], 2.HENNE[2], 1.SIMON[1]) was born 1872 in PROBABLY VA. He married **HELEN WILLIAMS.**

They had 3 children:

342.　m　i.　**MAXWELL ORENDORFF**, born 1 May 1907 in ASHLAND, BOYD CO KY.
MAXWELL'S NAME APPEARS AS "ORNDORFF".

343.　m　ii.　**RUSSELL ORENDORFF**, born in AFTER 1885.
RUSSEL'S NAME APPEARS AS "ORNDORFF".

344.   m   iii.   **ALVIN ORENDORFF**, born in AFTER 1890.

DIED AT AGE I ALVIN'S NAME APPEARS AS "ORNDORFF".

Notes for Helen:
Moved to KY.

Notes for Walter:
Moved to KY. Walter N.'s name appears as "Orndorff". Was known to have lived in Ashland, Boyd Co KY in 05-01-1907. He may have also been married to a Helen Esteridge.

- - - - - - - - - - -

197. PHILIP P.[10] **ORENDORFF** (112.JACOB[9], 70.JACOB[8], 59.PHILIP[7], 50.PHILIP[6], 26.THEISS[5], 9.LUDWIG[4], 3.HUBERT[3], 2.HENNE[2], I.SIMON[1]) was born 1856 in PROBABLY VA. PHILIP died 11 November 1926 in PROBABLY VA, at the age of 70. He married **MARGARET REBECCA HIMMELRIGHT** 25 December 1877 probably in VA. She was born 1859. MARGARET died 20 March 1937 probably in VA, at the age of 78.

They had 5 children:

345.   m   i.   **FORD ORENDORFF**, born 1901 in CIRCA.

346.   f   ii.   **EFFA C. ORENDORFF**, born 1885 in CIRCA/POSS. VA.

EFFA C.'S NAME APPEARS AS "ORNDORFF".

347.   f   iii.   **DORA ORENDORFF**, born 1883 in CIRCA/VA.

DORA'S NAME APPEARS AS "ORNDORFF".

+ 348.   m   iv.   **CONRAD ORENDORFF**, born 1881.

349.   f   v.   **FRANCIS L. ORENDORFF**, born 1893 in CIRCA/POSS. VA.

FRANCIS L.'S NAME APPEARS AS "ORNDORFF".

Notes for Philip:
Philip P.'s name is listed as "Orndorff".

- - - - - - - - - - -

198. EARLY LEE[10] **ORENDORFF** (112.JACOB[9], 70.JACOB[8], 59.PHILIP[7], 50.PHILIP[6], 26.THEISS[5], 9.LUDWIG[4], 3.HUBERT[3], 2.HENNE[2], I.SIMON[1]) was born 1867. He married **SARA BELLE RACEY.** She was born 1870 probably in VA.

They had 6 children:

350.   f   i.   **FANNY T. ORENDORFF,** born 1896 probably in VA.
FANNY T.'S NAME APPEARS AS "ORNDORFF".

351.   m   ii.   **MILES R. ORENDORFF,** born 1903 probably in VA.

352.   m   iii.   **PAUL C. ORENDORFF,** born 1893 probably in VA.
PAUL C.'S NAME APPEARS AS "ORNDORFF".

353.   f   iv.   **NELLIE R. ORENDORFF,** born 1894 probably in VA.
NELLIE R.'S NAME APPEARS AS "ORNDORFF".

354.   f   v.   **GLADYS E. ORENDORFF,** born 1895 probably in VA.
GLADYS E.'S NAME APPEARS AS "ORNDORFF".

355.   f   vi.   **MILDRED L. ORENDORFF,** born 1898 probably in VA.

Notes for Early:
Early Lee's name appears as "Orndorff".

- - - - - - - - - - -

201. JOSEPH WILLIAM[10] **ORENDORFF** (112.JACOB[9], 70.JACOB[8], 59.PHILIP[7], 50.PHILIP[6], 26.THEISS[5], 9.LUDWIG[4], 3.HUBERT[3], 2.HENNE[2], 1.SIMON[1]) was born 1862 in PROBABLY VA/POSS. 1861. JOSEPH died 1908 in PROBABLY VA, at the age of 46. He married **LAURA LEE SNYDER (See number 422)** 24 November 1886 in WOODSTOCK, SHENANDOAH CO VA. She was born 1868. She was the daughter of MARTIN V B SNYDER and MAHALA ORENDORFF. LAURA died 1957, at the age of 89.

They had 4 children:

356.   f   i.   **NAOMI ORENDORFF**, born 19 September 1890 in PROB. VA OR W. VA, died in OR NEAR HAMPSHIRE, CO W. VA.
NAOMI'S LAST NAME APPEARS AS "ORNDORFF". SHE IS BURIED IN OR NEAR HAMPSHIRE CO W. VA.

357.   f   ii.   **IRENE ORENDORFF**, born 1894 in VA, died in VA.
UNMARRIED IRENE'S NAME APPEARS AS "ORNDORFF".

358.   m   iii.   **JACOB MARTIN ORENDORFF**, born 1902 in VA. He married ELIZABETH FOSTER.
Notes for JACOB:
JACOB MARTIN'S NAME APPEARS AS "ORNDORFF".

359.   m   iv.   **JOSEPH WILLIAM JR ORENDORFF**, born 1896 in VA. He married NELLIE BENJAMIN.
Notes for JOSEPH:
Married twice. Joseph William's name appears as "Orndorff", he was married twice and his second wife was named Rebecca last name unknown.

Notes for Joseph:
Joseph William's name appears as "Orndorff".

- - - - - - - - - - -

204. CEATTA[10] **BRILL** (114.MARY[9], 70.JACOB[8], 59.PHILIP[7], 50.PHILIP[6], 26.THEISS[5], 9.LUDWIG[4], 3.HUBERT[3], 2.HENNE[2], 1.SIMON[1]). CEATTA died April 1913 in POSSIBLY NOT HER DEATH, DATE. She married **ADDISON T. ORENDORFF** 11 March 1875 in POSS. VA. He was born 15 October 1851 in VA. ADDISON died 20 March 1935 in FREDERICK CO VA, at the age of 83.

They had 5 children:

360.	m	i.	**IKY G. ORENDORFF**, born 1879 in POSS. VA.

IKY G.'S NAME APPEARS AS "ORNDORFF".

361.	m	ii.	**MAYNARD ORENDORFF**, born 1880 in POSS. VA.

MAYNARD'S NAME APPEARS AS "ORNDORFF".

362.	m	iii.	**NORTHEN GOHENE ORENDORFF**, born 1877 in POSS. VA, 1876, died in PROB. NEAR HAMPSHIRE, CO W. VA.

Also called Nort, Northia Northen Gohene's name appears as "Orndorff". He is buried with his parents in Union Cemetery, the Star Tannery area north of the old Hampton School in a field, Frederick Co VA. This cemetery is clean, well kept and fenced. There are many graves with just a plain stone (Gravel Springs area). Next to his grave are two unidentified stones, maybe children?

363.	f	iv.	**BESSIE L. ORENDORFF**, born 3 February 1888 in VA, died in FREDERICK CO VA.

Bessie L. is buried in Union Cemetery in the Star Tannery area north of the old Hampton School in a field Frederick Co VA. This cemetery is clean, well kept, and fenced. There are many graves with just plain stones. (Gravel Springs area).

364.	m	v.	**WILTON A. ORENDORFF**, born 4 October

1885 in PROBABLY FREDERICK CO, VA, died in FREDERICK CO VA.

Buried with parents Wilton A. is buried at Union Cemetery in the Star Tannery area north of the old Hampton School. This cemetery is clean, well kept, and fenced. There are many graves with just a plain stone. (Gravel Springs area).

Notes for Ceatta:

2nd wife. Ceatta apparently married a cousin of her mothers. Ceatta is buried in an unmarked grave next to her husband and family at Union Cemetery in the Star Tannery area north of the old Hampton School in a field. Frederick County VA. This cemetery is clean, well kept, and fenced. There are many graves with just a plain stone. (Gravel Springs area).

- - - - - - - - - - -

205. OCTAVIA[10] **BRILL** (114.MARY[9], 70.JACOB[8], 59.PHILIP[7], 50.PHILIP[6], 26.THEISS[5], 9.LUDWIG[4], 3.HUBERT[3], 2.HENNE[2], I.SIMON[1]) was born 6 February 1854 in PROBABLY VA. OCTAVIA died 19 October 1930 in VA OR W. VA, at the age of 76. She married **AARON R. ORENDORFF** 27 November 1879 in POSS. VA OR W. VA. He was born 20 May 1857 probably in VA. AARON died 22 December 1912 in OR 12-11-1912, VA OR W. VA, at the age of 55.

They had 4 children:

365.   f   i.   **FLORENCE ORENDORFF**, born 1892 in POSS. VA.

FLORENCE'S NAME APPEARS AS "ORNDORFF".

366.   f   ii.   **ROSA B. ORENDORFF**, born 1886 in POSS. VA.

ROSA B.'S NAME APPEARS AS "ORNDORFF".

367.   f   iii.   **MARY S. ORENDORFF**, born 1883 in POSS. VA.

     MARY S. NAME APPEARS AS
     "ORNDORFF".

368. m iv. **WILLIE HOLLIS ORENDORFF**, born 1880 in
     POSS. VA.
     WILLIE HOLLIS' NAME APPEARS AS
     "ORNDORFF".

Notes for Aaron:
Aaron R.'s name appears as "Orndorff".

Notes for Octavia:
Octavia apparently married a cousin of her mothers. Buried with her husband.

---

207. BARZELLA B.[10] **ORENDORFF** (116.HEZEKIAH[9], 71.PHILIP[8], 59.PHILIP[7], 50.PHILIP[6], 26.THEISS[5], 9.LUDWIG[4], 3.HUBERT[3], 2.HENNE[2], 1.SIMON[1]) was born 3 September 1884 in PROBABLY WEST VA. BARZELLA died in PROBABLY WEST VA. His spouse has not been identified.

 They had 1 child:

369. m i. **KERMIT BLAINE ORENDORFF**, born
     7 September 1910, died in POSS. W. VA NEAR
     WARDENSVILLE.
     Kermit Blaine is buried in a cemetery near
     Wardensville, his name appears as "Orndorff".
     His mother was Edith, and he is buried with
     his wife named Virginia b. 06-02-1913 and
     12-09-1972.

Notes for Barzella:
Barzella B. is buried with his family in West VA, his name appears as "Orndorff". He apparently married a cousin.

---

213. MINERVA[10] **ORENDORFF** (120.LEMUEL[9], 72.SAMUEL[8], 59.PHILIP[7], 50.PHILIP[6], 26.THEISS[5], 9.LUDWIG[4], 3.HUBERT[3], 2.HENNE[2], I.SIMON[1]) was born November 1868. She married **ASHBY MARION ORENDORFF (See number 193)**. He was born 1864. He is the son of ANDREW ADDISON ORENDORFF and RACHEL ANN CRETSINGER. **See number 193** listed above.

- - - - - - - - - - -

217. RHESA ALLEN[10] **ORENDORFF** (121.MEGUS[9], 72.SAMUEL[8], 59.PHILIP[7], 50.PHILIP[6], 26.THEISS[5], 9.LUDWIG[4], 3.HUBERT[3], 2.HENNE[2], I.SIMON[1]) was born 8 April 1866 in PROB W. VA, POSS. 1886. RHESA died IN OR NEAR HAMPSHIRE, CO W. VA. He married **EMMA SARAH HILL**. She was born 27 November 1871. EMMA died in OR NEAR HAMPSHIRE, CO W. VA.

They had 8 children:

370. m i. **NORMAN R ORENDORFF**, born 11 December 1889 in PROB VA OR W. VA, died in OR NEAR HAMPSHIRE, CO W. VA. NORMAN'S NAME APPEARS AS "ORNDORFF". HE IS BURIED IN OR NEAR HAMPSHIRE CO W. VA.

371. f ii. **RENA ORENDORFF**, born 1892.

372. f iii. **MINNIE B. ORENDORFF**, born 1896.

373. m iv. **DALE C. ORENDORFF**, born 1900. DALE C.'S NAME APPEARS AS "ORNDORFF".

374. f v. **ESTHER ORENDORFF**, born 1902.

375. m vi. **GORDON GEORGE ORENDORFF**, born 1905. He married ELSIE IRENE PEER.

376. m vii. **CLYDE C. ORENDORFF**, born 1908.

377. f viii. **LENA F. ORENDORFF**, born 13 October 1894. LENA F.'S NAME APPEARS AS "ORNDORFF".

Notes for Emma:
Emma Sarah Hill is buried in or near Hampshire Co W. VA with her husband. Poss died 04-23-1953.

Notes for Rhesa:
Rhesa Allen's name appears as "Orndorff". Also called Reese, buried in or near Hampshire Co W. VA.

- - - - - - - - - - -

218. REUBEN LOSTON[10] ORENDORFF (121.MEGUS[9], 72.SAMUEL[8], 59.PHILIP[7], 50.PHILIP[6], 26.THEISS[5], 9.LUDWIG[4], 3.HUBERT[3], 2.HENNE[2], 1.SIMON[1]) was born 1869 in POSSIBLY 1870/VA. REUBEN died in OR NEAR HAMPSHIRE, CO W. VA. He married **CLARA JANE ORENDORFF**. She was born 1873 probably in VA. CLARA died in OR NEAR HAMPSHIRE, CO W. VA.

They had 3 children:

378.	m	i.	**WARD W. ORENDORFF**, born 1898 in PROBABLY VA, died in OR NEAR HAMPSHIRE, CO W. VA. WARD W.'S NAME APPEARS AS "ORNDORFF". HE IS BURIED WITH HIS PARENTS IN OR NEAR HAMPSHIRE CO VA. POSS. DIED IN 1908.
379.	m	ii.	**GLENN G. ORENDORFF**, born 1903 in PROBABLY VA. GLENN'S NAME APPEARS AS "ORNDORFF".
380.	m	iii.	**ARBUTUS A. ORENDORFF**, born 1908 in PROBABLY VA. He married _____ BOWEN. Notes for ARBUTUS: ARBUTUS A.'S NAME APPEARS AS "ORNDORFF".

Notes for Clara:

Clara Jane's name appears as "Orndorff". She is buried in or near Hampshire Co W. VA with her husband and son.

Notes for Reuben:

Reuben's name appears as "Orndorff", he apparently married a cousin of his. He is buried with his wife in or near Hampshire Co W. VA.

- - - - - - - - - - -

220. SIDNEY CLINTON[10] **ORENDORFF** (122.LEWIS[9], 72.SAMUEL[8], 59.PHILIP[7], 50.PHILIP[6], 26.THEISS[5], 9.LUDWIG[4], 3.HUBERT[3], 2.HENNE[2], 1.SIMON[1]) was born December 1876. SIDNEY died May 1964, at the age of 87. He married **LYDIA C. PENNYWITT.**

They had 2 children:

381.　　m　i.　**LORING P. ORENDORFF,** born 1907.

382.　　m　ii.　**COURTNEY L. ORENDORFF,** born 1908. MARRIED A GWEN. COURTNEY L'S NAME APPEARS AS "ORNDORFF".

- - - - - - - - - - -

221. LUTHER S.[10] **ORENDORFF** (122.LEWIS[9], 72.SAMUEL[8], 59.PHILIP[7], 50.PHILIP[6], 26.THEISS[5], 9.LUDWIG[4], 3.HUBERT[3], 2.HENNE[2], 1.SIMON[1]) was born 5 September 1880. LUTHER died in MAYBE 03-26-1957. He married **NORA BELL SWARTZ.** She was born 1889.

They had 5 children:

+ 383.　　m　i.　**GERALD LUTHER ORENDORFF,** born 1910.

384.　　m　ii.　**MARTIN LEE ORENDORFF,** born 1 October 1913. MARTIN LEE'S NAME APPEARS AS "ORNDORFF".

+ 385.　　m　iii.　**KARL LINNAS ORENDORFF,** born 6 May 1917.

386. f iv. **MARY VIRGINIA ORENDORFF**, born 8 September 1920.
MARY VIRGINIA'S NAME APPEARS AS "ORNDORFF", SHE MARRIED DONALD CALVIN SHEELY BORN 1921.

387. f v. **SARA ELIZABETH ORENDORFF**, born 8 June 1923.
SARA ELISABETH'S NAME APPEARS AS "ORNDORFF", SHE MARRIED VINTON MCCLELLAN III BORN 1917.

Notes for Nora:
Possibly married 1907.

Notes for Luther:
Possibly married 1907. Luther S.'s name appears as "Orndorff".

- - - - - - - - - - -

222. HUGH CALVIN[10] **ORENDORFF** (122.LEWIS[9], 72.SAMUEL[8], 59.PHILIP[7], 50.PHILIP[6], 26.THEISS[5], 9.LUDWIG[4], 3.HUBERT[3], 2.HENNE[2], 1.SIMON[1]) was born 12 August 1888. HUGH died 13 August 1961, at the age of 73. He married **LENA MAE SWARTZ**. She was born 31 May 1891.
They had 6 children:

388. m i. **EDWIN CALVIN ORENDORFF**, born 10 October 1914. He married ELSIE VIRGINIA CONNER (FORTNEY). She was born 9 February 1915. Notes for EDWIN: EDWIN CALVIN'S NAME APPEARS AS "ORNDORFF".

389. f ii. **MARTHA ALICE ORENDORFF**, born July 1916.
MARTHA ALICE'S NAME APPEARS AS "ORNDORFF", SHE MARRIED ERNEST HOWARD NEWTON.

+ 390.   m   iii.   **LEWIS SWARTZ ORENDORFF**, born 1 February 1918.

391.   f   iv.   **ALBERTA ELIZABETH ORENDORFF**, born 8 February 1920.
ALBERTA ELIZABETH'S NAME APPEARS AS "ORNDORFF", SHE MARRIED MICHAEL YOURSHAW BORN 1917. THEY HAD THE FOLLOWING CHILDREN: A) MICHAEL C. YOURSHAW BORN 09-05-1941. B) MARTHA ELIZABETH YOURSHAW BORN 05-04-1944, C) MARY KATHLYNN YOURSHAW BORN 02-21-1948, D) BARBARA ANN YOURSHAW BORN 01-29-1958.

+ 392.   m   v.   **JAMES HUGH ORENDORFF**, born 25 July 1925.

393.   f   vi.   **CHARLENE MAE ORENDORFF**, born 15 June 1931.
CHARLENE MAE'S NAME APPEARS AS "ORNDORFF", SHE MARRIED REGIS EUGENE PENLEY BORN IN 1930. THEY HAD THE FOLLOWING CHILDREN: A) KAREN JEAN PENLEY BORN 11-08-1953, B) SUSAN CAROL PENLEY BORN 11-23-1954, C) MARTHA ANN PENLEY BORN 10-07-1955, D) ROBERT LEONARD PENLEY BORN 09-30-1957, E) WILLIAM LEWIS LEE PENLEY BORN 11-14-1962.

Notes for Hugh:
Hugh Calvin's name appears as "Orndorff".

- - - - - - - - - - -

227. MARTHA MAHALA[10] **ORENDORFF** (128.BENJAMIN[9], 73.LEWIS[8], 59.PHILIP[7], 50.PHILIP[6],

26.THEISS[5], 9.LUDWIG[4], 3.HUBERT[3], 2.HENNE[2], I.SIMON[1]) was born 1855. She married **LEWIS ORENDORFF (See number 122)** 15 October 1874 in POSS. VA. He was born 5 April 1847 in PROBABLY VA. He was the son of SAMUEL ORENDORFF and COMFORT JANE PEER. **See number 122** listed above.

- - - - - - - - - - -

230. CHARLES MONROE[10] ORENDORFF (128.BENJAMIN[9], 73.LEWIS[8], 59.PHILIP[7], 50.PHILIP[6], 26.THEISS[5], 9.LUDWIG[4], 3.HUBERT[3], 2.HENNE[2], I.SIMON[1]) was born 28 December 1856 in PROBABLY VA. CHARLES died 23 January 1927 in OR NEAR HAMPSHIRE, CO W. VA, at the age of 70. He married **EMMA LEE MCINTURFF** 2 June 1881 probably in VA. She was born 1 November 1863 in POSS. VA. EMMA died 29 February 1932 in OR NEAR HAMPSHIRE, CO W. VA, at the age of 68.

They had 4 children:

+ 394. m i. **LESTER G. ORENDORFF,** born 1884.

395. f ii. **MAUD V. ORENDORFF,** born 1893 in PROBABLY VA.
MAUD V'S NAME APPEARS AS "ORNDORFF".

396. f iii. **WINNIE D. ORENDORFF,** born 7 November 1896 in PROBABLY VA.
WINNIE D'S NAME APPEARS AS "ORNDORFF", SHE MARRIED LUTHER EDWARD SWARTZ.

397. m iv. **WELDON C. ORENDORFF,** born 1905.
WELDON C'S NAME APPEARS AS "ORNDORFF".

Notes for Emma:
Emma Lee Mcinturff is buried with her husband in or near Hampshire Co W. VA; she may have died 02-27-1932.

Notes for Charles:

Charles Monroe's name appears as "Orndorff". He is buried in or near Hampshire Co W. VA with his wife.

- - - - - - - - - - -

232. REBECCA ELLEN[10] **ORENDORFF** (128.BENJAMIN[9], 73.LEWIS[8], 59.PHILIP[7], 50.PHILIP[6], 26.THEISS[5], 9.LUDWIG[4], 3.HUBERT[3], 2.HENNE[2], I.SIMON[1]) was born 18 December 1852 in PROBABLY VA. REBECCA died 25 December 1908 in POSS. VA, at the age of 56. She married **GEORGE WASHINGTON ORENDORFF (See number 124)** 20 June 1872 probably in VA. He was born 15 October 1838 possibly in VA. He was the son of SAMUEL ORENDORFF and COMFORT JANE PEER. **See number 124** listed above.

- - - - - - - - - - -

238. WILLIAM ALLEN[10] **ORENDORFF** (132.HARRISON[9], 76.PHILIP[8], 60.JOHN[7], 50.PHILIP[6], 26.THEISS[5], 9.LUDWIG[4], 3.HUBERT[3], 2.HENNE[2], I.SIMON[1]) was born 28 May 1840 in LICKING CO OHIO. WILLIAM died 5 September 1914 in LAMAR, BARTON CO MO, at the age of 74. He married **SARAH JANE RALLS** 14 March 1867 in SULLIVAN/DAVIES CO MO. She was born 16 February 1850 in ADAIR CO MO. SARAH died 16 June 1924 in LAMAR, BARTON CO MO, at the age of 74.

They had 9 children:

398.   f   i.   **ZULA BELLE ORENDORFF**, born 22 September 1869 in GRUNDY CO MO, died 13 October 1933 in SKIATOOK, OSAGE CO OK, at the age of 64.

Zula married James Grant Ridennoure born 09-15-1866 in Mercer Co MO died 04-25-1950 in Hillsborough Co FL, son of Martin Ridennoure and Esther Frances Coon. Her 2nd husband was Porter or Peter Moss and the 3rd was Edward Fox. Her children were

Gertrude Gail 05-04-1891 Jasper Co MO died 09-11-1971 CA married 12-10-1910 Texas to Charlie E. Robinson. Martin Allen born 01-10-1893 in Jasper Co MO died 04-20-1971 Wichita Co Texas married to 09-30-1911 at Osage Co OK to Jennie Ethel Brown. Lawrence Culberson born 03-13-1895 in Barton CO MO died 08-08-1975 Otero County CO married 01-30-1922 Otero County CO to Etha Lynn Taylor. Winfield Carl born 06-23-1897 MO died 05-27-1976 Wash. Co OK married 07-27-1922 to Mildred Rosetta Saxton. Gerald Irvin born 09-15-1899 in MO died 08-10-1964 in Osage Co OK-married Rachel Madole. Sarah Frances born 12-25-1901 in Chatauqua Co KS married 08-06-1923 in Ill to Ansel Lindley. Theodore Roosevelt born 03-19-1904 in Chautauqua Co KS died 12-03-1904 Chautauqua Co KS. Ruby Leota born 06-12-1905 Chautauqua Co KS died 07-18-1974 in Rogers Co OK married #1 06-15-1927 Joe Vinson and #2 Mr. Smith. Otis Earl born 02-15-1908 in Taney Co MO married 05-23-1933 in Sperry, Tulsa Co OK to Eva Marie Ervin.

399.   f   ii.   **NOLA LEE ORENDORFF**, born 24 May 1871 in MO, died in MO.
DIED YOUNG

400.   m   iii.   **CLARENCE ALLEN ORENDORFF**, born 5 December 1872 in MO, died in MO.
DIED YOUNG

401.   f   iv.   **BIRTIE GAIL ORENDORFF**, born 28 February 1879 in LAMAR, BARTON CO MO, died 14 December 1969 in CA, at the age of 90.
Married twice Birtie Gail's name appears as

"Orndorff". Married first to Andrew Walter Bradford and secondly to Frank Osbourn. Child with first Elsie May 05-20-1896 died 07-27-1938. Children with second husband-Jessie Marie "Peggy" B. 05-12-1899, Nola Lee born 04-01-1902 died 1960, Grace Leora born 03-04-1905, and Arthur Allen born 02-10-1909.

402.   f   v.   **ANNIE DEE ORENDORFF**, born 31 May 1881 in LAMAR, BARTON CO MO, died 26 August 1923, at the age of 42.

Married John R. Clements. Annie Dee's husband was born in 1878 in IL. They had a child in 1903 named Clarence in MO in 1903 died in Ill, Huber born 1905 in MO, Theodore born 1907 in MO died 1932 in Lamar, Barton Co MO and who married Ruby, Eva J. born in 1909 in MO.

403.   f   vi.   **CLARA MAUDE ORENDORFF**, born 10 August 1874 in LAMAR, BARTON CO MO, died 9 October 1948 in NEVADA, MO, at the age of 74.

Married William Arthur Vincent. Clara Maude's name appears as "Orndorff", her husband was born 05-28-1871 in Galena, Kansas, died 05-28-1936 Hume, MO he was the son of Merrick Vincent and Nancy Beaston. Children-William Albert 11-24-1894 Lamar, Barton Co, MO died 11-18-1975 married Gladys Schultz. Rene May born 01-30-1896 Lamar, Barton Co MO died 04-13-1971 in CA married John William Murphy. Wilmer Allen born 07-09-1898 Lamar, Barton Co MO died 07-03-1966 never married. Vernaileta born 06-09-1903 Lamar, Barton Co MO married 09-13-1963 Jack Campbell. Roy Lee born 08-11-1905 born

09-00-1972 married Ethel Adams. Arthur Ray born 03-24-1907 died 08-08-1969 married #1 Pearl Waltz #2 03-00-1926 Sadie Barker. Lula Bell born 10-07-1908 married #1 James Walton Thornburn #2 George Edward Adams. Viola Fay born 06-19-1910 married 05-10-1927 Homer R. Miller.

+ 404. m vii. **IRA IRVIN ORENDORFF,** born 20 October 1875, died 23 February 1959.

+ 405. m viii. **ELMER LLOYD ORENDORFF.**

+ 406. m ix. **GEORGE WASHINGTON ORENDORFF,** born 2 January 1868, died 20 March 1938.

Notes for Sarah:
Sarah Jane Ralls was the daughter of Morgan Ralls and Lydia Abbott.

Notes for William:
William Allen resided in Lamar, Barton Co, MO in 1880. Moved to Barton Co in 1874 with family.

- - - - - - - - - -

239. LORENZO DOW[10] ORENDORFF (132.HARRISON[9], 76.PHILIP[8], 60.JOHN[7], 50.PHILIP[6], 26.THEISS[5], 9.LUDWIG[4], 3.HUBERT[3], 2.HENNE[2], 1.SIMON[1]) was born 2 April 1839 in COLUMBUS, LICKING CO OHIO. LORENZO died 1 March 1923 in MERCER CO, MISSOURI, at the age of 83. He married **MARY ANN GLASS** 14 April 1859 in KEOKUK CO, IOWA. She was born 1 September 1840 in South Carolina. MARY died in MERCER CO, MO.

They had 7 children:

407. f i. **INA FLORENCE ORENDORFF,** born 13 December 1862 in MARTINSBURG KEOKUK CO, IOWA, died 24 January 1940 in TRENTON, GRUNDY CO MISSOURI, at the age of 77.

Married Hiram E. Cooksey. Ina's name is spelled "Orndorff" in the Iowa genealogical index. Hiram was born 12-25-1848 in Dewitt, IL died 10-05-1933 Trenton, Grundy Co, MO son of John Cooksy and Sarah Martin.

408. f ii. **ALFRETTA ORENDORFF**, born 18 January 1864 in KEOKUK CO IA.
MARRIED WILLIAM VAN WINKLE ALFRETTA'S NAME APPEARS AS "ORNDORFF".

409. f iii. **OCTAVA FRANCES ORENDORFF**, born 3 March 1870 in MO.
MARRIED E.M. BRAHAM OCTAVA'S NAME APPEARS AS "ORNDORFF".

410. f iv. **DAISY DEAN ORENDORFF**, born 28 October 1872 in MISSOURI.
MARRIED MR. JONES

411. m v. **EMERY OLIVER ORENDORFF**, born 26 July 1871 in MO. He married LILLIAN MILNER.
EMERY died 4 February 1914, at the age of 42.
Notes for EMERY:
EMERY OLIVER'S NAME APPEARS AS "ORNDORFF".

+ 412. m vi. **LEANDER BOND ORENDORFF**, born SEE NOTES, died 1929.

413. m vii. **WILLIAM H. ORENDORFF**, born 29 June 1861 in KEOKUK CO IA. He married ROBERTA BRIDGES 1883 in POSS. IA.
WILLIAM died 21 April 1923 in POSS. IA, at the age of 61. Notes for WILLIAM:
William H.'s name appears as "Orndorff".

Notes for Mary:

Mary Ann was the daughter of James Glass and Hannah Freeman.

Notes for Lorenzo:
Lorenzo is listed in an Iowa genealogical index, the spelling is "Orndorff".

- - - - - - - - - - -

245. DANIEL M.[10] **ORENDORFF** (132.HARRISON[9], 76.PHILIP[8], 60.JOHN[7], 50.PHILIP[6], 26.THEISS[5], 9.LUDWIG[4], 3.HUBERT[3], 2.HENNE[2], 1.SIMON[1]) was born 16 May 1854 in IA. He married **EVANGALINE RUSELTON.**

They had 1 child:

414.　　m　i.　　**HARRISON ORENDORFF,** born 1879 in MO.
HARRISON'S NAME APPEARS AS "ORNDORFF".

Notes for Daniel:
Daniel M.'s name appears as "Orndorff".

- - - - - - - - - - -

260. LUTHER EDGAR[10] **ORENDORFF** (143.PHILIP[9], 78.LEVI[8], 60.JOHN[7], 50.PHILIP[6], 26.THEISS[5], 9.LUDWIG[4], 3.HUBERT[3], 2.HENNE[2], 1.SIMON[1]) was born 17 August 1860. LUTHER died in POSSIBLE DEATH DATE. His spouse has not been identified.

They had 1 child:

415.　　f　i.　　**LUCILE K. ORENDORFF,** born 1897 in PROBABLY VA.
LUCILE K.'S NAME APPEARS AS "ORNDORFF".

Notes for Luther:
Luther Edgar's name appears as "Orndorff". He married an Annie L. born 1867.

- - - - - - - - - - -

264. BRUCE MORGAN[10] **ORENDORFF** (143.PHILIP[9], 78.LEVI[8], 60.JOHN[7], 50.PHILIP[6], 26.THEISS[5], 9.LUDWIG[4], 3.HUBERT[3], 2.HENNE[2], 1.SIMON[1]) was born in 1870 POSS. 1874, POSS. VA. He married **BERTHA GIFFIN**.

They had 6 children:

416.   m   i.   **MILTON ORENDORFF**, born 10 April 1900 in POSS. VA, died in POSS. VA.
DIED YOUNG.

417.   m   ii.   **DELMAS ORENDORFF**, born 18 December 1907 in POSS. VA.
DELMAS' NAME APPEARS AS "ORNDORFF".

418.   m   iii.   **MARVIN ORENDORFF**, born 6 November 1910 in POSS. VA. He married RUTH SNYDER.

419.   m   iv.   **BRUCE WOODROW ORENDORFF**, born 17 August 1917 in POSS. VA.
BRUCE WOODROW'S NAME APPEARS AS "ORNDORFF".

420.   f   v.   **INA LEE ORENDORFF**, born in POSS. VA.
INA LEE MARRIED UZELL C. PEER, HER NAME APPEARS AS "ORNDORFF".

421.   f   vi.   **WINFRED ORENDORFF**, born 28 August 1905 in POSS. VA.
WINFRED MARRIED LOIS CAMPBELL, HER NAME APPEARS AS "ORNDORFF".

Notes for Bertha:

Father was a Confederate soldier. Bertha Giffin was the daughter of David W. Giffin (son of James Giffin and Eliza Keckley) and Margaret Secrest (daughter of Joseph and Christina Secrest). Her brothers and sister were: Mollie Giffin, Isiah Giffin, Lena Giffin who was married, Cline Giffin who lived in Maryland, Retta Giffin who married Alex Long. The other children of James Giffin and Eliza Keckley were: Margaret Giffin married to Elkanoh Ridway, living in

Cumberland Maryland, John R. Giffin married to Sallie Eaton, Susie Giffin married to Thornton Fletcher, Edward R. married to Ann Elizabeth McIntyre.

Notes for Bruce:
Bruce Morgan's name appears as "Orndorff".

- - - - - - - - - - -

277. MAHALA[10] **ORENDORFF** (149.MAHALA[9], 85.DAVID[8], 60.JOHN[7], 50.PHILIP[6], 26.THEISS[5], 9.LUDWIG[4], 3.HUBERT[3], 2.HENNE[2], I.SIMON[1]) was born 1848. MAHALA died 1919, at the age of 71. She married **MARTIN V B SNYDER**. He was born 1848. MARTIN died 1896, at the age of 48.

They had 1 child:

+ 422.   f   i.   **LAURA LEE SNYDER**, born 1868, died 1957.

Notes for Mahala:
Married Martin V. Snyder Mahala had a total of 9 children, her name appears as "Orndorff". One of the 9 married an Orendorff, the rest are as follows: 1) Wade H. Snyder 1866-1875,3) William M. Snyder 1870-1938 who married Harriet Strosnider, 4) Fannie E. (Pink) Snyder who married Daniel Selden, 5) James S. Snyder 1874-1949 who married Roberta Scott, 6) Sudie B. Snyder 1876-1956 who married Banks Gilbert, 7) Harry J. Snyder 1879-1942 who married Claudia Sone, 8) Mary V. Snyder 1882- , who married first Madison Kerney, and secondly Elmer Crutchfield, and 9) Grover C. Snyder 1885-1948 who married Mabel Holt.

- - - - - - - - - - -

281. BAKER C.[10] **ORENDORFF** (150.HARRISON[9], 85.DAVID[8], 60.JOHN[7], 50.PHILIP[6], 26.THEISS[5], 9.LUDWIG[4], 3.HUBERT[3], 2.HENNE[2], I.SIMON[1]) was born 1860 probably in VA. BAKER died in OR NEAR HAMPSHIRE, CO W. VA. His spouse has not been identified.

They had 3 children:

423.　　m　i.　**WATSON V. ORENDORFF**, born 1886.
　　　　　　　POSSIBLY BORN 1888
424.　　f　ii.　**LENA ORENDORFF**, born 1890.
　　　　　　　POSSIBLY BORN 1891
425.　　m　iii.　**"NO NAME" ORENDORFF**, born 1898.
　　　　　　　FIRST NAME UNKNOWN/3RD CHILD

　　Notes for Baker:
　　Baker C.'s name appears as "Orndorff", he married a Martha born 1866 died 1909. He is buried with his wife in Hardy Co W. VA.

- - - - - - - - - - -

　　283.　　HARRISON　RILEY[10]　**ORENDORFF** (150.HARRISON[9], 85.DAVID[8], 60.JOHN[7], 50.PHILIP[6], 26.THEISS[5], 9.LUDWIG[4], 3.HUBERT[3], 2.HENNE[2], 1.SIMON[1]) was born 20 March 1854 probably in VA. HARRISON died in or NEAR HAMPSHIRE, CO W. VA. He married **LORENA E. CALVERT**. She was born 1876. LORENA died in or NEAR HAMPSHIRE, CO W. VA.

　　They had 4 children:

426.　　m　i.　**HOYT ORENDORFF**, born 1893.
　　　　　　　CIRCA B. DATE HOYT'S NAME APPEARS AS "ORNDORFF".
427.　　m　ii.　**DECIL ORENDORFF**, born 1898.
　　　　　　　CIRCA B. DATE
428.　　f　iii.　**EUNICE ORENDORFF**, born 1904.
　　　　　　　CIRCA B. DATE EUNICE'S NAME APPEARS AS "ORNDORFF".
429.　　f　iv.　**MATTIE ORENDORFF**, born 1892.
　　　　　　　CIRCA B. DATE MATTIE'S NAME APPEARS AS "ORNDORFF".

Notes for Harrison:

Harrison Riley's name appears as "Orndorff". He is buried in Hardy Co W. VA.

- - - - - - - - - - - -

284. AMANDA M.[10] **ORENDORFF** (150.HARRISON[9], 85.DAVID[8], 60.JOHN[7], 50.PHILIP[6], 26.THEISS[5], 9.LUDWIG[4], 3.HUBERT[3], 2.HENNE[2], 1.SIMON[1]) was born 1849. AMANDA died in PROBABLY HARDY CO W., VA. She married **TILBERRY ORENDORFF**. He was born 1845 in VA. He was the son of JONAH ORENDORFF and CHRISTINA ORENDORFF. TILBERRY died in WEST VA.

They had 7 children:

430. f i. **RUBY ORENDORFF**, born 1873 in PROBABLY VA.
POSS. 3RD CHILD BORN RUBY'S NAME APPEARS AS "ORNDORFF'. SHE MARRIED JAMES TEETS AND HAD ONE CHILD.

431. f ii. **MINNIE ORENDORFF**, born 1871 in WEST VA, POSS. 1870.
MINNIE'S NAME APPEARS AS "ORNDORFF". SHE IS BURIED IN WEST VA.

432. f iii. **DAISY ORENDORFF**, born 1875 in PROBABLY VA.
MARRIED ANGUS WALKER DAISY'S NAME APPEARS AS "ORNDORFF". SHE HAD 6 CHILDREN.

433. f iv. **SPRING ORENDORFF**, born 1878 in WEST VA, died in WEST VA.
UNMARRIED SPRING'S NAME APPEARS AS "ORNDORFF". SHE IS BURIED IN HARDY CO WEST VA. HER NAME MAY HAVE BEEN SPRIGG.

434.   f   v.   **HATTIE ORENDORFF**, born 1881 in WEST VA, died in PROBABLY WEST VA. HATTIE'S NAME APPEARS AS "ORNDORFF". SHE IS BURIED IN HARDY CO WEST VIRGINIA.

435.   f   vi.   **LYNN ORENDORFF**, born 1885 in WEST VA, POSS. 1884. LYNN'S NAME APPEARS AS "ORNDORFF". SHE IS BURIED IN WEST VA.

436.   f   vii.   **DORA ORENDORFF**, born in POSS. VA, died in POSS. VA OR W. VA. DIED YOUNG DORA'S NAME APPEARS AS "ORNDORFF".

Notes for Tilberry:

Poss. spelled Tilbury/soldier Tilberry was a 1st private in company d 62nd VA infantry CSA. He enlisted 08-20-1862 in Hardy Co West Virginia. Present for duty as of 09-01-1862. Transferred to company I 18th VA cavalry. Captured 01-03-1864. Released from Ft Delaware, Delaware 06-20-1865. He was a farmer. He had a light complexion, light hair, and blue eyes. He was 5' 9" and is buried in Wardensville Cemetery, Wardensville, Hardy Co West VA. Tilberry was married to a woman named Amanda M. born 1847(8) died 1932. They had 8 children. Sources-confederate military records, tombstone inscription.

Notes for Amanda:

Amanda's name appears as "Orndorff", she may have married a Tilbury Orendorff. Poss born 1847, she is buried with her husband in Hardy Co W. VA. Source-tombstone inscription.

- - - - - - - - - - -

288. ROBERT FRANCIS[10] **ORENDORFF** (165.JOSEPH[9], 89.JOHNATHAN[8], 60.JOHN[7], 50.PHILIP[6], 26.THEISS[5],

9.LUDWIG[4], 3.HUBERT[3], 2.HENNE[2], I.SIMON[1]) was born 1832. He married **SALINA P. HUBBELL** 20 November 1858 in DELAWARE CO OHIO. She was born 1840.

They had 2 children:

+ 437.   m   i.   **HOWARD S. ORENDORFF**, born 1864.

438.   m   ii.   **ORVILLE H. ORENDORFF**, born 1868 in PROBABLY VA.

ORVILLE H'S NAME APPEARS AS "ORNDORFF".

Notes for Robert:

Farmer Robert Francis's name appears as "Orndorff". He appears in the 1850 census for Frederick Co VA, the towns of Newton and Stephensburg living with his parents. His name appears as "Orndorff" and his age is listed as 17.

- - - - - - - - - - -

292. WILLIAM B.[10] ORENDORFF (165.JOSEPH[9], 89.JOHNATHAN[8], 60.JOHN[7], 50.PHILIP[6], 26.THEISS[5], 9.LUDWIG[4], 3.HUBERT[3], 2.HENNE[2], I.SIMON[1]) was born 1834 in VA. He married **CATHERINE LOREN** 1856 in PROBABLY VA.

They had 3 children:

439.   m   i.   **FRANK C. ORENDORFF**, born 1863 in POSS. VA.

440.   f   ii.   **ADA E. ORENDORFF**, born 1870 in POSS. VA.

ADA E.'S NAME APPEARS AS "ORNDORFF".

441.   m   iii.   **JOSEPH W. ORENDORFF**, born 1866 in POSS. VA.

JOSEPH W.'S NAME APPEARS AS "ORNDORFF".

Notes for Catherine:
Name possibly Loring.

Notes for William:
Farmer. William B.'s name appears as "Orndorff". He is shown to be living with his parents in the 1850 census for Frederick Co VA towns of Newton and Stephensburg, his age is listed as 15.

- - - - - - - - - - - -

293. ROBERT HOUSTON[10] **ORENDORFF** (166.WILLIAM[9], 90.JESSE[8], 65.CHRISTIAN[7], 54.CHRISTIAN[6], 48.JOHANN[5], 25.HERMANN[4], 7.STEPHEN[3], 2.HENNE[2], 1.SIMON[1]) was born 1847 in BRECKINRIDGE CO., KY. He married (1) **FANNY HAMPTON** 9 September 1868. She was born 5 May 1851 in FANNIN CO TX. FANNY died 13 October 1873 in WESTON TX, at the age of 22.

They had 2 children:

+ 442.   m   i.   **DEE ORENDORFF.**
+ 443.   f   ii.   **NOVA ORENDORFF**, born 27 December 1871, died 8 March 1958.

Notes for Fanny:
First wife of R. H. Orendorff. Marriage license book no. 3, April 5, 1867-Feb. 6, 1876 lists R.H. Orenduff, groom and Fanny Hampton, bride. Date of their marriage is 9 Sept. 1868 with marriage performed by E.W. Morton. Fanny was Sue Hampton's younger sister who married Jesse Orenduff (Robert's brother).

ROBERT married (2) **AMANDA JANE CULWELL** 3 August 1876 in COLLIN COUNTY TEXAS. She was born 23 March 1860 in TEXAS, PROBABLY COLLIN CO. She was the daughter of ANDREW JACKSON CULWELL. AMANDA died 10 May 1938, at the age of 78.

They had 3 children:

+ 444.   m   iii.   **STEPHEN HAMILTON ORENDORFF,**

born 17 December 1878, died 9 April 1944.

445.   m   iv.   **ED ORENDORFF**, born 11 January 1881, died 4 October 1919 in PLAINVIEW OKLAHOMA, at the age of 38.

Ed Orenduff was born on January 11,1881, the third child of Robert Houston and Amanda Jane Culwell Orenduff. He was a barber by trade and while working in El Paso, Texas he contacted tuberculosis and returned to Plainview, Oklahoma where he was cared for by his brother Stephen Hamilton and family until his death on October 4, 1919 at thirty eight years of age. Source: Velma Thacker.

446.   f   v.   **LENA ORENDORFF**. She married JOHN SLIMP. Notes for LENA:

Lena was the first child born to Robert Houston and Amanda Jane Culwell Orenduff. She later changed her name to the Orendorff spelling. She married John Slimp. Source: Velma Thacker

Notes for Amanda:

2nd wife of R.H. Orendorff. Amanda's father was Andrew Jackson (Caldwell) Culwell. He was born in Alabama on 04-06-1817 and died on 06-07-1903 in Weston Texas. There were Culwells living in Weston Texas. According to the 1900 census for Collin Co. Amanda's parents were both born in Arkansas. After her husband Robert Houston disappeared she married John A. Dorsey, b. August 1859 in South Carolina (1900 census index). They were probably married around 1895 and lived in Weston Texas where he had a store. The 1900 census lists them as living together along with a stepson Stephen Orendorff. Apparently John A. was a grocer and sold jewelry from his store also. It might have been a general store. Also on the census John A. is shown to have owned his own home without a mortgage. Robert S. Caldwell (Culwell) died in Collin Co Texas in October of 1860 of unknown causes, he was born in Texas and died after being sick for 4 weeks at the age of 3/12, probably meaning 3 months and 12 days. J.W. Culwell appears in a Collin Co Texas bond book as a constable appointed November 6, 1894.

Notes for Robert:
Religion: Methodist.
Confederate soldier/policeman (from family accounts), in Gainesville, Texas around the year 1880. He joined the 6th regiment Texas cavalry as a private in company d while it was in Harrisonburg, Catahoula Co Louisiana on March 13 in 1863 by Lt. Murchison. He fought in miss, Tenn., Georgia, and was in the battle of Atlanta. He apparently was captured at Coahoma Co Mississippi on Feb 17 1865. Coahoma Co is in northwestern Mississippi and it borders the Mississippi River, about 50-miles south west of Memphis Tennessee. It has been stated that he fought under the "black flag". He was captured in Coahoma Co Mississippi on February 17 1865 and was taken to Helena Arkansas. He arrived in camp Douglas IL on 03-05-1865 from Helena Ark. He was then forwarded to New Orleans LA on 05-04-1865 and confined on 05-11-1865. Next he was exchanged on May 23 1865 by order of union Maj. General E.R.S. Canby. His daughter Lena describes him as being 6 feet tall, curly auburn hair, blue eyes, and very fair complexion. Many people have said he was very handsome and that he was honest and knew no fear. She also says that her mother told her he idolized his children, the night was never too hot, dark, or cold if a child wanted anything he was the first to it's bedside. He was nicknamed Howt. She also said that he did not use tobacco, coffee, or whiskey, just could not take. R.H. disappeared in 1881. His son Stephen Hamilton recalled being outside at their home with his father when a gang of "ruffians" rode up. As they approached, R. H. jumped on his horse, bounded over a fence and that was the last time that he was ever seen. It is believed that this was a gang of outlaws out for revenge. It is still uncertain as to what happened to Robert Houston. Some have thought that in trying to escape this gang, he made it to New Orleans where he died due to a cholera epidemic and was buried in a mass grave. Another story of speculation is that he

escaped to China via California and married a Chinese princess, these stories were told to me by Mary Ann Thacker who had heard these accounts from her mother and other family members. Apparently his sister Lena had hired a private detective to track him down and the detective found him still living in China during the 1930's. Robert Houston married Fannie Hampton firstly on 09-09-1868 ceremony performed by E. W. Morton. Secondly married Amanda Jane Culwell married by F.M. Bounds. The marriage record was filed by the county clerk, J.M. Benge on August 3, 1876. Robert is shown to have attended school when he was 13 years old. He is listed as "Howerton" in an old Collin Co newspaper article about his brother Jesse and is also refered to as R.H (Howerton) in the obituary of his eldest brother, John Hayes Orenduff. Sources-Marriage license book no. 3, April 5, 1867-Feb. 6, 1876 (Orenduff-Hampton marriage certificate (Orenduff-Culwell) J.H.O. obituary, various family members, Civil war enlistment papers, Collin Co TX census)

- - - - - - - - - - -

295. JESSE WILLIAM[10] **ORENDORFF** (166.WILLIAM[9], 90.JESSE[8], 65.CHRISTIAN[7], 54.CHRISTIAN[6], 48.JOHANN[5], 25.HERMANN[4], 7.STEPHEN[3], 2.HENNE[2], 1.SIMON[1]) was born 19 March 1843 in BRECKINRIDGE CO KY, WEBSTER. JESSE died 17 July 1928 in MELISSA TX, at the age of 85. He married **SUE G. HAMPTON** 27 April 1865 in MELISSA TX. She was born 27 April 1842 in LEWIS CO MISSOURI. SUE died 30 August 1922 in MELISSA TX, at her home, at the age of 80.

They had 7 children:

+ 447.   m   i.   **ARBA ORENDORFF**, born 24 March 1866, died 10 October 1919.

+ 448.   f   ii.   **JENNIE IONE ORENDORFF**, born 18 July 1868.

449.   f   iii.   **KAY ORENDORFF**, born in PROBABLY MELISSA TEXAS.
BORN BETWEEN 1868 AND 1879 KAY MARRIED FRANK BOONE. HAD THE

FOLLOWING CHILDREN: ARBY BOONE, BEATRICE BOONE, JENNIE BOONE, BUFORD BOONE, AND ORTHELL BOONE.

+ 450.   m   iv.   **JESSE ORENDORFF**, born 1874.

451.   f   v.   **LEONA ORENDORFF**, born in BETWEEN 1880 AND 1885.

LEONA WAS MARRIED TO OTHA C. HARRIS, THEY HAD ONE CHILD WHO DIED YOUNG. ALSO A LEONA MARRIED HENRY C. ROACH.

+ 452.   m   vi.   **ROSS ORENDORFF**, born 22 February 1886.

+ 453.   m   vii.   **MONROE ORENDORFF**, born 30 April 1879, died 18 November 1959.

Notes for Sue:

Suzannah moved to Texas from Missouri when she was 4 years old with her parents. Her family first settled at Bonham, then moving to Weston. Both of her parents are also buried in the Chambersville Cemetery. Her family is related to that of General Wade Hampton, the noted South Carolina confederate general and leader. Sue G. Hampton married Jesse William Orenduff on April 27, 1865 the marriage was performed by Buford Henry. She and her husband lived on their farm all their lives except when they moved to McKinney for three years to give better school advantages for their children. She was known as "Miss Sue" and was buried at the Chambersville cemetery with her family. Chambersville is near Melissa TX and Sue is buried next to her husband Jesse Orendorff. It is a small town; there is a church and a couple of houses. Her father was William Hampton, a pioneer of Collin co Texas. She and Jesse had a mutual agreement that whichever of them died first would be buried in his or her own respective family plot. Her father William Hampton came to Collin Co Texas in 1846 from Missouri and was also one of the early settlers of Fannin Co TX, he operated the grist mill and cotton gin at Squeezepenny for a number of years. During the civil war the mill was converted to make cloth for confederate soldiers uniforms. A quote from a newspaper carrying news of her death "her intellectual face beamed intelligence, enthusiasm, love and graciousness on all the world about her. She was worshipped by her children and descendants and devotedly loved and respected by her neighbors and every acquaintance. She delighted in service to others, to her church and to her god. She often remarked that old age was in the midst of her loved ones and friends and Christian influences, was the happiest period of her life. She enjoyed life and wanted to live as long as it was her master's will that she should live, but felt prepared to go any time. Her memory will linger as a benediction upon her community where her long life was busily and happily spent. Her example will be an inspiration to all who knew her to live noble lives and like herself leave the world brighter, happier and better." from another Collin Co newspaper in a Chambersville column-"the remains of Mrs. Jesse Orenduff of trinity were brought here and laid to rest in the Chambersville cemetery on last Friday afternoon. In the presence of a large concourse of friends and relatives. Her sudden passing away was a shock to her many friends and acquaintances here, where she was so well known and beloved. the grave was a mound of the most fragrant flowers. Among them was a sheaf of golden wheat entwined with flowers. It seemed to us it was a fitting symbol of her life of usefulness, scattering love and sunshine all along her pathway and now her master had called her home and to her reward. To her children and aged husband we extend our sympathy." From a Collin Co newspaper-"pioneer Collin county woman dies suddenly. Mrs. Sue Orenduff passed away. (photo) Mrs. Sue Orenduff. After an illness of less than twelve hours, Mrs. Sue Hampton Orenduff, beloved wife of Jesse W. Orenduff, died at the family home in the trinity schoolhouse community, five miles north of McKinney, at five minutes after 4 o'clock, Thursday afternoon, august 30. Her sudden passing came as a shock to her immediate family, relatives and friends. She was in the enjoyment of her usually good health for one of her advanced years and on the evening and night before she went auto driving in company with her daughter, Mrs. O. C. Harris, who lives on a farm nearby the old family homestead and who has been a daily visitor and companion of her dear old parents ever since her marriage. Mrs. Orenduff retired Wednesday night seemingly as well as usual and at 12:30 her youngest son, Ross Orenduff, who with his wife resided with his aged parents, went into her room and asked her if she wanted a drink of water. She replied no. He asked her then how she was feeling. She replied that she was feeling all right. About 5 o'clock the next morning a slight groan was the first indication to her husband and son of her illness. When they reached her bedside she was unable to speak. The family physician was quickly summoned and remained with her almost constantly until she quietly breathed her last at the above stated hour". Buford Henry married Sue and Jesse. Sources: Marriage records: Collin Co. obituary, interview with Ross Orenduff, Collin Co newspaper clippings from family scrapbook donated for use by my cousin Arba Orenduff)

Notes for Jesse:
Religion: Methodist.
Orenduff spelling. Confederate soldier\farmer. Jesse William enlisted in the 6th regiment, company d Texas cavalry in Dallas Texas on Sept. 10, 1861 to serve 12 months. His horse was valued at $130.00 and his equipment at $15.00, he also had a db gun (double barrel shotgun) and a 6 shooter and rode 50 miles to enlist. Captain Thomas H. Bowen commanded his company in 1861. From November to December 1861 he was detached from service at Cantonment Washington. From January to March 1862 he was absent on sick furlough. Then from April to December 1862 he was on furlough back in Texas. From January to February 1863 he was dropped from the muster roll due to his inability to serve. Then in March 1863 he returned to service with a surgeons certificate. He had blue eyes, had light complexion, and fair hair. Jesse came to Texas with a wagon train; William Henry, Mary E, and Cora came by boat to New Orleans. From there they came in a carriage (Cora on horseback) to north of McKinney Texas in 1855. Jesse went to war on a fine Kentucky bred horse, which was lost, when the regiment dismounted to fight. After the war when he married Sue Hampton he wore his Confederate uniform

and borrowed a shirt from his father. Some 300 people attended the wedding at Grandpa Hampton's plantation "Squeze Penny", which was 7 miles north of McKinney. Parson Buford Henry of McKinney officiated. Returning soldiers whom heard about the wedding came. They were served mutton, turkey, etc. Jessie regretted that a guest stole the beautiful knitted gloves made for him by his bride. Had an adjoining farm in McKinney Texas with his brother John Hayes Orendorff. The old Orendorff graveyard was established on his farm, he was also a Methodist. Jesse passed away at 8:10 PM on a Tuesday evening at his home in the Orendorff community five miles north of McKinney on his farm. He suffered a paralyzing stroke while sitting in his chair and lingered fourteen days until he passed away. He was apparently a member of the Confederate Veterans. Funeral services were held at 4:00 on Wednesday at his home. His pastor Rev J.T. Wilson of the church located at the Melissa and south Wilcox street church in McKinney assisted by Rev J.A. Old. He was buried with his wife at the Chambersville cemetery under the direction of the Kelher-Crouch funeral home. Some of the pallbearers were Earl Orendorff, Jesse orendorff iii, Monroe Orendorff JR, Oren Boone of Austin, Mulkey, and O. Boone. The Daughters of the Confederacy were honorary pallbearers. Jesse lived at his home for the 5 years after his wife died and was taken care of by his youngest son, Ross Orendorff. He often drove into McKinney in his auto with his daughter O. C. Harris. On Feb. 20 1865 Jesse was furloughed, at this time an officer of the Ross brigade named D.L. Rosamond gave the following description of him. "Aged 21 years, fair complexion, blue eyes, light hair, and by occupation a farmer, is hearby permitted to go to Collin co Texas". He was somewhere in Mississippi at this time. Jesse often wrote poetry in his letters to Miss Sue, such as the following. "Had I the wings of a beautiful dove, I'd soar across the deep, I'd fondly whisper to my love, before I'd go to sleep." he often wrote letters and the ones he received were a great comfort to him. Jesse was camped near Vernon Mississippi on October 26, 1863. He wrote Miss Sue the following letter: "again with pleasure I take my seat to answer your welcome letter, which I received on the fifteenth. We were in line of battle about 9 o'clock at night. Some had become sleepy and had lain down on the damp ground to take rest, when to our astonishment a voice was heard, saying how are you bear skins, it was _____ wilmoth. We soon had a fire built and we were all reading letters from our friends and relations. I can assure you yours was read with interest and pleasure as I think you one of my most worthy friends. Sue you said you would close for fear you had already wearied my patience I hope that thought will vanish from your mind, as I never tire reading letters from one so worthy my attention. If you could only see me persuing your letters over and over you would be reconciled to think that I appreciate them very much. I received several letters _____ ____ _____. I think that pulling ears to make friends think of me is quite a treat as I have received a letter since. You spoke of the association at _ _____. I wish I had been there, but would not have been _____ _____ _ _____ _____ for the world. (Jesse Orenduff) we see _____ _____ ____ _____ nearly every day _____ gathering _____ blackberries _____ and apples yesterday I have one in my pocket now I wish you had. You spoke of some of my Kentucky friends being there I wish it was so I could go home too. I would like to have seen my old friend _____ but much rather see my Texas friends. I have written to several who I thought were my friends, but am fearful I was mistaken. I wrote two or three letters to Miss _____, but received no answer. Tell the girls to neglect one if they wish to. I have met with several in Miss. and Tenn. that appear to be very intimate, at least. They give me to understand they wished to go to Texas as soon as the war is over. Sue I hope it will not be so with you, I want you to write every convienant oppertunity and excuse this as I have nothing to write on, I am writing on my cartridge box and it is very awkward as I have to hold it on my lap and it has 40 rounds of cartridges in it. I heard that Mrs. Ohio mallow was married to a deserter Mr. brake, if it is so I wish her a happy life. I can sympathize with anyone that is ignorant enough to even speak well of deserters much less marry one. Give my best respects to all inquiring friends, as ever Jesse Orenduff." The following is from an old Collin Co newspaper "a delightful anniversary dinner was served at the home of Jesse Orenduff ii at his hospitable farm home in the trinity community five miles north of McKinney, Friday, April 27th. The occasion celebrated the 58th wedding anniversary of Jesse Orenduff I and his wife, who were married April 27, 1865. The children, grandchildren, and great-grandchildren of this splendid old couple united in honoring them. A most happy day spent. The children present were: Mrs. O.C. Mulkey of commerce, Mrs. Frank Boone of Melissa, Jesse Orenduff II of Melissa, Mrs. O.C. Harris of Melissa, and Ross Orenduff of Melissa. One son, Monroe Orenduff, of Bonham, could not be present. The wedding cake was baked by Mrs. J.W. Wilmeth and decorated by Ed Seeger, the McKinney baker, in a most artistic way with white roses on stems and a miniature bride and groom mounted on its summit. Mrs. Leon Rutledge, formerly Miss Sue Etta Mulkey, of Commerce, a granddaughter, sent beautiful flowers for the occasion. Mrs. Jesse Orenduff II was assisted in serving by Mrs. Frank Boone, Mrs. O.C. Mulkey, Mrs. Rose Orenduff, Mrs. O.C. Harris and three grand-daughters, Mrs. O.C. Stevens and the misses Arlye and Beatrice Boone. The bride's book brought out was the same one used on the occasion of the golden anniversary of this worthy, old couple, which took place eight years before. Toast to grandfather. Jesse Orenduff III, little 12 year old grandson, delivered the following toast to his grandfather: to dear grandpa. This day I'm sure means much to you. The day you won your bride so true, to us, it is a pleasure rare to honor our grandparents whose love and care, has blest our lives and guided us, to nobler things and put our trust in him who has the power divine, to keep us pure in heart and mind. You have given us a heritage greater than fame; you have given us a good and honorable name. Jesse Orenduff the first is a man of his word, not aught against him has ever been heard, Jesse Orenduff the second that's dear old dad, I think he is the best child you ever had. He has followed the example that you set; he has lived a life you won't regret. Your life has been so honest and true, I wish I could be just like you. There is no fame, no honor revered, that I'd exchange for my name-Jesse Orenduff the third. Toast to grandmother. Arthelle Boone, twelve years old, gave the following toast to the beloved old grandmother: to dear grandma. Just 58 years ago today, there was a bride, beautiful and gay: her eyes as bright as the morning dew, her cheeks were tinted with a rosebud hue. As we look you in the face today, though time has changed the raven locks to Grey, those eyes are still bright, that face is still fair, and grandma's sweet smile is always there. Dear grandma, your life and your love to me, will be beautiful and great to eternity." Jesse was shown to be attending school at age 17. The following was printed in a Collin county newspaper along with an aged picture of Jesse. It is in his own words "this little sketch of my life during the war of '61-65, which I had never even thought of writing, is written at the request of my beloved daughter, Leona. My first experience as a soldier was responding to a call for volunteers to go to Fort Arbuckle and Fort Cobb, situated in Indian Territory. These forts were then occupied by United States soldiers for the purpose of guarding the frontier against the frequent raids of the Indians. These soldiers were well equipped with firearms, some cannon, ammunition, provisions, plenty of forage, good horses, wagons, tents, medicines, and in fact everything the United States soldiers stood in need of. So some of the leading men on the southern side thought to capture these forts and equip a southern regiment or two with the spoils, would not only aid the south materially, but add a crown of fame to those who would undertake the supposed perilous adventure. Be it remembered that a lot of poorly armed and untrained men and boys to storm a fort supplied with well drilled soldiers and the very best of modern arms, would take men of courage as well as strategy. After various suggestions and discussions, it was finally agreed to place in command of the expedition, Col. Bourland who then resided northwest of Sherman on red river-a man with a military bearing who had proved his worth as a frontiersman in fighting Indians. So the volunteers were ordered to report, without delay to Col. Bourland at Borland's ferry on Red River. I suppose that inside of two days there were about a thousand men and boys from sixty years old down to fifteen-all anxious and willing to show their patriotism. The older men while in camp on the march were talking about the soldiers in the forts. Some even thought they might be in favor of the south and would surrender without any resistance whatever. After a forced march we came in sight of fort Arbuckle-all was quiet. Col. Bourland sent some scouts on ahead of the command to find out their intentions at the fort, whether they would surrender peaceably or by fore of arms. While waiting for the scouts to report, Col. Bourland made a display of his command. We were about one mile from the fort and on a rolling prairie. We formed in line of battle and paraded in plain view of the fort to show our strength and intimidate the officers to surrender. While we were thus engaged, the scouts returned and reported, "fort evacuated". Not a soldier of the fort was seen. They had heard of our intentions and had left in haste, taking everything of value with them except a supply of corn and hay. So we captured the fort without any laurels, but our jaded horses enjoyed the good corn and hay, while the men and boys enjoyed a rest. The friendly Indians were carrying the corn away. After a nights rest we went on toward fort Cobb, but found out after some hard riding, that the place also had been evacuated. So we were disbanded and had to shift for ourselves, which meant, "get home the best way you can". We received no pay, no thanks, but had a foretaste of there responsibility and need of self-confidence. When we returned from this trip, we found there was a general call for volunteers. Then excitement and anxiety was at every home. The citizens were called together frequently to hear someone speak and urge the young men to volunteer. Most of the talking was done by old men who thought perhaps the war would last three to six months. This prophecy was fulfilled by adding three and a half years more; as experience and history have both taught us. I joined a company that was being made up at Mantua, Collin County, Texas. After we had organized and had been drilled to some extent, we then went to Dallas county, near Lancaster, where we were joined by nine other companies, making a little over one thousand men and boys. This was then commissioned and known as the sixth Texas cavalry, Col. B.W. Stone in command. After several days of drilling, we started north, crossing Red River at old Fort Warren, and proceeded leisurely through the Indian Territory. On this march we were continually being drilled in the tactics of war. We were sent out as scouts, picket guards, chain guards, and camp guards. Many amusing things happened during this trip. The officers would test the privates in many ways, merely to see if they would remember their orders. For instance, they would place a man on guard with instructions to let no one pass unless they could give the password, which was not given until (missing a sentence) out in to the camp, when the guard would halt this person and ask "who comes there?" the usual response would be, "a friend." Then the guard would say "advance friend and give the password." then the fun would begin. This friend, already posted, would give some other password, and then start on. If the guard let him pass, then came the trouble: for he had forgotten the password or was not doing his duty and he was sure to get a severe reprimand and sometimes put on extra duty. On the other hand, if he had not forgotten, and the "friend" insisted on passing, being on important business and sometimes offering bribes, but could not, then that guard was known as one in whom they could trust. By this means the officers would sometimes send for a certain soldier if they wanted to learn something definite. Another plan was to put out what was known as chain guards or post guard, when a number of the post and the hour of the night had to be called every hour. That was a trick to see if any soldier slept while on duty. That became so common that the boys (as they were called) decided to put a stop to it. The officer in charge of the guard always called from no. 1 then on it went from one guard to another "post no. --, 9 o'clock and all is well!" so one could night the boys changed the call to "post no -- and cold as h-e-l-l!" with a loud and long sound. This put a stop to post calling. Afterwards they would send out spies to see if any slept while on duty. Finally this was abandoned and left to the honor and patriotism of the soldier, which proved the best. On our march through the Indian Territory we passed Col. Stan Waity's regiment of full blooded Indians, they were out on parade and were drawn up in line of battle as we passed before them. They were in full war paint with all manner of trophies hanging from their heads, such as scalps, eagle's claws, ear rings, and some had rings in their noses-the most hideous and barbarous looking set of human beings I ever saw. Our men could scarcely their contempt and hatred they had for this motley regiment, who could blame them? Perhaps some of those very Indians were then wearing as a trophy the scalp of a relative or friend whom they had murdered in Texas. We heard afterwards that the majority of this command proved to be torries and went to the federal army at the first opportunity. We crossed the Arkansas River at Fort Smith, then on north over the Boston Mountains to Elkhorn. We then began to learn the realities of war. After some skirmishing and much marching, winter coming on, we were ordered to go into winter quarters on big mulberry creek, about 18 miles east of Van Buren, Ark. Here pneumonia and typhoid fever broke out in camp and caused a heavy mortality. Seldom a day went by without some comrade buried with military honors, which consisted of the firing of a volley of 8 to 12 guns at a given signal. I was a victim of typhoid-was not able to walk for several months without using crutches. I came home in spring of 1862, was discharged in the fall, but I improved in health and in March '63, I went back to my old command, then in the northern part of Mississippi, but when I got there they had been ordered to Tennessee. I went on and joined them near Franklin. From that time on, we had all the fighting and hardships that were necessary to satisfy and soldiers ambition. History gives our brigade credit of participating in one hundred and twenty-five engagements, including skirmishing. While in Tennessee, we were on the march, or being drilled or fighting continually. We were then under the command of the fighting and dashing General Vandorn. While camped at Springhill Tennessee, there were some sad things occurred as well as amusing incidents. Gen. Vandorn's headquarters were in the town and he became very much attached to one Mrs. Dr. Peters, so much so that the doctor forbade him coming to his house, but Mrs. Peters being one of the leading society ladies, encouraged the General regardless of her husband's objections. So one evening on returning from a call in the country and finding Vandorn at his home, the doctor deliberately took his six-shooter and killed our General. Under the excitement, he mounted his horse and made for the Yankees, as it was about two miles to the picket lines. He knew that he could get through, as all the guards were instructed to let doctors pass. So that was the last of the doctor for some time, but he was finally caught by some of the scouts, brought back and tried by a military court and was honorably acquitted. I heard afterwards that he and his wife were living happily together. The next evening after the death of General Vandorn, the whole command that he had charge of were ordered put on dress parade to pay their last respects to their brave little General. I remember as the funeral procession passed, his little bay horse was tied to the vehicle that bore his corpse, the one saddle with pistols and sword fastened thereon, and his boots finely polished, with the spurs buckled on, tied in the stirrups. So passed one brave Confederate General that his soldiers all loved and would have followed to the very jaws of death. While at this camp (Springhill Tenn.) the picket lines were skirmishing nearly every day, just enough to keep up excitement and keep the soldiers all in camp, expecting to have to go to the front at any time. There were strict orders to always heap our guns as soon as we entered camp, after being out either on the skirmish line or out as scouts. One evening while everybody was enjoying the nice spring weather-some of the soldiers writing, some joking, some playing cards, etc. there came the clear quick call of the bugle. "Boots and saddle and fall into line", all in the time call. We had saddled our horses in a hurry and were putting on our cartridge boxes as some scouts came dashing up. As they dismounted one of them let his gun off, the ball striking one of my mess mates center in the forehead. He never knew what hit him as his brains were scattered for several feet around. At the time, he and I were standing talking, about four feet apart. He was a good boy and a good soldier. His name was Harry Vardaman. One of the boys that buried Harry Vardaman told me they carried him to the railroad, got a hand card, and took him about two miles to a country cemetery: said when they got there he was still breathing and they had to wait awhile for him to die. This was the second young man I had seen killed accidentally and it hurt me much worse than to see them fall in battle. Quite a difference in this young man's funeral and that of General Vandorn, but such is life and will be to the end of time. While we were at this place, fighting became almost an every day occurrence. So much so that it was necessary to send the whole regiment to the front at night to strengthen the picket line and prevent a surprise. One night when the third Texas or legion, as it was called, was on duty, the Yankees captured the outer pickets and just at daylight dashed in on the main camp, scattered the command. The command went on "doublequick" i.e. at a gallop, for about two miles, and after some maneuvering found out that it was only some Yankee scouts. It had been reported the Yankees were moving south. So we returned to our camp and the boys piled together what saddles, blankets and guns the boys had left and burned them. So they went by the name of the burnt legion. Colonel Brooks succeeded in rallying enough of his men to hold the Yankees in check until he received assistance. After everything quieted down and the legion all got together again, the Colonel called his regiment to form a square, so they could all hear him talk. He made quite a severe speech, reprimanded the officers as well as the private soldiers, called them cowards to run off and leave their commands and in the close of his remarks said: "in the discharge of your duty as a soldier, if one comes, whip him: if two comes, fight them: yes, if a whole troop comes I tell you to skirmish with them until hell freezes over and then skirmish with them on the ice!" That last remark raised the southern yell and closed the speech. We were transferred back to Mississippi for the purpose of relieving the situation at Vicksburg, which place was under the control of Gen. Pemberton. The federal gunboats had succeeded in running the blockade at that place which gave them control of the Mississippi River, had landed a considerable force, and had the place surrounded. So there we were: at every approach we made toward the town, we were confronted with breastworks and heavy artillery and about five or six soldiers to our one. We were just enough to keep them harassed and every time they would send out a command to get forage or reconnoiter, we would surely drive them back to their breastworks. Still this was no relief to Gen. Pemberton and we knew that he would finally have to surrender, as they had no way of getting supplies. So the fort was captured or starved out, and to add to the humility of the situation, Gen. Pemberton surrendered on the fourth of July. After the fall of Vicksburg we were fighting and skirmishing every day and sometimes at night, especially along Black and Yazoo rivers. The federals were advancing on Jackson. We had a considerable army of infantry at Jackson and some of the largest cannon I ever saw: but the Yankees outnumbered us to such an extent that it was impossible to hold them in check. I know that our little brigade did some hard service. We fought them at a little place called Starkville and near there for five days. And at night we would slip down on Black River and lay in ambush to watch their gunboats and see what was going on generally. As they were patrolling the river every two hours, we would fire a volley at their portholes. We knew we could not do much harm to their boats but thought we might kill some through the portholes. While we were in these swamps, the yanks got between us and another brigade (I think it was an Alabama brigade). After Gen. Ross had stayed in these swamps for seven days, and had received no orders at all for five days, he concluded it was time to act on his own responsibility. The Alabama command was in the same condition as ours. So Gen. Ross held a consultation with the Alabama general and they concluded to take their commands and report to general headquarters, which was then at Jackson, Miss. Gen. Ross was to be in command of two brigades until they got to their respective commands. So we started for Jackson, not expecting anything unusual to occur. We knew by the occasional report of cannon that the front of the federal army was near Jackson. As the Alabama general had shown courtesy to Ross by requesting him to take charge of the command, Ross returned the compliment by asking him to lead the way. In the early afternoon the advance guard discovered that the federals had possession of our road to Jackson. After the Alabamians had exchanged a few shots with them, they reported the road was full of federals and that we would have to flank them and go way round and come into Jackson from the east. That report didn't set well with Gen. Ross so he sent a courier in full haste to the Alabama general to give him the road. The Alabamians got out of the way, and Gen. Ross called for fifty volunteers to clear the road, and fifty more to keep it clear, while our brigade passed through. Those Alabama soldiers seemed perfectly amazed to see so many men tender their services to go into a fight: however, as soon as the road was cleared of the Alabamians, Gen. Ross gave the command to his men to "close up and keep in time" and to the volunteers to "clear the road of all yanks". In a very few minutes we were in full charge. We never even halted, but raised the "rebel yell" and went through that line of federal soldiers, as some of the boys said afterwards, like greased lightening. Of course, that was a pretty daring adventure but that was the way to accomplish the act. Gen. Ross knew that to take them on surprise that way, we could get through by the time they would get over the surprise that the charge from their rear would cause. So went our brigade into Jackson! We had been without any rations for five days, except roasting ears and what little we could find, such as potatoes and peanute, and but very little of them. We had no salt for our corn, so the boys were about half sick and the others, half mad-just in the right humor to fight. We were sent into camp and some rations issued us, which put the soldiers in better spirits. The Yankees were pressing their way slowly upon our soldiers, who were putting up a stubborn resistance. Our command was sent out south of the town where they had driven our infantry from their position, and had placed some artillery. The shells were doing so much damage to the fort, it was thought best to try to drive them from the field or capture them. So a considerable force of our infantry were quietly sent out there, and our command was ordered to advance as though we were going to charge their guns. This was for the purpose of drawing their fire, while the infantry was to make the real charge. We certainly did draw their fire as was intended: for the shot and shell fell thick and fast for awhile, but when the infantry raised a yell and charged them, they soon turned their attention to them. They were driven back and both their guns captured, but they soon received reinforcements and made a charge with such a large force, that we only succeeded in getting off the field with one of their guns. I remember that some of the boys remarked that they did not mind to fight." There is a Jesse W. Orenduff listed for Collin Co Texas as receiving a pension #21940 book #3. Sources: Tombstone dates at Chambersville TX, marriage records; Collin Co. TX. Newspaper articles, Confederate service papers, poems and letters shared by Arba and Ross Orenduff.

- - - - - - - - - - -

296. JOHN HAYES[10] ORENDORFF (166.WILLIAM[9], 90.JESSE[8], 65.CHRISTIAN[7], 54.CHRISTIAN[6], 48.JOHANN[5],

25.HERMANN[4], 7.STEPHEN[3], 2.HENNE[2], I.SIMON[1]) was born 4 July 1837 in KENTUCKY, PROB. BRECKINRIDGE CO. JOHN died 6 June 1913 in ON HIS FARM NORTH OF, MCKINNEY, at the age of 75. He married **NANCY COFFMAN** 6 January 1859 in TEXAS. She was born 20 February 1842. NANCY died 13 June 1878 in COLLIN CO TEXAS, at the age of 36.

They had 8 children:

454.　　f　i.　**MARY E. (BOONE) ORENDORFF.**
RESIDED IN ALDONSON OK. IN 1913.
MARY MARRIED TOM C. BOONE.

455.　　m　ii.　**JOHN W. ORENDORFF**, born in COLLIN CO TX, probably at MELISSA.
Constable of Melissa TX sur. Mastin Hardin, married by Rev. Richard Elliott. Resided in Henryetta OK in 1913. John was also Mayor of Henryetta OK at the time of his wife's death. This was in mid June 1925.

+ 456.　m　iii.　**VIVIAN WAVERLEY (MAJOR) ORENDORFF**, born 7 November 1869, died 6 March 1948.

457.　　f　iv.　**NORA ORENDORFF.**
RESIDED IN ROCKFORD ILLINOIS 1913.
NORA MARRIED A MR. ADAIR AND HAD AT LEAST 1 CHILD NAMED MARY LOU WHO MARRIED A MR. CLARK. HER NAME IS MARY LOU CLARK.

458.　　m　v.　**JAMES ORENDORFF.**
POSSIBLY ALSO CALLED JACK. JAMES MARRIED A WOMAN NAMED MINNIE AND HAD 4 CHILDREN.

459.　　f　vi.　**Lula ORENDORFF.**
RESIDED IN TERRELL TEXAS IN 1913. LULA WAS MARRIED TO A.C. SIMMONS.

460.　　f　vii.　**MARTHA ORENDORFF**, born 1 December 1861 in PROBABLY TEXAS, died in PROBABLY COLLIN CO TEXAS.

MARTHA IS BURIED IN THE OLD ORENDORFF CEMETERY IN TEXAS. SHOWN TO BE BORN IN 1861. HER NAME APPEARS AS "ORENDUFF".

461.   m   viii.   **GEORGE H. ORENDORFF**, born 11 March 1863 in COLLIN CO TEXAS, died in COLLIN CO TEXAS.
GEORGE IS BURIED IN THE OLD ORENDORFF CEMETERY IN MELISSA, TEXAS. GEORGE DIED AT THE AGE OF 2 YEARS 10 DAYS. HIS NAME APPEARS AS "ORENDUFF".

Notes for Nancy:

Nancy Coffman Orenduff was born on February 20, 1842. She was called Nannie. Her husband John Hayes's obituary states that she is the sister of Hogue Coffman and the late George Coffman. Jesse C. Portman married Nancy and John. She is buried in the Orenduff Cemetery outside of Melissa, Texas. Sources: obituary

Notes for John:

Religion: Presbyterian.

John Hayes Orenduff was born in Kentucky July 4, 1837, to William Henry Orenduff and Mary E. Hayes Orenduff. He moved from Kentucky to Texas when he was eighteen years of age. John joined the 20th regiment Texas cavalry, company c, on March 10, 1862. This unit was commanded by Captain J.R. Johnson, also known as the Bass regiment. He rode twelve miles in order to join and was enlisted by T.C. Bass. He was a farrier and blacksmith. His horse was valued at two hundred dollars, and equipment at twenty dollars. Mustered in on March 15 at Camp Bass Texas. Enlisted as a private for 12 months and appears on a receipt roll for commutation of rations, dated July 30, 1862. The amount paid was $8.33. He was severally wounded and discharged under a surgeon's certificate of disability. Around March of 1864, the regiment was reduced to a battalion of four companies and designated Johnson's battalion, 20th regiment Texas dismounted cavalry. The following information is from John Hayes's obituary. John was a farmer and a stock raiser all his life, for a brief time he operated the old city hotel, a noted hostelry for nearly half a century. He was a member of the Melissa Presbyterian Church and had great renown socially, religiously, and intellectually. John was an extensive reader whose mind was stored with a varied knowledge and he always took a lively interest in keeping up with current affairs both local and global. People enjoyed his company and his hospitality was unmatched and people said he was almost liberal to a fault. No traveler was ever turned away from his door without food or shelter. John married firstly, Nancy Coffman on 01-06-1859, marriage performed by Jesse C. Portman. John's second wife was Mattie J. Claycomb who survived him. They were married on 07-13-1880 at the residence of Silas Jordan in KY. The marriage bond was filed 06-12-1880 and the bondsman was P.J. Henderson. All of his children but James were at his side when he passed away on Thursday, June 6, 1913 at 7:10 PM after a two-year period of declining health. Rev. M. Fincher of Mckinney conducted John's funeral at 4:00 in the afternoon and the burial took place in the old Orendorff graveyard. Sources: Collin Co TX obituary, Breckenridge County KY marriage records 1800's, Confederate Service papers.

CHAPTER ELEVEN

GENERATION NO. 11

331. LUTHER MILTON[11] **ORENDORFF** (186.JOHN[10], 108.LEWIS[9], 68.JOHN[8], 59.PHILIP[7], 50.PHILIP[6], 26.THEISS[5], 9.LUDWIG[4], 3.HUBERT[3], 2.HENNE[2], 1.SIMON[1]) was born 14 June 1882 in VA. LUTHER probably died in WEST VA. He married **EDNA M. ORENDORFF**. She was born 28 October 1894 probably in VA. EDNA probably died in WEST VA.

They had 4 children:

462.	f	i.	**ARLEEN ORENDORFF**, born in VA/ AFTER 1900. ARLEEN'S NAME APPEARS AS "ORNDORFF".
463.	m	ii.	**BRANSON ORENDORFF**, born in VA\ AFTER 1900. BRANSON'S NAME APPEARS AS "ORNDORFF".
464.	m	iii.	**MITCHELL ORENDORFF**. MITCHELL'S NAME APPEARS AS "ORNDORFF".
465.	m	iv.	**MARVIN ORENDORFF**, born in POSS. VA. MARVIN'S NAME APPEARS AS "ORNDORFF".

Notes for Edna:

Edna M.'s name appears as "Orndorff", she apparently married a cousin.

Notes for Luther:

Luther Milton's name appears as "Orndorff". Luther is buried in West VA with his wife.

- - - - - - - - - - -

333. WILLIAM THEODORE[11] **ORENDORFF** (186.JOHN[10], 108.LEWIS[9], 68.JOHN[8], 59.PHILIP[7], 50.PHILIP[6], 26.THEISS[5], 9.LUDWIG[4], 3.HUBERT[3], 2.HENNE[2], 1.SIMON[1]) was born 1879 in POSS. VA. WILLIAM died in VA or W. VA. He married **MYRTLE CATHERINE MCILWEE**. She was born 20 July 1885 in VA or W. VA. MYRTLE died in VA or W. VA.

They had 3 children:

466.   m   i.   **IRVING ORENDORFF.** IRVING NEVER HAD ANY CHILDREN, HIS NAME APPEARS AS "ORNDORFF".

467.   m   ii.   **CLAUDE ORENDORFF.** CLAUDE'S NAME APPEARS AS "ORNDORFF". HE WAS MARRIED TO A WOMAN NAMED JUANITA.

468.   m   iii.   **CLARKE ORENDORFF**, born 30 August 1927 in VA or W. VA, died in VA or W. VA. BURIED W/MOTHER CLARKE'S NAME APPEARS AS "ORNDORFF".

Notes for William:

William Theodore's name appears as "Orndorff".

- - - - - - - - - - -

340. MELVIN ADDISON[11] **ORENDORFF** (194.ADAM[10], 111.ANDREW[9], 70.JACOB[8], 59.PHILIP[7], 50.PHILIP[6], 26.THEISS[5], 9.LUDWIG[4], 3.HUBERT[3], 2.HENNE[2], 1.SIMON[1]) was born 1897. He married **MINNIE BELLE CONNER**. She was born 6 October 1895.

They had 5 children:

469.   m   i.   **ARTHUR JAMES ORENDORFF**, born 25 January 1920.

470. f ii. **ELSIE MARIE ORENDORFF**, born 19 November 1922.
ELSIE MARIE'S NAME APPEARS AS "ORNDORFF", SHE MARRIED A MR. HOTTEL.

471. f iii. **ANNA LEE ORENDORFF**, born 3 November 1926 probably in VA OR W. VA, died in or near HAMPSHIRE, CO W. VA.
ANNA LEE IS BURIED IN OR NEAR HAMPSHIRE CO W. VA. HER NAME APPEARS AS "ORNDORFF".

472. m iv. **ERMA ADDISON ORENDORFF**, born 25 February 1930. He married HELEN PEER.
Notes for ERMA:
ERMA ADDISON'S NAME APPEARS AS "ORNDORFF".
473. m v.
ORLANDO JACK ORENDORFF, born 23 October 1931.

Notes for Melvin:
Melvin's name appears as "Orndorff".

- - - - - - - - - - -

341. DELLA M.[11] **ORENDORFF** (194.ADAM[10], 111.ANDREW[9], 70.JACOB[8], 59.PHILIP[7], 50.PHILIP[6], 26.THEISS[5], 9.LUDWIG[4], 3.HUBERT[3], 2.HENNE[2], I.SIMON[1]) was born 1891 possibly in W. VA OR VA. DELLA died IN OR NEAR HAMPSHIRE, CO W. VA. She married **LESTER G. ORENDORFF (See number 394)**. He was born 1884 probably in W. VA OR VA. He is the son of CHARLES MONROE ORENDORFF and EMMA LEE MCINTURFF. LESTER died IN OR NEAR HAMPSHIRE CO, VA.
They had 7 children:

474. m i. **ROY ORENDORFF**. He married CHRISTY JEWEL.

475.   m   ii.   **DONALD ORENDORFF**, born 9 April 1918.
He married EDITH MCILWEE. She was born
20 August 1922. Notes for DONALD:
DONALD'S   NAME   APPEARS   AS
"ORNDORFF".

476.   m   iii.   **BENJAMIN V. ORENDORFF**, born 1922 in
PROBABLY W. VA.
BENJAMIN'S   NAME   APPEARS   AS
"ORNDORFF". HE IS BURIED IN OR
NEAR HAMPSHIRE CO W. VA.

477.   f   iv.   **EMMA ORENDORFF**.
EMMA'S   NAME   IS   LISTED   AS
"ORNDORFF", SHE MARRIED A MR.
GOOD.

478.   m   v.   **ROBERT ORENDORFF**, born 1924. He
married RUTH FOLTZ. Notes for ROBERT:
CIRCA BIRTH DATE ONLY ROBERT'S
NAME APPEARS AS "ORNDORFF".

479.   f   vi.   **RUTH ORENDORFF**.
RUTH'S   NAME   APPEARS   AS
"ORNDORFF", SHE MARRIED A MR.
LONG.

480.   m   vii.   **PHIL ORENDORFF**.

Notes for Lester:
Lester G.'s name appears as "Orndorff", he was apparently a
cousin of his wife. He is buried in or near Hampshire Co West VA
with his wife. Poss died in 1936.

Notes for Delia:
Apparently married a cousin Della M.'s name appears as
"Orndorff", she married Lester G. Orndorff 1884-1926. She is
buried with her husband in or near Hampshire Co West VA.

- - - - - - - - - - -

348. CONRAD[11] **ORENDORFF** (197.PHILIP[10], 112.JACOB[9], 70.JACOB[8], 59.PHILIP[7], 50.PHILIP[6], 26.THEISS[5], 9.LUDWIG[4], 3.HUBERT[3], 2.HENNE[2], 1.SIMON[1]) was born 1881 possibly in VA. His spouse has not been identified.

They had 1 child:

481.　　m　i.　**GERALD W. ORENDORFF**, born 1906 in POSS. VA.
　　　　　　　GERALD W.'S NAME APPEARS AS "ORNDORFF".

Notes for Conrad:
Conrad's name appears as "Orndorff". Married to Maude m-, born 1881 died 10-28-1966.

- - - - - - - - - - -

383. GERALD LUTHER[11] **ORENDORFF** (221.LUTHER[10], 122.LEWIS[9], 72.SAMUEL[8], 59.PHILIP[7], 50.PHILIP[6], 26.THEISS[5], 9.LUDWIG[4], 3.HUBERT[3], 2.HENNE[2], 1.SIMON[1]) was born 1910. He married **ROMAINE E. STAUFFER**. She was born 1910.

They had 1 child:

482.　　f　i.　**CHARLOTTE ROMAINE ORENDORFF**, born 26 May 1939.
　　　　　　　CHARLOTTE ROMAINE'S NAME APPEARS AS "ORNDORFF".

Notes for Gerald:
Gerald Luther's name appears as "Orndorff".

- - - - - - - - - - -

385. KARL LINNAS[11] **ORENDORFF** (221.LUTHER[10], 122.LEWIS[9], 72.SAMUEL[8], 59.PHILIP[7], 50.PHILIP[6], 26.THEISS[5], 9.LUDWIG[4], 3.HUBERT[3], 2.HENNE[2], 1.SIMON[1]) was born 6 May 1917. He married **ELDA MARIE OSMAN**. She was born 1915.

They had 4 children:

483.   f   i.   **JANET LOUISE ORENDORFF**, born 1941. JANET LOUISE'S NAME APPEARS AS "ORNDORFF", SHE MARRIED LEROY ESWORTHY II BORN IN 1934.

484.   m   ii.   **WALLACE WAYNE ORENDORFF**, born 1943. WALLACE WAYNE'S NAME APPEARS AS "ORNDORFF".

485.   f   iii.   **CAROLE JEANNE ORENDORFF**, born 1946.

486.   f   iv.   **CYNTHIA ANN ORENDORFF**, born 1955. CYNTHIA ANN'S NAME APPEARS AS "ORNDORFF".

Notes for Karl:
Karl Linnas' name appears as "Orndorff".

- - - - - - - - - - -

390. LEWIS SWARTZ[11] **ORENDORFF** (222.HUGH[10], 122.LEWIS[9], 72.SAMUEL[8], 59.PHILIP[7], 50.PHILIP[6], 26.THEISS[5], 9.LUDWIG[4], 3.HUBERT[3], 2.HENNE[2], I.SIMON[1]) was born 1 February 1918. He married **GEORGIE ETHEL HODGES**. She was born 1927.

They had 5 children:

487.   m   i.   **CHARLES LEWIS ORENDORFF**, born 3 June 1952. CHARLES LEWIS' NAME APPEARS AS "ORNDORFF".

488.   m   ii.   **DAVID ALVIN ORENDORFF**, born 19 September 1954.

489.   m   iii.   **WALTER HUGH ORENDORFF**, born 28 June 1957.

490.   f   iv.   **LORETTA MAE ORENDORFF**, born 26 August 1958.

LORETTA MAE'S NAME APPEARS AS "ORNDORFF".

491.　f　v.　**JEANETTE ORENDORFF**, born I June 1961.
JEANETTE'S NAME APPEARS AS "ORNDORFF".

Notes for Lewis:
Lewis Swartz's name appears as "Orndorff".

- - - - - - - - - - -

392. JAMES HUGH[11] ORENDORFF (222.HUGH[10], 122.LEWIS[9], 72.SAMUEL[8], 59.PHILIP[7], 50.PHILIP[6], 26.THEISS[5], 9.LUDWIG[4], 3.HUBERT[3], 2.HENNE[2], I.SIMON[1]) was born 25 July 1925. He married **DORRIS BEA SULLIVAN**. She was born 1928.

They had 5 children:

492.　m　i.　**DONALD JAMES ORENDORFF**, born 4 July 1950.

493.　f　ii.　**SHARON LEA ORENDORFF**, born 21 September 1951.
SHARON LEA'S NAME APPEARS AS "ORNDORFF".

494.　m　iii.　**MARK STEPHEN ORENDORFF**, born 25 May 1955.
MARK STEPHEN'S NAME APPEARS AS "ORNDORFF".

495.　f　iv.　**JUDITH MARIE ORENDORFF**, born 18 June 1958.
JUDITH MARIE'S NAME APPEARS AS "ORNDORFF".

496.　f　v.　**CINDY LOUISE ORENDORFF**, born 29 October 1960.
CINDY LOUISE'S NAME APPEARS AS "ORNDORFF".

Notes for James:
James Hugh's name appears as "Orndorff".

- - - - - - - - - - -

394. LESTER G.[11] **ORENDORFF** (230.CHARLES[10], 128.BENJAMIN[9], 73.LEWIS[8], 59.PHILIP[7], 50.PHILIP[6], 26.THEISS[5], 9.LUDWIG[4], 3.HUBERT[3], 2.HENNE[2], 1.SIMON[1]) was born 1884 probably in W. VA or VA. LESTER died in or near HAMPSHIRE CO, VA. He married **DELLA M. ORENDORFF (See number 341)**. She was born 1891 possibly in W. VA or VA. She is the daughter of ADAM DECALB ORENDORFF and EMMA F. PEER. **See number 341** listed above.

- - - - - - - - - - -

404. IRA IRVIN[11] **ORENDORFF** (238.WILLIAM[10], 132.HARRISON[9], 76.PHILIP[8], 60.JOHN[7], 50.PHILIP[6], 26.THEISS[5], 9.LUDWIG[4], 3.HUBERT[3], 2.HENNE[2], 1.SIMON[1]) was born 20 October 1875 in LAMAR, BARTON CO, MO. IRA died 23 February 1959 in ENID, GARFIELD CO, OK, at the age of 83. He married **SADIE OLIVE FAST** 4 February 1900 in LAMAR, BARTON CO, MO. She was born 3 September 1880 in FAIRFIELD, JEFFERSON CO, IA. SADIE died 1 October 1971 in INDEPENDENCE, MONTGOMERY CO, KS, at the age of 91.

They had 3 children:

497.   f   i.   **OLIVE OLEANE ORENDORFF**, born 10 December 1901 in LAMAR, BARTON CO MO.

Married Roy Irvin Rathbun. Olive Oleane's name appears as "Orndorff", her husbands last name was Rathvin. Born 10-24-1902 in Newton KS son of Marshall Riley Rathvin and Mary Elizabeth Kline. The children were Joann Oleene Merdice born 10-20-1926 in Independence KS, she married Samuel A. Bush on 04-02-1949 and her second husband was Oliver Holcomb.

Marshall Irvin was born 11-09-1936 and married first Peggy Bullock 06-05-1960 and then Elizabeth Foster.

+ 498. m ii. **ELMER LEROY ORENDORFF**, born 20 December 1918.

+ 499. m iii. **HOWARD ALLEN ORENDORFF**, born 31 March 1916.

Notes for Sadie:

Sadie Olive was the Daughter of John Milton Fast and Mary Isabelle Bales.

- - - - - - - - - - -

405. ELMER LLOYD[11] ORENDORFF (238.WILLIAM[10], 132.HARRISON[9], 76.PHILIP[8], 60.JOHN[7], 50.PHILIP[6], 26.THEISS[5], 9.LUDWIG[4], 3.HUBERT[3], 2.HENNE[2], 1.SIMON[1]). He married **RUBY IRENE RUSSELL (BRITTON)**.

They had 3 children:

500. f i. **DEBRA MICHELLE ORENDORFF (BRITTON).**

        ADOPTED BY ELMER L. ORENDORFF

501. f ii. **ROSLEE IRENE ORENDORFF**, born 11 July 1958 in ROCKY FORD, CO.

502. f iii. **DEBRA MICHELLE ORENDORFF**, born 14 July 1954 in ELKHART, KANSAS.

        Adopted. Debra Michelle's name appears as "Orndorff".

- - - - - - - - - - -

406. GEORGE WASHINGTON[11] ORENDORFF (238.WILLIAM[10], 132.HARRISON[9], 76.PHILIP[8], 60.JOHN[7], 50.PHILIP[6], 26.THEISS[5], 9.LUDWIG[4], 3.HUBERT[3], 2.HENNE[2], 1.SIMON[1]) was born 2 January 1868 in MO. GEORGE died 20 March 1938 in SPRINGFIELD, BACA COUNTY, CO, at the age of 70. He married **CORA ELIZABETH HILTON** 17 April 1898 in

NEWPORT, BARTON CO, MO. She was born 6 October 1879 in HARDINSBURG, BRECKINRIDGE CO, KY. CORA died 5 July 1931 in LAMAR, POWERS COUNTY, CO, at the age of 51.

They had 7 children:

503.　　m　i.　**WORTHY HILTON ORENDORFF**, born 4 January 1906 in KANSAS CITY, CLAY CO MO.

Worthy's name appears as "Orndorff" and he is the son of George Washington Orendorff and Cora Elizabeth Hilton.

+ 504.　m　ii.　**HILTON GEORGE ORENDORFF**, born 20 October 1908, died 28 April 1970.

505.　　m　iii.　**EMERY WILSON ORENDORFF**, born 14 March 1915 in SPRINGFIELD, BACA CO, CO. He married ALICE MARIE EDEN 24 August 1939 in CO. She was born 18 February 1923 in ELKHART KS. Notes for ALICE:

Alice Marie was the daughter of Oscar S. Eden and Lillie Mccallum. Notes for Emery:

Emery Wilson's name appears as "Orndorff".

506.　　f　iv.　**REBA MAY ORENDORFF**, born 28 May 1899 in LAMAR, BARTON CO, MO. Died in SALT LAKE CITY UT.

Married twice. Reba May's name appears as "Orndorff", she was married to Red Clark first and then to Wellington "Deet" Vanderhoof.

507.　　f　v.　**ELSIE HAZEL ORENDORFF**, born 2 November 1901 in LAMAR, BARTON CO MO, died 12 October 1970 in SPRINGFIELD, BACA CO CO, at the age of 68.

Elsie Hazel married Wallace Nidey b. 12-21-1896 in West York, Ill d. 06-07-1981 in Springfield, Baca Co, MO. He was the son of Thomas Vincent Nidey and Eva May Wheeler.

They had the following children: Paul Ray b. 12-27-1919 in Campo, Co d. 04-04-1941 Lamar, Co. married to Olive Elizabeth Mayhan.

+ 508.   m   vi.   **WILLIAM HARRISON ORENDORFF**, born 4 January 1906, died 11 April 1971.

509.   f   vii.   **DELORES IONE ORENDORFF**, born 27 September 1904 in LAMAR, BARTON CO, MD, died 6 February 1973 in PUEBLO, COLORADO, at the age of 68.

Delores Ione's name appears as "Orndorff". She married Wade Ralph Henderson b. 07-20-1895 d. 03-14-1976 La Junta, Colorado. Children: Henry Rudolph b. 01-03-1923 Ralston OK, Wade Ralph Jr 02-06-1926 Springfield, Baca Co, Colorado, Earl George 08-31-1928 Ralston OK, and Keith Sidney b. 10-12-1933.

Notes for Cora:
Cora Elizabeth was the daughter of John Hilary Hilton and Mary Greene.

Notes for George:
George Washington's name appears as "Orndorff".

- - - - - - - - - - -

412. LEANDER BOND[11] **ORENDORFF** (239.LORENZO[10], 132.HARRISON[9], 76.PHILIP[8], 60.JOHN[7], 50.PHILIP[6], 26.THEISS[5], 9.LUDWIG[4], 3.HUBERT[3], 2.HENNE[2], 1.SIMON[1]) was born (SEE NOTES) in MO. LEANDER died 1929. He married **MARGARET S. DOUGHTERY.** She was born SEE NOTES in KS.

They had 4 children:

510.   m   i.   **BESSIE ORENDORFF**, born 10 April 1882 in STEPHANS CITY, FREDERICK CO, VA, died in STEPHANS CITY, FREDERICK CO, VA.

MAY NOT BE THE RIGHT PARENTS. BESSIE WAS BURIED IN THE SALEM BRETHREN CEMETERY, STEPHANS CITY VA. MAYBE BORN IN MAY 1891.

511.   m   ii.   **OTTIE ORENDORFF**, born January 1889 in MO.

OTTIE'S NAME APPEARS AS "ORNDORFF".

512.   f   iii.   **DELLA ORENDORFF**, born February 1898 in MO.

DELLA'S NAME APPEARS AS "ORNDORFF".

513.   m   iv.   **ORVILLE RAY ORENDORFF**, born 18 January 1896 in RAVANNA, MERCER CO, MO. He married HAZEL D. COLLINS. Notes for ORVILLE:

ORVILLE RAY'S NAME APPEARS AS "ORNDORFF".

Notes for Margaret:
Birth: 10/00/1868.

Notes for Leander:
Leander Bond was also called "Lee", his name appears as "Orndorff".
Birth: 02/00/1867.

- - - - - - - - - - -

422.   LAURA   LEE[II] **SNYDER**   (277.MAHALA[10], 149.MAHALA[9], 85.DAVID[8], 60.JOHN[7], 50.PHILIP[6], 26.THEISS[5], 9.LUDWIG[4], 3.HUBERT[3], 2.HENNE[2], 1.SIMON[1]) was born 1868. LAURA died 1957, at the age of 89. She married **JOSEPH WILLIAM ORENDORFF (See number 201)** 24 November 1886 in WOODSTOCK, SHENANDOAH CO VA. He was born 1862 in PROBABLY VA/POSS. 1861. He was the son of JACOB J. JR

ORENDORFF and RACHEL REGINA WILLIAMS. **See number 201** listed above.

- - - - - - - - - - -

437. HOWARD S.[11] **ORENDORFF** (288.ROBERT[10], 165.JOSEPH[9], 89.JOHNATHAN[8], 60.JOHN[7], 50.PHILIP[6], 26.THEISS[5], 9.LUDWIG[4], 3.HUBERT[3], 2.HENNE[2], 1.SIMON[1]) was born 1864 in VA. He married **JESSIE TULLER**.

They had 1 child:

+ 514.   m   i.   **RICHARD BOOKMAN ORENDORFF**.

Notes for Howard:
Howard S.'s name appears as "Orndorff".

- - - - - - - - - - -

442. DEE[11] **ORENDORFF** (293.ROBERT[10], 166.WILLIAM[9], 90.JESSE[8], 65.CHRISTIAN[7], 54.CHRISTIAN[6], 48.JOHANN[5], 25.HERMANN[4], 7.STEPHEN[3], 2.HENNE[2], 1.SIMON[1]). DEE died in VAN ALSTYNE TEXAS on a Sunday. He married **NANCY LULA THOMPSON**.

They had 1 child:

515.   f   i.   **Maie ELIZABETH ORENDORFF**, born 31 December 1896 in McKinney TX. - Collin, Co.
Information obtained from: Texas Dept. of Health, Bureau of Vital Statistics, Certificate of Birth Vol.-16-514

Notes for Nancy:
Occupation: Housewife
Listed as living in Grayson Co, VanAlstyne, TX. No street address was given. Nancy Lula's age at the time of daughter Maie's birth was 24. Her name is listed in Stephen Hamilton Orendorff's obituary. It states "Relatives and friends from out of town expected for the services include Mrs. Lula Orendorff, Van Aylstine, Texas;" Sources : Birth Certificate, Collin Co TX Obituary.

Notes for Dee:

Occupation: Dry Good Sales.

Dee was living in Van Alstyne, Texas and was the uncle of a Mrs. H. Grady May. He died at his home on a Sunday morning. Mrs. May and Mrs. Monroe Orenduff attended the services held at 3 o'clock in the afternoon. This information came from an old newspaper clipping, unnamed, presumably from a Bonham, Texas newspaper.

- - - - - - - - - - -

443. **NOVA**[11] **ORENDORFF** (293.ROBERT[10], 166.WILLIAM[9], 90.JESSE[8], 65.CHRISTIAN[7], 54.CHRISTIAN[6], 48.JOHANN[5], 25.HERMANN[4], 7.STEPHEN[3], 2.HENNE[2], 1.SIMON[1]) was born 27 December 1871 in WESTON TEXAS. NOVA died 8 March 1958 in DENTON TX, at the age of 86. She married **Dr. WILLIAM HENRY LITTLE** 18 November 1891 in Weston, TX.

They had 5 children:

+ 516.　　f　i.　　**JEWEL LITTLE**, born 13 August 1892.

517.　　f　ii.　　**EDITH LITTLE**, born 22 February 1894.

518.　　m　iii.　　**AUSTIN FLINT LITTLE**, born 3 October 1898.

519. m　iv.　　**ROBERT W. LITTLE**, born 6 October 1900.

+ 520.　　m　v.　　**DEE ORENDORFF LITTLE**, born 13 December 1903.

Notes for Nova:

Nova was born Dec. 27, 1871, the second child of Robert Houston and Francis Hampton Orenduff. Married Dr. William Henry Little. Resided in Maple Texas for a time. She had the following children- Jewel Little b. 08-13-1892, Edith Little b. 02-22-1894, Austin Flint Little b. 10-03-1898, Robert William Little b. 10-06-1900 in Maple Texas, he was a journalist who died in an auto accident in 1939, Dee Orendorff Little b. 12-13-1903. Nova is buried in Sherman, TX.

- - - - - - - - - - -

444.   STEPHEN   HAMILTON[11]   **ORENDORFF** (293.ROBERT[10], 166.WILLIAM[9], 90.JESSE[8], 65.CHRISTIAN[7], 54.CHRISTIAN[6], 48.JOHANN[5], 25.HERMANN[4], 7.STEPHEN[3], 2.HENNE[2], 1.SIMON[1]) was born 17 December 1878 in COLLIN CO., TX. STEPHEN died 9 April 1944 in MANGUM OK, at the age of 65. He married **MARY ALLIE CUNNINGHAM** 11 November 1911 in MARTHA OK. She was born 10 January 1886 in SOUTH OF DUBLIN, TX. She was the daughter of HUIE WASHINGTON CUNNINGHAM and MARY ARZONA STEPHENS. MARY died 10 November 1963, at the age of 77.

They had 6 children:

+ 521.   m   i.   **EDDIE   DEE   ORENDORFF,**   born 10 December 1922, died 8 May 1976.

+ 522.   f   ii.   **EDNA   DEAN   ORENDORFF,**   born 10 December 1922.

+ 523.   f   iii.   **MILDRED JEANNETTE ORENDORFF,** born 5 March 1920.

+ 524.   f   iv.   **MAMIE   BELLE   ORENDORFF,**   born 7 August 1918, died 17 May 1997.

+ 525.   f   v.   **VELMA   FAYE   ORENDORFF,**   born 11 January 1915.

+ 526.   f   vi.   **LENA   JEWEL   ORENDORFF,**   born 26 February 1913, died 20 October 1998.

NOTES for MARY:
Religion: SO. BAPTIST.

Mary Allie Cunningham Orendorff was born January 10, 1886, south of Dublin Texas. She was the second child of Huie Washington Cunningham and Mary Arzona Stephens Cunningham. Mary passed away on November 10 at Scott's rest home after an extended illness. She was an active member of the first Baptist church up until the time of her illness. She moved with her parents in the 1890's to Martha OK. They also lived in Plainview OK for a year before moving to Mangum in about 1918. She was buried in the Riverside Cemetery under the direction of Johnson mortuary. The service was held at 10 am in the first Baptist church on November 14 with Rev. Haston Brewer and Rev. Bob Evans officiating. (Source: obituary) Called "Allie" and "grannie" she was very hard working and always did things to save money around the house. Allie did a lot of canning and she would take gallon-sized jars out to Oregon for Eddie and his family. She would can fruit from her son Eddie's trees and local vegetables when visiting in Oregon. Allie helped her husband Stephen with his work when he was a paperhanger. Belle and Ross hart have said that Allie was a "chatterbox". Allie would always help people, if somebody was sick she would help take care of them. When Allie homesteaded she did it alone, living in a small dugout home while she made improvements on the land, it was about 135-160 acres near Clovis new Mexico. Allie loved to cook and could make "anything from scratch" according to her daughter Belle. Allie worried that her children might catch TB while Ed was living with them. Mary's sisters were Ina, Minnie, Lilly, and Mamie. There is a picture of them taken together in 1964 after Mary Allie's funeral. She was much loved by her family. In a letter written shortly after her passing, Mildred wrote "I miss that precious mother of ours." This letter also tells of a book placed in the Baptist church library in her memory titled, "This Gold is Mine". Sources: interviews with Ross and Belle Hart.

Notes for Stephen:
Religion: Southern Baptist.
Stephen Hamilton Orendorff was born on December 17, 1878 in Collin Co Texas, the second child of Robert Houston and Amanda Jane Caldwell Orenduff. Stephen recalled to his family that at about five years of age, he was playing in the yard and his father Robert Houston was outside with him when a gang of "ruffians" rode up. Robert Houston jumped on his horse and rode off. The last he saw of his father was him bounding over a low stone wall on his horse. He also told them that his father was a sheriff at the time and that the men were a gang. After this happened his grandparents, A. J. and Clarissa Calwell in Weston, Texas raised him. This is shown in a 1900 census for Collin Co. Texas stating the following: occupation-day laborer, 0 months unemployed, reads, writes< speaks English, owns no home. He

died of a heart attack at 10:25 at his home at 327 West Tyler Street in Manugm Oklahoma. Services were held in the Baptist church at 4:00 PM and he was buried in the Riverside Cemetery. He and his wife were both Methodist before moving to Mangum and there began attending the Baptist church. (Source: obituary). Mildred, Belle, and Stephen were all baptized at the same time. Stephen was a rodeo rider until he was injured badly. He and his wife moved to Mangum in 1920, shortly before this they lived near Jester OK. He was called "bop" by John who was his first grandchild and the name stuck. Mildred and Belle said that when Stephen was about 5 years old he was playing in the yard and Robert Houston Orendorff was outside with him when a gang of "ruffians" rode up. R.H. jumped on his horse and rode off. The last he saw of his daddy was him jumping over a low stone wall with his horse. They were told this by their father and also that R.H. was a sheriff at that time and that the men were a gang. After this happened Stephen was raised by his grandparents, A.J. and Clarissa Calwell who lived in Weston, Texas as is shown in a 1900 census for Collin County which states the following of him: occupation-day laborer, 0 months unemployed, reads, writes, speaks English, owns no home. When Stephen met Allie she had just started to homestead her land. They met in Martha, Oklahoma when Stephen had just helped bring in a cotton crop with the Bunches family with whom he lived. One of his friends, a Mr. Saunders who also lived in Weston was with him at the time. They had also worked in the fields around Weston and McKinney at this time. They married and lived in Martha, OK, where their daughter Velma was born. They later moved onto the homestead which was near Clovis, New Mexico. To get there they went by train, probably the Rock Island R.R., which ran through Mangum. They lived in a dugout that was carved into a hill. It had a wood frame across the front with a couple of rooms. There were a lot of rattlesnakes, Allie said "more than you could shake a stick at" and were very fearful for the children to play in the yard. During this time they had at least twenty horses. They then moved to Plainview, Oklahoma where they lived for a few years. While there Stephen was injured with a "rupture" and it was never medically tended to. His daughters remember him going into town in a wagon and bringing back " about a nickels worth of candy " for them. After selling the homestead at Plainview, they rented a house on North Byers Street in Mangum, OK. It was there that they bought their first car. Stephen along with another man continued to take their horses and cattle up to Plainview. These cattle were later on caught in an "awful snowstorm" and froze to death. It was while he was in Plainview tending to his stock that he received word of the twins' birth. Always worked hard and was always in demand to work in the finer homes in the area. Belle also said that he had blue eyes, was short and a little hard of hearing and "one of the best men that ever lived." Belle also said that Stephen was just to sweet to discipline his children so Allie had to do it. Stephen H. loved to get a cold bottle of beer after work on a warm day. One time Uncle Ross Hart took some "wild concord grapes" and put them in Allie's churn with sugar etc. He made it into wine and Stephen would come down the street everyday to his house and ask Belle if she had "any of that soda pop". He did not like flies and would not eat out of anything that had been left open. He was a paperhanger and painter and was contracted by loan companies in Mangum to work on their vacant houses. His expertise in this area was much sought after by the community. Many times he worked long into the night in order to complete these jobs on time. His wife Allie would help on many of the jobs. One time he was going to paint a woman's house and needed something to use for the color match so the lady brought him a fountain pen that was the color she wanted and he was able to match it perfectly. He always wore white overalls while on the job. Two things he didn't like were a thief and a liar. He enjoyed playing dominos and when Pete and Raymond would come to his house Stephen would ask Raymond if he wanted to play dominos and they would sit at the kitchen table to play. Stephen lived with his family next at 327 West Tyler in Mangum and owned almost an entire city block, part of which they sold. They used some of the land for a large garden. A portion of this ground next to the Orendorff home later became a home site for their daughter Jewel and her family. Stephen has been described as "a whole lot like Eddie" because he seldom got angry. He attended church with his family often but occasionally, always desiring for his family to go, he would say "I'll wash the dishes while you girls get ready for church." Sources: 1900 Collin Co. census, obituary, interviews with Mildred Brewer, Velma Thacker, Dorothy Orendorff, Ross & Belle Hart.

- - - - - - - - - - -

447. ARBA[11] ORENDORFF (295.JESSE[10], 166.WILLIAM[9], 90.JESSE[8], 65.CHRISTIAN[7], 54.CHRISTIAN[6], 48.JOHANN[5], 25.HERMANN[4], 7.STEPHEN[3], 2.HENNE[2], I.SIMON[1]) was born 24 March 1866 in 5 MILES NORTH OF MCKINNEY, TX. ARBA died 10 October 1919 in BONHAM, TEXAS, at the age of 53. He married **HENRIETTA FITZHUGH** 6 December 1887 in TEXAS, PROBABLY MCKINNEY.

They had 1 child:

527.   f   i.   **SUSAN ORENDORFF.**

Adopted: Susan was married to a Mr. Herbert Norman and they lived in Oklahoma.

Notes for Henrietta:

Lived in Bonham Texas. Henrietta was married to Arba by A.M. Douglas. William F. Fitzhugh married Mary Rattan daughter of Thomas Rattan. They were the parents of seven children: John, George, Robert, Mrs. John W. Moore, Mrs. Sally Herndon, Mrs. Joe Skelton, and Henrietta Fitzhugh who married Arba "Orenduff". Mrs. Fitzhugh died in September of 1904.

Notes for Arba:

Harness and saddle maker. The following is Arba's obituary from a Mckinney newspaper- "In the passing away of Arba Orenduff at his home in Bonham, November 10th, inst, a notice of which appeared in this paper much genuine regret is heard expressed on every hand by many staunch friends in this city. He with his parents once lived here and he attended our schools. Many of his boyhood friends still reside here and are grieved to learn of his untimely death. He was born on the old homestead five miles north of the city, march 24, 1866, where his aged parents, Mr. and Mrs. Jesse W. Orenduff still reside and whose hearts are broken by this great sorrow. Arba was the eldest of seven children and the first to be called by the grimreaper. Thirty-two years ago he was married to Mrs. Spurietta Fitzhugh, daughter of the late Col. Fitzhugh, one of Collin County's earliest and most influential citizens. Mrs. Orenduff's devotion to him during the five of his incurable illness was sublime, refusing the help of a trained nurse and caring for him so tenderly her. No truer or more generous hearted man ever lived than Arba Orenduff. Of a retiring disposition, liberal to a fault as he made friends everywhere and held them and the good deeds he did will never be known until the books are opened. He was a member of the oddfellows, eagles and woodmen. Rev. Fincher of this city and a personal friend of the deceased went over to Bonham and with the Rev. O'Malley conducted impressive funeral services at the home Monday afternoon. The services were largely attended by friends and relatives in Bonham and elsewhere, attesting to the high esteem in which the deceased was held. On Tuesday the body was laid to rest in Fairview cemetery at Denison under a bank of loveliest autumn blossoms to await the resurrection." another- "Arba Orenduff dies at Bonham. Arba Orenduff, 55 years old, died at his home in Bonham at 6 o'clock Monday morning, following a protracted illness. The body was shipped to Denison where the burial took place at 10'o clock Tuesday morning. The funeral services were held by Dr. E. B. Fincher, pastor of the Presbyterian Church of this city. His wife and one daughter, Mrs. Herbert Norman, of Bonham, survive him. He is also survived by three brothers and three sisters as follows: Monroe Orenduff, Bonham: Ross Orenduff, Melissa: Jesse J. Orenduff, Melissa: Mrs. O. C. Harris, Melissa: Mrs. O. C. Mulkey, Commerce: Mrs. Frank Boone, Melissa, and his parents Mr. and Mrs. J.W. Orenduff of Melissa. He was born and reared on the Orenduff homestead near Mckinney. He formerly lived in this city about eight years ago and was employed by the Massie Harness Store." Sources: Marriage Record, Collin Co TX Obituary.

- - - - - - - - - - -

448. JENNIE IONE[11] ORENDORFF (295.JESSE[10], 166.WILLIAM[9], 90.JESSE[8], 65.CHRISTIAN[7], 54.CHRISTIAN[6], 48.JOHANN[5], 25.HERMANN[4], 7.STEPHEN[3], 2.HENNE[2], 1.SIMON[1]) was born 18 July 1868 in MELISSA TEXAS. She married **OLIVER CLARK MULKEY**.

They had 5 children:

+ 528.	f	i.	**MUNA MAE MULKEY**, born 17 August 1889.
529.	m	ii.	**JESSE MULKEY**, born 1892, died in childhood 1894, at the age of 2.
530.	f	iii.	**SUETTA MULKEY**, born 20 December 1895.
531.	f	iv.	**MAURINE IONE MULKEY**, born 14 September 1902.
532.	m	v.	**OLIVER CLARK MULKEY JR.**, born 29 July 1908.

Notes for Oliver:
Occupation: County Judge, Texas State Rep.

Notes for Jennie:
Jennie married Oliver Clark Mulkey who was a county Judge and a Texas State Representative. Jennie was also a member of the DAR. Their children are: Muna Mae Mulkey b. 08-17-1889, Jesse Mulkey b. 1892 d. 1894, Suetta Mulkey b. 12-20-1895, Maurine Ione Mulkey b. 09-14-1902, and Oliver Clark Mulkey JR b. 07-29-1908. Her husband died on October 27 1942 at a hospital after a 2-week illness and was buried on October 28, 1942. The following is from his obituary: "Coming to Commerce 48 years ago from Melissa, Collin Co, Judge Mulkey had practiced law here all during his long residence. Served 10 years as Mayor of Commerce, represented this district in the Texas legislature for four years and occupied the hunt county bench four years. Twice a master of the commerce Masonic lodge, he also served as district deputy grand master of the grand lodge of Texas and as grand orator of the grand royal arch chapter of Texas. Before

coming to commerce he had been president of the Estacado Institute of Plainview. At one time Judge Mulkey held a temporary appointment as an Associate Justice of the State Supreme Court.

- - - - - - - - - - -

450. JESSE[11] **ORENDORFF** (295.JESSE[10], 166.WILLIAM[9], 90.JESSE[8], 65.CHRISTIAN[7], 54.CHRISTIAN[6], 48.JOHANN[5], 25.HERMANN[4], 7.STEPHEN[3], 2.HENNE[2], 1.SIMON[1]) was born 1874, probably in MELISSA TEXAS. He married **MARY MAGNESS**.

They had 2 children:

| 533. | m | i. | **JESSE ORENDORFF**, born 9 January 1912 north of MCKINNEY TEXAS, died in EL PASO, EL PASO CO, TEXAS. |
| 534. | f | ii. | **LILA ORENDORFF**. LILA MARRIED O. C. STEVENS. |

Notes for Jesse:
Born around 1874.

- - - - - - - - - - -

452. ROSS[11] **ORENDORFF** (295.JESSE[10], 166.WILLIAM[9], 90.JESSE[8], 65.CHRISTIAN[7], 54.CHRISTIAN[6], 48.JOHANN[5], 25.HERMANN[4], 7.STEPHEN[3], 2.HENNE[2], 1.SIMON[1]) was born 22 February 1886 in MELISSA TEXAS. ROSS died in MCKINNEY TEXAS. He married **MARGUERITE HUGHES**.

They had 2 children:

| + 535. | m | i. | **ROSS JR ORENDORFF**, born 25 August 1924. |
| 536. | f | ii. | **PATSY ORENDORFF**, born 25 January 1928 in SHERMAN TEXAS. |

Notes for Ross:
Might have been named after General Ross. He worked in the automotive parts business all his life. His nephew remembers going

to visit him and listening to him play his trombone and putting on minstrel shows in black face. Source: book "Hayes and Allied Families", interview with Ross Orenduff.

- - - - - - - - - - -

453. **MONROE**[11] **ORENDORFF** (295.JESSE[10], 166.WILLIAM[9], 90.JESSE[8], 65.CHRISTIAN[7], 54.CHRISTIAN[6], 48.JOHANN[5], 25.HERMANN[4], 7.STEPHEN[3], 2.HENNE[2], I.SIMON[1]) was born 30 April 1879 in MELISSA, TX. MONROE died 18 November 1959 in BONHAM, TX, at the age of 80. He married **MINNIE ANNIE WILMETH** 24 December 1905. She was born 11 October 1884. MINNIE died 5 January 1964, at the age of 79.

They had 3 children:

+ 537. m i. **MONROE WILMETH ORENDORFF**, born 14 October 1906, died October 1986.

538. f ii. **BESSIE MAE ORENDORFF**, born 5 November 1916 in BONHAM, TX, died 25 May 1993, at the age of 76.
Orenduff spelling. Bess graduated from Bonham Texas high school in 1934. Attended college in Denton for two years 1935-36. During the war she worked as a machinist for the South West Pump Company in Bonham. Later she worked for her brother in a store in Sherman. She worked for her brother Arba in his store in Bonham for 10 years. After he closed his store she worked at JB White Department Store for 25 years. She never married. Sources: Arba R. Orenduff - Family Bible Registers (copies), S.S Death Index

539. m iii. **ARBA RAYMOND ORENDORFF**, born 18 January 1920 in BONHAM, TX, died 30 November 1994, at the age of 7

Notes for Arba: Orenduff spelling. Arba owned a store in Bonham, Texas for many years. He was instrumental in getting information and photos to his cousin Stephen Bradley Orendorff for use in this book. - Source Social Security Death Index

Notes for Monroe:
Occupation: Worked for Bonham Wholesale Grocery. Orenduff spelling. Monroe finished high school in Sherman Texas. Graduated from Austin College in Sherman Texas in 1934. During WWII he was a in the Civilian Air patrol out of Carlsbad New Mexico. Birth, Marriage and Death dates - Family Bible Register given to me by my cousin Arba Orenduff.

Notes for Minnie:

- - - - - - - - - - -

456. VIVIAN WAVERLEY (MAJOR) [11] **ORENDORFF** (296.JOHN[10], 166.WILLIAM[9], 90.JESSE[8], 65.CHRISTIAN[7], 54.CHRISTIAN[6], 48.JOHANN[5], 25.HERMANN[4], 7.STEPHEN[3], 2.HENNE[2], I.SIMON[1]) was born 7 November 1869 in MELISSA TEXAS. VIVIAN died 6 March 1948, at the age of 78. He married **CLARA BYRNE** 14 June 1892 in MCKINNEY TEXAS. She was born 10 July 1872 in UNION CITY INDIANA. She was the daughter of JAMES EDWARD BYRNE and MIMA. CLARA died 15 November 1897, at the age of 25.

They had 3 children:

+ 540.   m   i.   **VIVIAN BYRNE ORENDORFF**, born 23 December 1892.

541.   f   ii.   **BONNIE MIMA ORENDORFF**, born 1 March 1897.
Bonnie married Wilbur Carmack and had 2 children. Fay Louise b. 11-25-1920 married Wayne Thomas and had Wayne JR, Brian, and Douglas. Donna Jane b.1205-1924 married to Richard Halterman.

542.   f   iii.   **NANCY   FAY   ORENDORFF,**   born 7 November 1899.

Nancy married Thomas Mervyn Kaney and had 2 children. Katherine Eileen b.10-31-1924 who married David Morrison and had Patricia Eileen, John Thomas, David Paul, she then married Charles Griggs. Thomas Mervyn b. 06-22-1926 died in 1992 married 2 wives, both unknown. Had 4 children by his first wife, Lynn Ann, Nancy Louise, and Teresa Eileen and Kimberly Leigh who were twins.

Notes for Clara:

Clara's father is buried in the old Orenduff/Orendorff cemetery in Texas. This cemetery also has allied families of the Orendorffs in it, such as the Byrne family. A 1900's Census record showed that a Mrs. Mima Byrne was a widow and living on a farm with her five sons. Her sixth child was Clara who was already married to Vivian (Major) Orendorff and living elsewhere.

Notes for Vivian:

Vivian W. moved to Chico CA in the early 1900's. His brother James also moved there along with his wife Clara's brothers Charles and Homer Byrne. The clergyman at Vivians wedding was A. M. Douglas and the witnesses were Frank H. Boone, John W. Orendorff, and Mark Byrne.

CHAPTER TWELVE

GENERATION NO. 12

498. ELMER LEROY[12] **ORENDORFF** (404.IRA[11], 238.WILLIAM[10], 132.HARRISON[9], 76.PHILIP[8], 60.JOHN[7], 50.PHILIP[6], 26.THEISS[5], 9.LUDWIG[4], 3.HUBERT[3], 2.HENNE[2], 1.SIMON[1]) was born 20 December 1918 in PERU, CHATAUQUA CO, KS. ELMER died in OKLAHOMA CITY, OK. He married **HELEN MCNARY.**

They had 1 child:
+ 543.   m   i.   **TERRY OWEN ORENDORFF.**

HELEN also married (2) TERRY OWEN ORENDORFF **(See number 543).** He was the son of ELMER LEROY ORENDORFF and HELEN MCNARY.

- - - - - - - - - - -

499. HOWARD ALLEN[12] **ORENDORFF** (404.IRA[11], 238.WILLIAM[10], 132.HARRISON[9], 76.PHILIP[8], 60.JOHN[7], 50.PHILIP[6], 26.THEISS[5], 9.LUDWIG[4], 3.HUBERT[3], 2.HENNE[2], 1.SIMON[1]) was born 31 March 1916 in PERU, CHAUTAUQUA CO, Kansas. He married **ANN ELENE QUATTLEBAUM.**

They had 2 children:
544.   f   i.   **RITA ORENDORFF.**
                    Rita's name appears as "Orndorff".
545.   m   ii.   **DAVID ORENDORFF.**
                    David's name appears as "Orndorff".

Notes for Howard:
Had 2 children Howard Allen's name appears as "Orndorff".

- - - - - - - - - - -

504. HILTON GEORGE[12] **ORENDORFF** (406.GEORGE[11], 238.WILLIAM[10], 132.HARRISON[9], 76.PHILIP[8], 60.JOHN[7], 50.PHILIP[6], 26.THEISS[5], 9.LUDWIG[4], 3.HUBERT[3], 2.HENNE[2], 1.SIMON[1]) was born 20 October 1908 in BARTON CO, MO. HILTON died 28 April 1970 in DENVER, CO, at the age of 61. He married **BEAULAH FERN PEMBERTON**. She was born 1 January 1916 in BEAVER CO, OK.

They had 4 children:

546.	m	i.	**DOYLE LEE ORENDORFF**, born 8 March 1936 in ROSTEN, OK. DOYLE LEE'S NAME APPEARS AS "ORNDORFF".
+ 547.	m	ii.	**MADISON DOW ORENDORFF**, born 11 December 1940.
+ 548.	m	iii.	**ROGER ARNOLD ORENDORFF**, born 6 January 1938.
549.	m	iv.	**DENNIS K. ORENDORFF**, born 10 September 1949 in CANON CITY, CO. He married RAMONA LYNN STOCK.

Notes for Beaulah:
Beaulah Fern was the daughter of Fred Cason Pemberton and Lucinda Despain.

Notes for Hilton:
Hilton George was called "bud", his name appears as "Orndorff".

- - - - - - - - - - -

508. WILLIAM HARRISON[12] **ORENDORFF** (406.GEORGE[11], 238.WILLIAM[10], 132.HARRISON[9],

76.PHILIP[8], 60.JOHN[7], 50.PHILIP[6], 26.THEISS[5], 9.LUDWIG[4], 3.HUBERT[3], 2.HENNE[2], I.SIMON[1]) was born 4 January 1906 in KANSAS CITY, CLAY CO, MO. WILLIAM died 11 April 1971, at the age of 65. He married **MARY JOSEPHINE HUBER.**

They had 2 children:

+ 550.   m   i.   **ROBERT DEANE ORENDORFF,** born 26 March 1933.

+ 551.   m   ii.   **CARL JOSEPH ORENDORFF,** born 16 July 1936.

Notes for William:
William Harrison's name appears as "Orndorff".

- - - - - - - - - - -

514.   RICHARD   BOOKMAN[12]   **ORENDORFF** (437.HOWARD[11],   288.ROBERT[10],   165.JOSEPH[9], 89.JOHNATHAN[8],   60.JOHN[7],   50.PHILIP[6],   26.THEISS[5], 9.LUDWIG[4], 3.HUBERT[3], 2.HENNE[2], I.SIMON[1]) was born probably in VA. His spouse has not been identified.

They had 1 child:

552.   m   i.   **RICHARD ORENDORFF,** possibly born in VA.
Richard's name appears as "Orndorff".

Notes for Richard:
Richard Bookman's name appears as "Orndorff".

- - - - - - - - - - -

516.   JEWEL[12]   **LITTLE**   (443.NOVA[11],   293.ROBERT[10], 166.WILLIAM[9], 90.JESSE[8], 65.CHRISTIAN[7], 54.CHRISTIAN[6], 48.JOHANN[5],   25.HERMANN[4],   7.STEPHEN[3],   2.HENNE[2], I.SIMON[1]) was born 13 August 1892 in Weston, TX. She married **GEORGE FITZGERALD BRYANT.** He was born 15 September 1892. He was the son of CHARLES WESLEY BRYANT and SARAH FRANCES FITZGERALD. GEORGE died 24 October 1949, at the age of 57.

They had 4 children:

553.   f   i.   **FRANCES BRYANT**, born 19 September 1914.

554.   m   ii.   **GEORGE F. Jr. BRYANT**, born 31 December 1915.

555.   f   iii.   **NOVA BRYANT**, born 28 August 1917.

556.   m   iv.   **WILLIAM HENRY BRYANT**, born 24 January 1920.

- - - - - - - - - - -

520. DEE ORENDORFF[12] LITTLE (443.NOVA[11], 293.ROBERT[10], 166.WILLIAM[9], 90.JESSE[8], 65.CHRISTIAN[7], 54.CHRISTIAN[6], 48.JOHANN[5], 25.HERMANN[4], 7.STEPHEN[3], 2.HENNE[2], 1.SIMON[1]) was born 13 December 1903 in Maple, TX. He married **Christiana BARRETT** 16 July 1949 in Sherman, TX. She was born 24 March 1916.

They had 3 children:

557.   m   i.   **BARRETT DEE LITTLE**, born 18 January 1951.

558.   m   ii.   **ROBERT RANDOLPH LITTLE**, born 27 September 1952.

559.   m   iii.   **DAVID RAY LITTLE**, born 24 March 1954.

Notes for Christiana:
Occupation: Retired schoolteacher.

Notes for Dee:
Occupation: Retired Pharmacist.

- - - - - - - - - - -

521. EDDIE DEE[12] ORENDORFF (444.STEPHEN[11], 293.ROBERT[10], 166.WILLIAM[9], 90.JESSE[8], 65.CHRISTIAN[7], 54.CHRISTIAN[6], 48.JOHANN[5], 25.HERMANN[4], 7.STEPHEN[3], 2.HENNE[2], 1.SIMON[1]) was born 10 December 1922 in MANGUM, GREER CO, OK. EDDIE died 8 May 1976 in EUGENE, OR, at the age of 53. He was buried 11 May 1976 in ALFORD CEMETERY at HARRISBURG, OR. He married **DOROTHY LEE ANGLIN** 1941. She was born 13 November 1922 in MANGUM, OK. She was the daughter of MARVIN EDGAR ANGLIN and EVA MAE SULLIVAN (O'Sullivan). DOROTHY died 8 July 1996 in JUNCTION CITY, LANE CO, OR at the age of 73. She was buried 11 July 1997 in ALFORD CEMETERY at HARRISBURG, OR.

They had 5 children:

+ 560.   m   i.   **STEPHEN MARVIN ORENDORFF**, born 1 June 1953.

+ 561.   m   ii.   **EDDIE DAVID ORENDORFF**, born 7 March 1942, died 7 May 1990.

+ 562.   f   iii.   **NANCY LEE ORENDORFF**, born 8 December 1945.

563.   f   iv.   **SHARON ROSE ORENDORFF**, born 16 May 1950 in ALBANY OR.
Religion: Protestant.
Sharon Rose Orendorff was born in Eugene, Oregon on May 16, 1950. The fourth child born to Eddie Dee Orendorff and Dorothy Lee Anglin Orendorff. She worked for the first National Bank in Harrisburg for many years and is now an office employee for a water purification company in Junction City, Oregon. She married Raymond Halsey firstly and later married James Singletery. Her three children were born in Eugene OR and are as follows-Carleen Halsey b. 03-28-70, Brandon Halsey b. 05-11-1973 and Heather Singletery b. 11-23-1978.

564.   f   v.   **ANITA SUE ORENDORFF**, born 24 August 1944 in EUGENE, LANE CO, OR and died in HARRISBURG, LINN CO, OREGON, buried in RIVERSIDE CEMETERY MANGUM, OK.
Anita Sue Orendorff was the second child born

to Eddie Dee and Dorothy Anglin Orendorff. She was born on Aug. 24,1944 in Eugene, Or. Her parents called her Susie. The baby died in her sleep at seventy-two days old. Sources-Dorothy Orendorff, birth announcement.

Notes for Dorothy:

Religion: Protestant.

The first child born to Edgar Marvin Anglin and Eva Mae Sullivan Anglin. Born on Nov 13, 1922 in Mangum, OK. She grew up in Mangum and attended school there. She and Eddie married there and moved to Oregon shortly afterwards. She taught Sunday school classes for many years. She was an artist and it was said that even as a child she could draw anything. Her talents as an artist led her into painting with oils, which became a favorite hobby. She also loved to sing. The Anglin family came to America in 1844 or 1846 from Sheffield England and settled in Tennessee. William Thomas Anglin joined the army of the Tennessee in 1863 at the age of 15 giving his age as 18. Thomas was born in 1848. He married a civil war widow with one child named John Chaffin. To them was born William Marvin Anglin who married Huldah Jane Elliot in Marrietta, OK around 1891. Their son Marvin was Dorothy's father who married Eva Sullivan. Marvin and Eva lived in Harrisburg, OR before moving to Brownsville, OR. An American flag belonging to Marvin was given to his great -grandson, Stephen Bradley Orendorff. Murphy's Funeral Home in Junction City, OR handled the services. A graveside service was held at Alfred Cemetery near Harrisburg, OR. Pastor Albert Erickson, a close family friend, directed it. Sources: Birth Certificate, Obituary, interview with Dorothy and Eva Anglin.

Notes for Eddie:

Religion: Protestant.

Eddie Dee Orendorff (twin) was born on December 10, 1922 in Mangum, Oklahoma, the last child born to Stephen Hamilton Orendorff and Mary Allie Cunningham Orendorff. He was born in his parent's home on North Byers Street in Mangum. His father was in Plainview, Oklahoma tending to his cattle when he received word and immediately returned home. He was met by the doctor who told him that he had a girl. The family has enjoyed telling of the fun and excitement, which transpired when their daddy learned there were two and that one was a boy. Shortly after the twins birth, the family moved to 327 West Tyler street where the family settled. Eddie and his twin Edna were absolutely adored and were pampered as children since they were the babies of the family. The older girls helped care for the twins. Jewell helped with Eddie and velma helped tend to Edna. Velma said they would feed the babies their oatmeal "then finish up the dish." His sister Mildred recalled a time when Eddie, at about eight years of age, had broken his leg while swinging at the park and was in a splint with the injured leg elevated in the air. In this unfortunate and precarious predicament, the family of course tended to his every need. This constant care and concern is no doubt the reason for Mildred sleepwalking into Eddies room one night and fortunately awakening right before attempting to attend to her brothers broken leg! His other sister Belle said she always wanted to be near her brother. Edna's closeness to her twin brother was always apparent even though they teased each other relentlessly. Edna loved to remind her little brother that she was the eldest! Once as a young boy Eddie was told not to mess around with the battery on model t car his folks had. But he did so anyway and ended up getting the shock of his life. However, that wasn't nearly as shocking as the time he tried to look into the gas tank with a match and had his eyebrows burnt off. Also at some point in his younger life he drove a car into a river. One time Belle's husband, Ross had gone with Eddie for a job interview at a large dairy and was talking to the manager. Ross was smoking a cigar and bragging about how well Eddie had done with testing and pasteurizing at another plant. The manager said he would like to give him a job and started to show them around. Ross soon noticed that Eddie was gone and told the manager that he thought Eddie had gone to the restroom and went to find him. The place was too big and Eddie didn't like it so he had gone out a window and escaped to the car. Eddie was always quiet about who he was dating because his sisters would always tease him about girls. The family never knew whom their brother was dating until he met Dorothy. They married and stayed in Mangum a few years before moving to Oregon where her parents had already located. He worked for the railroad. He was a reserve city police officer for the town of Harrisburg, OR, and a plywood mill worker, pulp and paper worker. Eddie was very jealous when he was younger. Once while vacationing in old Mexico with Belle and Ross, Eddie got very upset because a man was looking at his wife while they were walking down the street. If the man hadn't fled, Eddie would have fought him. After moving to Los Angeles, Eddie was on his way to a job and got lost in the city until the next morning. He never did get to the place he was trying to find. Belle said that her brother "cheated no one in is life". Eddie loved sugar cookies and anything that had nuts in it. His grandson Stephen remembers the following: "my granddaddy used to always have candy in the glovebox of his truck, I especially remember the caramel squares, and he would always give them to me. He would come over and mow our lawn when I was about four years old and we lived at the "rent house" across from him in Harrisburg. It was a riding lawn mower and he would let me ride on it with him. He passed on before I turned five and he left a strong impression on me to this day. Many times I have talked to him at his grave about my problems or just about how much I miss him. If I can be just half the man he was I will be satisfied with my life." Eddie also built a church in Harrisburg, which was donated to the four square church organization in the late 1980's. Once when he was working at the mill he had some problems with a man who also worked there. He told Eddie to meet himm after work down by the river. When Eddie got down there he fought the man and also got jumped by the man's friend who had hidden in the bushes. He whipped them both. He is listed in the 1994 social security death index, his SSI # was 447-16-7035. Eddie bought the house on 554 1/2 Territorial St in Harrisburg in 1951. In 1942 Eddie and Dorothy came to Oregon on a greyhound bus, Dorothy's parents lived in Harrisburg on Territorial St in a house which no longer stands. They stayed with them for a few months before moving to an apartment on the corner of 3rd and LaSalle St. in Harrisburg. They lived there during the winter of 1943. Eddie worked in the woods logging for a short time in the Belfountain area with his father -in -law Marvin Anglin. Inducted into the US army in 1943 as a private at Portland, Oregon then to Fort Lewis, Washington, then to camp Berkley, Texas. Stationed in Abilene, Texas. Ross went and saw him there and found him playing craps with other soldiers. Shortly before he was to be shipped overseas he suffered a severe head injury and was transferred to a hospital in Colorado Springs, Colorado for specialized treatment. He nearly died from his injuries. Apparently he had fallen while crossing a riverbed by some system of ropes high over it and struck his head on rocks. He served 6 months before receiving an honorable discharge due to injury. A few years later he bought a farm in the little mountain town of Crow, Oregon. Crow is a community west of Eugene where he was employed with the railroad. The town was set in a beautiful wilderness area and their nearest neighbor was a government trapper named Mr. Lewis. Eddie hunted in the mountains behind the home place. A creek ran through the property that contained an abundance of trout. His daughter Nancy remembers him showing her the fish while standing over it on a fallen log. Eddie's sister Belle and her husband Ross lived in one of the two houses on the land. There was a large fruit orchard and several large buildings equipped for the commercial raising of chickens. A dairy cow provided fresh milk and the garden provided an abundant variety of delicious vegetables that were canned in preparation for the harsh winter months. Many hardships were created because of weather. The snow and ice made the mountain road they lived on impassable much of the time. Since his work with the railroad was based from Eugene travel to and from work became a major problem and was the foremost reason for moving from the area. The Hart's eventually returned to Texas and Eddie moved to Harrisburg. Although in town, the house and property that he purchased was secluded and private with many fruit and nut trees surrounding it. When the family came for summer visits, his mother enjoyed canning the cherries, apples, pears and plums from the trees in the yard. There he centered his life around his family. He was much loved and respected by all. Everyone knew of his integrity and honesty. He was absolutely fearless and his life was an example to all that knew him. If Eddie said he would do something everyone knew he would do it. Sources: Social Security death index, interviews with family.

- - - - - - - - - - -

522. EDNA DEAN[12] **ORENDORFF** (444.STEPHEN[11], 293.ROBERT[10], 166.WILLIAM[9], 90.JESSE[8], 65.CHRISTIAN[7], 54.CHRISTIAN[6], 48.JOHANN[5], 25.HERMANN[4], 7.STEPHEN[3], 2.HENNE[2], 1.SIMON[1]) was born 10 December 1922 in MANGUM OK, GREER CO. She married **JOE WAYNE MORRIS** 29 March 1945 in MANGUM, OKLAHOMA. He was born 23 April 1922 in Erick, OKLAHOMA. JOE died 13 July 1998, at the age of 76, and was buried in Riverside National Cemetery.

They had 2 children:

+ 565.　　m　　i.　　**EDDIE WAYNE MORRIS**, born 26 April 1951.

July 31 1969.

+ 566.　　f　　ii.　　**MARY SUE MORRIS**, born 5 August 1957.

1975.

NOTES for JOE:

Religion: Baptist

Joe Wayne Morris was born April 23,1922 in Erick, OK, the third of seven children born to Charlie and Ruth Morris. He grew up and graduated from high school in Mangum, OK, where he excelled in sports, especially football, basketball and golf.

His college tenure at Northwestern in Weatherford, OK was interrupted by World War Two. On November 11, 1942, Wayne was inducted into the United States Army and, after three months of training, was shipped overseas. He saw military action in Tunisia, Sicily, Normandy, Northern France, and Germany.

Wayne served his country gallantly and bravely, earning five Bronze Battle Stars, a Silver Battle Star, a Purple Heart, the Order of

Bronze Arrowhead, an EAME Campaign Ribbon, the Distinguished Unit Citation, the Combat Infantryman's Badge with the Oakleaf Cluster, and the Good Conduct Medal and Bar. On D-Day, June 6, 1944, he was awarded the Bronze Star for heroic achievement.

After being wounded twice and suffering from malaria, Wayne's feet were frozen during the Battle of the Bulge and he was shipped to England and then finally to a hospital in Colorado. While recuperating and on leave from the Army, Wayne returned to Mangum and married his high school sweetheart, Edna Dean Orendorff, on March 29, 1945. The couple settled in Altus, Oklahoma, where their three children, Eddie Wayne, Mary Sue, and Jean Ann were born. For a number of years, Wayne had a newspaper franchise in Oklahoma. Then, in 1963, the family moved to California where Wayne worked in the aircraft industry.

But by far, his most important and lifetime vocation was in the Church where he served so faithfully. With Edna by his side, Wayne was active in the First Southern Baptist Church of LaHabra from 1963 to 1987. Beloved by all, he taught adult Sunday school classes, conducted rest home ministries and was Chairman of the Board of Deacons. It was at the LaHabra church that he was ordained and licensed as a minister in 1986.

In 1987, Wayne and Edna moved to Moreno Valley, where Wayne again took up the mantle of deacon and served as Minister to Senior Adults at the First Baptist Church.

Wayne's ministry touched the lives of many people. He had the joy of baptizing grandson Greg and granddaughter Heather. One young man, Richard Bender of LaHabra, was confined to a wheelchair and had no transportation. Sunday after Sunday, for nine years, Wayne walked to his home and pushed Richard to church in his chair.

For the past few years, Wayne was a faithful caregiver to his invalid wife, never wanting to be apart from her. Still, the Lord enabled him to continue his ministry with the senior adults and even to teach his grandson Greg to play golf. One of Wayne's last pleasures was knowing that, as a high school freshman, Greg lettered in the game of golf.

Wayne is survived by his wife of fifty-three years, Edna Morris; his son, Ed Morris; his daughter, Mary Sue Nunnaly; four grandchildren. Greg and Heather Nunnally, Matt and John Wayne Morris; his brother, Doyle Morris; and his sisters, Jean Ellis and Sue Allen. Wayne was a beloved husband, father, grandfather and brother. Both in word and deed, he was a true servant of his Lord Jesus Christ.

Sources: Edna Morris, Nancy Cobb (Orendorff), obituary.

Notes for Edna:

Religion: Baptist

Twin sister of Eddie Dee Orendorff, delivered by E.W. Mabry. Edna married Wayne Morse and is living in Moreno Valley, CA. Source: birth certificate.

- - - - - - - - - - -

523. MILDRED JEANNETTE[12] **ORENDORFF** (444.STEPHEN[11], 293.ROBERT[10], 166.WILLIAM[9], 90.JESSE[8], 65.CHRISTIAN[7], 54.CHRISTIAN[6], 48.JOHANN[5], 25.HERMANN[4], 7.STEPHEN[3], 2.HENNE[2], I.SIMON[1]) was born 5 March 1920 in MANGUM OKLAHOMA Greer, Co. She married **HAROLD HASTON BREWER** 14 September 1942 in Ft. Belvoir, VA. He was born 12 February 1919 in CORINTH, MISS. He is the son of OSCAR S. BREWER and CHARLSIE C. GURLEY.

They had 4 children:

+ 567.   f   i.   **CAROLYN SUE BREWER**, born 15 December 1949.

+ 568.   f   ii.   **MARTHA ANN BREWER**, born 25 March 1952.

+ 569.   f   iii.   **JAN ELIZABETH BREWER**, born 27 March 1953.

+ 570.   f   iv.   **SARAH JEAN BREWER**, born 1 June 1954.

Notes for Harold:

Harold Haston Brewer was born February 14,1919 in Corinth, Mississippi, the third child of Oscar S. Brewer and Charlsie C. Gurley Brewer. Haston served in Burma during the war. He is a retired Baptist minister.

Notes for Mildred:

Religion: So. Baptist

Mildred Jeannette Orendorff, the 4th child born to Stephen Hamilton and Mary Allie Cunningham Orendorff on March 5, 1920 in Mangum, OK. She grew up in Mangum and worked as a telephone operator until her husband returned from the war. She and Haston, a retired Baptist minister, live in Cleburne, Texas. Mildred called Edward Orendorff "Uncle Ed" and she thought he had died during the 1920's.

- - - - - - - - - - -

524. MAMIE BELLE[12] **ORENDORFF** (444.STEPHEN[11], 293.ROBERT[10], 166.WILLIAM[9], 90.JESSE[8], 65.CHRISTIAN[7], 54.CHRISTIAN[6], 48.JOHANN[5], 25.HERMANN[4], 7.STEPHEN[3], 2.HENNE[2], I.SIMON[1]) was born 7 August 1918 in PLAINVIEW OKLAHOMA. MAMIE died 17 May 1997 in FT. WORTH, TX, at the age of 78. She married **WILLIAM ROSS HART** 28 August 1938 in Cheyenne, OK.

They had I child:

571.　　f　i.　**ROSSLYN KAYE HART.**

Adopted from family member.

Notes for Mamie and Ross:

Education: Wedford College.

Religion: Baptist.

Mamie married William Ross Hart; she also attended southwestern teachers college. William was a salesman for H.J. Hines Co. in Fort Worth Texas. They adopted one child, Rosslyn Kay Hart. Called "Belle". Belle and Ross kept Stephen Marvin Orendorff for awhile when he was small. Belle is a good cook and she has a date cake recipe that was handed down to her by her mother Allie who it is believed got it from her mother. Belle and Ross met through the Baptist church where Ross's father was a preacher. Belle has written a book called "Key to the Inner Chamber" which is a collection of her thoughts concerning the bible etc. She is also currently working on a similar book (1994). Once Belle made Ross move to Oregon just to be near Eddie since they missed each other so much. They lived in Eugene OR. Belle was once in Oregon on vacation for a week when she discovered Dorothy was giving away food, milk, etc. Belle had gone to bed and she got up for a drink in the night. She was sleeping in the room by the stairs. As she went by the front door she noticed a case of canned milk sitting below the dining room window and that the front door was unlocked. She knew what was going on and was so mad she got dressed and waited with her door open so she could see the front door. She also locked the front door. Opened sometime later she heard Elmer (E.W.) Anglin knocking and saying "dot", "dot". Belle the door and asked him what he wanted. He said he was taking the milk to sister so and so because her kids were hungry. Belle told him "over my dead body, this milk was paid for with my brothers money. If sister so and so's kids are hungry her husband should get out and work. E.W. would call her Belle to irritate her since only her friends called her that. He left and did not come back while she was there. Ross called in sick and they stayed an extra week. Belle also does not like flies and will not eat out of anything open if any are around, just like her father. Ross's grandparents were farmers all their lives and they had 13 children, one of which died early. Ross's mother was the oldest. His grandpa (Will Henderson) was tall, mustached, and had jet-black hair right up until his death at age 90. His grandma (Mattie Henderson) looked like an Indian, she lived to be 94 and died around 1992. They had a one-acre garden and his grandpa would not work on a Saturday or Sunday. He would take a cup of coffee to his wife every morning. They would work from just before day light until noon then take a break for lunch, about an hour. Sometimes his grandpa would rest on one of the tall straight back cane bottomed chairs by flipping it over and putting a pillow on the back. They owned 160 acres. In Mangum Belle went to Wedford College, a small college 7 blocks from the main part of town, and took beautician classes. Belle and Ross married north of Mangum in Cheyenne. After this Belle and Ross bought into an ice cream plant business for about $3,000.00 and were equal partners with Raymond Thacker. This was before Eddie moved to Oregon. Belle would make cookies for him often. Eddie delivered ice cream at this time. Belle uses the expression "putting a halo on" about people who try to make them selves look good.

- - - - - - - - - - -

525. VELMA FAYE[12] ORENDORFF (444.STEPHEN[11], 293.ROBERT[10], 166.WILLIAM[9], 90.JESSE[8], 65.CHRISTIAN[7], 54.CHRISTIAN[6], 48.JOHANN[5], 25.HERMANN[4], 7.STEPHEN[3], 2.HENNE[2], 1.SIMON[1]) was born 11 January 1915 in MARTHA, OKLAHOMA. She married **RAYMOND PAUL THACKER** 5 February 1938 in MANGUM, OK. He was born 16 June 1914 in Willow Grove, TENN. He was the son of WILLIAM MARTIN THACKER and IDA FLORENCE WATSON. RAYMOND died 26 September 1997 in Ardmore, OK, at the age of 83.

They had 1 child:

572.   f   i.   **MARY ANN THACKER**, born 14 January 1942 in GRANITE, OK, died 25 September 1993 in FORT WORTH, TEXAS, at the age of 51, and was buried in Rose Hill Cemetery.
Education: Univ. of Oklahoma Graduate, Texas Christian Univ. & Univ. of TX
Mary Ann Thacker was born on January 14, 1942, in Granite, Ok. She was the only child of Raymond Paul Thacker and Velma Faye Thacker. Reared in Ardmore, she graduated from the University of Oklahoma, received her masters degree in organ performance from Texas Christian University, and had earned a doctorate in humanities from the University of Texas. She taught music at Tarleton State University in Stephenville and was an archivist for the Chickasaw Indian Nations at Tishomingo. She was a prominent Fort Worth area antique dealer and shop owner and. As a young woman she became extremely interested in the family's

history and did extensive research on the Stephens, Orendorff's and Cunningham lines. She married Jerry Glasscock, then married secondly William Hornbuckle 09-19-1981. Mary Ann attended Texas Christian College and is a professor of organ at southwestern Adventist College in Keene Texas. She was murdered sometime between 1130 am and 1215 PM Saturday September 25 1993 by a single gunshot wound to the head. Mary Ann's service was held at 2 PM September 29 1993 at the first Baptist church with doctor Alton Fannin officiating. Interment was at Rose Hill Cemetery. Mary Ann was killed September 25 1993 at her Fort Worth business, the emporium antique shop. A segment about her death was run on the television show "Unsolved Mysteries". She lived in Fort Worth for 27 years and founded the Fort Worth antique dealers association. Mary Ann also taught music at Tarleton State University and was an archivist for the Chickasaw Indian nations at Tishomingo. Pallbearers were Craig Beskow, Rocky Bunting, Rev Franklin Krause, Henry Hogan, Charles and David Thacker. Craddock Funeral Home directed the services. At the time of this writing (07-18-94) there have been no arrests made for her murder. Lt. J.P. Foley has been assigned to the case; he works for the Fort Worth police departments homicide division.

Notes for Raymond:

Occupation: Retired agency manager for the Daily Oklahoman Newspaper

Raymond Paul Thacker was born on June 16, 1914, in Willow Grove, Tenn., the eighth child of William Martin Thacker and Ida Florence Watson Thacker.

Notes for Velma:
Velma married Raymond Paul Thacker. They had one child-Mary Ann Thacker born 01-14-1942 in Granite OK. Velma is nicknamed "Pete". Velma was born at Martha OK and then the family moved out to Allie's homestead shortly after.

- - - - - - - - - - -

526. LENA JEWEL[12] **ORENDORFF** (444.STEPHEN[11], 293.ROBERT[10], 166.WILLIAM[9], 90.JESSE[8], 65.CHRISTIAN[7], 54.CHRISTIAN[6], 48.JOHANN[5], 25.HERMANN[4], 7.STEPHEN[3], 2.HENNE[2], I.SIMON[1]) was born 26 February 1913 in MARTHA, OKLAHOMA. LENA died 20 October 1998 in MANGUM, OK, at the age of 85. She married **ROY CLAYBURN WILEMAN** 5 August 1939 in Sayer, OK. Beckham Co.

They had 4 children:

573.	m	i.	**JOHN CLAYBURN WILEMAN**, born 20 May 1940 in MANGUM, OK. Religion: Southern Baptist
574.	m	ii.	**JAMES STEPHEN WILEMAN**, born 8 February 1943.
575.	f	iii.	**JUDY KAY WILEMAN**, born 14 September 1946 in MANGUM, OK.
576.	f	iv.	**KATHY ANN WILEMAN**, born 28 December 1945 in MANGUM, OK.

Notes for Lena:
Religion: Baptist

Lena Jewel Orendorff was the first child of Stephen Hamilton and Mary Allie Cunningham Orendorff. She was born Feb 26, 1913 in Martha, OK. Married Roy Clayburn Wileman. Their children are as follows: John Clayburn Wileman born 05-20-1940 in Mangum OK, semi-retired from nursing. James Stephen Wileman-born 02-08-1943. Judy Kay Wileman-born 09-14-1946. Kathy Ann Wileman, born 12-28-1955. Source- book "Hayes of Virginia".

- - - - - - - - - - -

528. MUNA MAE[12] **MULKEY** (448.JENNIE[11], 295.JESSE[10], 166.WILLIAM[9], 90.JESSE[8], 65.CHRISTIAN[7], 54.CHRISTIAN[6], 48.JOHANN[5], 25.HERMANN[4], 7.STEPHEN[3], 2.HENNE[2], 1.SIMON[1]) was born 17 August 1889. Her spouse has not been identified.

They had 1 child:

577.   m   i.   **unknown.**

- - - - - - - - - - -

535. ROSS JR[12] **ORENDORFF** (452.ROSS[11], 295.JESSE[10], 166.WILLIAM[9], 90.JESSE[8], 65.CHRISTIAN[7], 54.CHRISTIAN[6], 48.JOHANN[5], 25.HERMANN[4], 7.STEPHEN[3], 2.HENNE[2], 1.SIMON[1]) was born 25 August 1924 in SHERMAN TEXAS. He married **ANN MCCUISTON** and died Feb 2000 in Texas.

They had 1 child:

578. f   i.   **NONA PAT ORENDORFF**, born 23 May 1947 in HOUSTON TEXAS.

Notes for Ross:

Ross worked for Westinghouse and lived on the old Orendorff/Orenduff land. Ross was very interested in family history and corresponded with Stephen B. Orendorff. Phone number as of 11-04-1993 was 214-562-1468.

- - - - - - - - - - -

537.   MONROE   WILMETH[12]   **ORENDORFF** (453.MONROE[11],   295.JESSE[10],   166.WILLIAM[9],   90.JESSE[8], 65.CHRISTIAN[7],   54.CHRISTIAN[6],   48.JOHANN[5], 25.HERMANN[4], 7.STEPHEN[3], 2.HENNE[2], 1.SIMON[1]) was born 14 October 1906 in MELISSA, TX. MONROE died October 1986, at the age of 80. He married **PEARL EUDORA ARMSPRING**.

They had 1 child:

579.   f   i.   **JANE PATRICIA ORENDORFF.**

Notes for Monroe:

Orenduff spelling - Lived in Claremore, OK. Source: S.S. Death Index.

- - - - - - - - - - -

540. VIVIAN BYRNE[12] **ORENDORFF** (456.VIVIAN[11], 296.JOHN[10], 166.WILLIAM[9], 90.JESSE[8], 65.CHRISTIAN[7], 54.CHRISTIAN[6], 48.JOHANN[5], 25.HERMANN[4], 7.STEPHEN[3], 2.HENNE[2], 1.SIMON[1]) was born 23 December 1892. He married **GERTRUDE SHEPHERD**. She was born 17 November 1893.

They had 5 children:

580.	f	i.	**CLARIBEL GERTRUDE ORENDORFF**, born 26 November 1914. CLARIBEL MARRIED HARRY LINDAHL AND HAD 3 CHILDREN. HARRY JR, MAURICE, AND ELIZABETH (LISA).
581.	f	ii.	**ANNA FAY ORENDORFF**, born 1 August 1916. ANNA MARRIED RALPH HORNER AND HAD 5 CHILDREN. JANET, DALE, NANCY, MARTHA, AND DEAN.
+ 582.	m	iii.	**JOHN EDWARD (JACK) ORENDORFF**, born 5 October 1918.
583.	f	iv.	**VIVIAN JEANNE ORENDORFF**, born 8 January 1921. VIVIAN J. MARRIED ROBERT UHTE AND HAD 2 CHILDREN JON AND DAVID.
584.	f	v.	**VIRGINIA MARIE ORENDORFF**, born 8 March 1928. VIRGINIA MARRIED CECIL THOMPSON AND HAD 3 CHILDREN, BRUCE, BRIAN, AND SCOTT.

CHAPTER THIRTEEN

GENERATION NO. 13

543. TERRY OWEN[13] ORENDORFF (498.ELMER[12], 404.IRA[11], 238.WILLIAM[10], 132.HARRISON[9], 76.PHILIP[8], 60.JOHN[7], 50.PHILIP[6], 26.THEISS[5], 9.LUDWIG[4], 3.HUBERT[3], 2.HENNE[2], 1.SIMON[1]). He married **HELEN MCNARY.**

No children have yet been identified.

HELEN also married (1) ELMER LEROY ORENDORFF **(See number 498).** He was born 20 December 1918 in PERU, CHATAUQUA CO KS. He is the son of IRA IRVIN ORENDORFF and SADIE OLIVE FAST.

Notes for Terry:
Terry Owen's name appears as "Orndorff".

- - - - - - - - - -

547. MADISON DOW[13] ORENDORFF (504.HILTON[12], 406.GEORGE[11], 238.WILLIAM[10], 132.HARRISON[9], 76.PHILIP[8], 60.JOHN[7], 50.PHILIP[6], 26.THEISS[5], 9.LUDWIG[4], 3.HUBERT[3], 2.HENNE[2], 1.SIMON[1]) was born 11 December 1940 in SPRINGFIELD, BACA COUNTY, CO. He married **DORIS ILENE SCHUSTER** 9 June 1963 in SPRINGFIELD, BACA COUNTY, CO.

They had 1 child:

585.   f   i.   **DAWN ORENDORFF,** born 8 June 1967.
                DAWN'S NAME APPEARS AS "ORNDORFF".

Notes for Doris:
Daughter of Frank Schuster Jr.

- - - - - - - - - - -

548. ROGER ARNOLD[13] **ORENDORFF** (504.HILTON[12], 406.GEORGE[11], 238.WILLIAM[10], 132.HARRISON[9], 76.PHILIP[8], 60.JOHN[7], 50.PHILIP[6], 26.THEISS[5], 9.LUDWIG[4], 3.HUBERT[3], 2.HENNE[2], I.SIMON[1]) was born 6 January 1938 in BUFFALO OK. He married **TERESA LEE PORTER**.

They had 2 children:

586.   m   i.   **ERIC ROGER ORENDORFF**, born 8 September 1960.
ERIC ROGER'S NAME APPEARS AS "ORNDORFF".

587.   f   ii.   **HEIDI LYN ORENDORFF**, born 11 February 1964.
HEIDI LYN'S NAME APPEARS AS "ORNDORFF".

- - - - - - - - - - -

550. ROBERT DEANE[13] **ORENDORFF** (508.WILLIAM[12], 406.GEORGE[11], 238.WILLIAM[10], 132.HARRISON[9], 76.PHILIP[8], 60.JOHN[7], 50.PHILIP[6], 26.THEISS[5], 9.LUDWIG[4], 3.HUBERT[3], 2.HENNE[2], I.SIMON[1]) was born 26 March 1933 in MINDEN, NE. He married **LILY AUDREY NIDEY**.

They had 4 children:

588.   f   i.   **PEGGY RUTH ORENDORFF**, born 15 November 1957 in POSS. NE.
PEGGY RUTH'S NAME APPEARS AS "ORNDORFF".

589.   f   ii.   **LADEANE FAY ORENDORFF**, born 27 October 1955 possibly in NE.
LADEANE FAY'S NAME APPEARS AS "ORNDORFF".

590.   m   iii.   **GLENN EDWIN ORENDORFF**, born 1 August 1962 possibly in VA.
GLENN EDWIN'S NAME APPEARS AS "ORNDORFF".

591.   m   iv.   **RICHARD PAUL ORENDORFF**, born 20 April 1959 possibly in NE.
RICHARD PAUL'S NAME APPEARS AS "ORNDORFF".

Notes for Lily:
Poss named Lila.

Notes for Robert:
Robert Deane's name appears as "Orndorff".

- - - - - - - - - -

551. CARL JOSEPH[13] **ORENDORFF** (508.WILLIAM[12], 406.GEORGE[11], 238.WILLIAM[10], 132.HARRISON[9], 76.PHILIP[8], 60.JOHN[7], 50.PHILIP[6], 26.THEISS[5], 9.LUDWIG[4], 3.HUBERT[3], 2.HENNE[2], 1.SIMON[1]) was born 16 July 1936 in LAMAR, BARTON CO, MO. He married **MARLENE KAY MYERS**.

They had 3 children:

592.   f   i.   **LORINDA KAY ORENDORFF**, born 14 July 1964 in POSS. VA.
LORINDA KAY'S NAME APPEARS AS "ORNDORFF". SHE WAS THE DAUGHTER OF CARL JOSEPH ORNDORFF.

593.   m   ii.   **CARL DOUGLAS ORENDORFF**, born 5 October 1959.
CARL DOUGLAS' NAME APPEARS AS "ORNDORFF".

594.   m   iii.   **HOWARD WILLIAM ORENDORFF**, born 7 July 1962.
HOWARD WILLIAM'S NAME APPEARS AS "ORNDORFF".

Notes for Marlene:
Marlene Kay was married to Carl Joseph "Orndorff".

Notes for Carl:
Carl Joseph's name appears as "Orndorff".

- - - - - - - - - - -

560. STEPHEN MARVIN[13] **ORENDORFF** (521.EDDIE[12], 444.STEPHEN[11], 293.ROBERT[10], 166.WILLIAM[9], 90.JESSE[8], 65.CHRISTIAN[7], 54.CHRISTIAN[6], 48.JOHANN[5], 25.HERMANN[4], 7.STEPHEN[3], 2.HENNE[2], I.SIMON[1]) was born 1 June 1953 in EUGENE, OR. He married **NELDA LOUISE GLOVER** born Apr 03, 1955 in Duncan, Stephens Co, OK. She was the daughter of HOMER DALE GLOVER b: January 16, 1926 in Pontotoc Co, OK m: May 17, 1946 in DUNCAN, STEPHENS CO, OK d: March 31, 1992 in SPRINGFIELD, LANE CO, OR and BETTY LOU HOWERTON b: February 14, 1929 in LOCO, STEPHENS CO, OK d: December 02, 1978 in EUGENE, LANE CO, OR.

They had 2 children:

595.   m   i.   **STEPHEN BRADLEY ORENDORFF**, born 21 June 1972 in EUGENE, OR. He married Joyce Elaine O'Connor daughter of John O'Connor and Joyce Elaine McKee born 31 January 1980 on November 4, 1998 in CRESCENT CITY, CA. They had a daughter Brittney Lynn Orendorff born July 31, 1999 at Medford, OR. Notes for STEPHEN: Occupation: Corrections Officer.

Notes for Stephen:
Stephen Bradley Orendorff was born June 21,1973 in Eugene, Oregon. The first child of Stephen Marvin and Nelda Louise Glover Orendorff. Stephen began working part time

at the Klickitat County Jail in August of 1991 and graduated from the Corrections Academy in Seattle, Washington in 1994. He became a full time officer in 1996, and later became training coordinator for the computerized L.E.T.N. for Klickitat Co, WA. Married to Jennifer Davis in 1996 and divorced in 1998, no children by that marriage. Stephen is a member of the Sons of Confederate Veterans, enjoys collecting military relics, reading, and family genealogy research.

Notes for Joyce:
Joyce works for the Northern Oregon Regional Correctional Facility (NORCOR) located in Wasco Co, The Dalles, OR. She currently resides in Wasco, Oregon with. Her parents were married at Walla Walla, WA. Her mother was married to the following: Ron Adams, Orval Zink, John O'Connor, Genero Trevino, and currently Dennis Combs. Her children are Connie Adams b. in Vancouver, WA; Sherry Adams b. Heidelberg, Germany; Dane Zink b. Nashville, TN; Willa Zink b. in Bristow, OK; Angela O'Connor b. Walla Walla, WA; Julie O'Connor b. Vancouver, WA; John O'Connor b. in Vancouver, WA; and Joyce Elaine O'Connor b. in Vancouver, WA. Her mother Joyce Elaine McKee was the daughter of James Elijah McKee b. 05-07-21 and Goldie Cook b. 03-24-1928 in Omaha, NB. They married at Sunnyside, WA on September 29, 1945. As a child he and his first cousin Frieda used to play tricks on his grandmother Eliza Williamson (his mothers mother). She lived with them for several years. One time James cut down a tree that had a lot

of pitch in it. Eliza loved honey, so he put the pitch in a jar and gave it to her as honey. She put some of it on bread and tried to eat it, but it got stuck in her false teeth! James spent some time logging old snag timber left over from the big fire that happened about 1900, he said they salvaged some good yellow fir wood. His father had mule teams but James preferred horses. He had one team of mules he hated. He used to take groceries to his mom and sisters every weekend while he was in his 20's. His parents divorced and both remarried. During WWII James served in the Naval Armed Guard protecting merchant shipping. He served in many theaters including the Mediterranean and the Pacific. While in Italy he befriended a young Italian boy who was hungry. They never were able to learn each others language but they left a lasting impression on each other. Before he left port there the boy gave him his Catholic medal. While in the pacific he helped feed some Japanese POW's that were starving. He spent some time in Australia and also Egypt. He served on board ship with a man named Thomas Lakey who became a lasting friend. After being reunited in the late 1990's James moved to Ashland, Benton Co, Mississippi where Thomas lives. After the war he spent 30 plus years as a mill worker before retiring. He was an outdoorsman and still enjoys fishing. He has a great sense of humor and is a joy to visit. A large photo of him in his uniform now hangs in the home of his granddaughter Joyce. The parents of James Elijah McKee were Andrew Ferdinand McKee b. near Amboy, WA circa 1892 d. circa 1979 of flu at a hospital in Vancouver, WA and Della Ann Hutchens, daughter of Elijah Hutchens and Eliza Williamson (see below). They had the following children: James Elijah McKee (only son), Minnie (oldest) b. circa 1916 still living in Vancouver, WA, Mary b. 4 miles east of Mabton, WA, still living in Vancouver, WA, and Anna b. north of Granger WA on 10 acres. Andrew Ferdinand was the son of James (Jim) Dean McKee from Joplin, Missouri. Andrew told his son James a story about being 6 years old and there was a big forest fire. He said it got so dark from all the ash in the air that the chickens went to sleep. He lived in Washington except for 2 years when the family lived near Medford, OR at Butte Falls on 40 acres rented from "an old indian". According to James McKee it was "wild country", you could hear cougar screaming at night and there were deer and bear on the property. The parents of Goldie were Amos Cook and the mothers maiden name was Davis. They had the following children: Joyce Elaine McKee b. 10-13-1947 in Sunnyside, WA; Linda Marlene McKee b. 01-19-1949 in Toppenish, WA; Gordon James McKee b. 02-06-1951 in Vancouver, WA; Jack Dean McKee b. 08-29-1954 in Vancouver, WA; and Donna Marie McKee b. 07-08-1958 in Vancouver, WA. The McKee family came to Virginia from Ireland and Scotland. The family followed the typical migration to Kentucky and Missouri, then from there they branched off to Texas and Washington. Three brothers, Arch, George, and Jim went to Amboy, WA by wagon train from St Joseph, MI about 1880. The other brother Bill moved to Jct City, Texas where he bought a large cattle ranch for .10 an acre. When he was 60 he sold the ranch, moved to town, and opened a bank. He married his secretary, a "good lookin woman" as his nephew said, about 35 years his junior. He wanted to have someone to leave his money to so his brothers would not fight over it. WILLIAMSON GENEALOGY-IV. Eliza Williamson b. 07-12-1855 in OR married Elijah Hutchens. They had the following children: Orph, Lenore, John, Minnie, Mary, and Della. III. Parents of Eliza were John Rush Williamson b. 12-13-1820 in W. VA d. 1892 in OR m. 1845 to Susan Olivia Martin b. 08-29-1825 in W. VA d. My 1871 in OR. They had the following children: Elizabeth b. Fed 1847, Ann b. 1849 in OR, Eliza b. 1852 in OR, Mary Emily b. July 12, 1855 in OR, and John Jr b. June 28, 1859 in OR. II. Parents of Susan Olivia Martin were Nathaniel Manning Martin b. Sept 24, 1802 in W. VA and Mary (Polly) Huffman b. mar 20, 1804 in W. VA. I. The parents of Nathaniel Manning Martin were Jephthan Martin b. April 2, 1767 in VA m. Sept 6, 1792 to Ollie Williamson b. March 3, 1776 in VA. The Williamson family came to America from England. John Williamson was born during the administration of George Washington, he was the father of the above mentioned John Rush Williamson. He had a large plantation in western VA growing tobacco and cotton. He had a large number of negro slaves which he freed in the 1820's, they stayed on and worked the land. He had 8 children, the eldest of which was John Rush. He died after a period of declining health when his son John Jr was 14. When John Jr was

25 he traveled to Missouri and spent the winter working on a farm. John has been described as having brown eyes, being tall, rather handsome, and that he showed his mother's French ancestry. He married pretty blue eyed, golden haired Susan Olivia Martin, daughter of a farmer formerly from VA. In the spring of 1846 they headed for the Chedlam Valley in Yamhill Co, OR.

596.   f   ii.   **SARAH JOY ORENDORFF**, born 5 March 1977 in EUGENE, OR.
Sarah Joy Orendorff was born March 5, 1977 in Eugene, OR. The second child of Stephen Marvin Orendorff and Nelda Glover Orendorff. She moved to McCall, Idaho in 1997 and worked in an insurance office. Married Richard Brian Kemp b. 1973.
Isaak Dylan Kemp b. Dec 7, 1999 at Ashland, OR.

Notes for Nelda:
Manager of Mt View Retirement in Ashland OR. Nelda worked for Sherman County Oregon District Attorney Ray English for about 6 years and began working at the Klickitat County jail in July of 1994. Nelda had an older sister named Carol who died of liver scirrosis at age 16, she contracted hepatitis at a young age. She also has a younger sister named Angie who has a twin brother named Carl, and two older brothers named Ronnie and Donnie. Carl Glover was nicknamed "butch" and lived in Goldendale, Klickitat Co, WA in 1996-97. In the early to mid 1990's he lived in Sherman Co, OR in the towns of Wasco and Rufus. Carl also was married in the 1980's and divorced with three children in that marriage, her name was Theresa. He also had one male child named Erik by his girlfriend Laura Lawrence when he lived in Wasco OR. He was living in Springfield, Lane Co, OR in 2000. The following is a list of Glover genealogy provided by her and her brother:

1 Caleb Carmen McClard b: June 04, 1848 in TN d: July 18, 1923 in Elmore City, OK.

. +Tabitha Donoho b: 1848 in TN m: Oct 25, 1870 in Macon County, TN d: Sept 24, 1882.

    2 Mills Fisher McClard b: Jan 27, 1873 d: Jan 27, 1873.

    2 Cora Frances McClard b: July 01, 1875 in Ark d: Aug 16, 1960.

      . +Willie O Shuffield b: 1873 m: July 09, 1891 in Garland County, Ark.

.... 3 Rosa Shuffield.

.... 3 Minnie Shuffield.

.... 3 Jennie Shuffield.

.... 3 Myrtle Shuffield.

.... 3 Argus Caleb Shuffield b: Sept 06, 1904 d: Oct 29, 1959.

.... +Vera Augustine Wagner b: Aug 13, 1908 d: Sept 28, 1987.

... *2nd Husband of Cora Frances McClard:

.... +Charles Isaac Farmer b: Aug 31, 1865 m: Dec 06, 1908 d: May 15,1958.

... *3rd Husband of Cora Frances McClard:

.... +Clyde Charles Isaac Farmer b: Aug 31, 1865 m: Dec 16, 1908 in Garland Co, Ark d: May 15, 1958.

... 2 William Charles McClard b: May 18, 1878 in Ark d: Nov 18, 1957 in CA.

.... +Elizabeth b: 1879 in Ark m: 1896.

.... 3 Wilburn H McClard b: 1900 in Ark.

.... +Opal M b: 1902 in OK.

.... 4 Berniy E McClard b: 1919 in OK.

... *2nd Wife of William Charles McClard:

.... +Mary Belle McCurtain m: Dec 02, 1902 in Bennington, OK d: 1904 in OK.

.... 3 Myrtle Blanche McClard b: Dec 13, 1900 in Bennington, Bryan Co, OK d: July 04, 1972 in Oklahoma City, OK.

.... +Mr. Kisten.

.... *2nd Husband of Myrtle Blanche McClard:

.... +Will Smith.

.... *3rd Husband of Myrtle Blanche McClard:

.... +Smith Melton James b: Feb 13, 1895 in Bonham, TX d: Feb 14, 1973 in Fort Supply, OK.

.... 4 Smith Melton James b: in OK d: in OK.

.... 4 Evelyn Ouida James b: Aug 06, 1916 in Bennington, OK d: Nov 18, 1996 in Altus, Jackson County, OK

.... 4 William Clinton James b: Nov 10, 1921 in Sulphur, OK

.... +Flora Mae Warren b: April 14, 1926 in Olustee, OK m: Dec 24, 1952 in Lawton, Comanche County, OK.

.... 4 Tiffany Joy James b: Nov 21, 1925 in Hugo, Choctaw County, OK.

.... +Robert Warren Hardy Benson b: 1921 in OK m: Nov 1940 in Cleveland County, OK.

.... 5 Ronald Jaroy Benson b: June 16, 1944 in Oklahoma City, Oklahoma d: March 13, 1987 in Fort Worth, TX.

.... +Charlotte Gorman.

.... 6 Randall Lee Benson b: Mar 18, 1967 in Arlington, TX.

.... +Judy

.... 7 Jana Jay Benson b: May 24, 1991 in Fort Worth, TX.

.... 7 Lauren Brook Benson b: Sep 11, 1992 in Fort Worth, TX.

.... 7 Ryan Keith Benson b: Jan 19, 1994 in Fort Worth, TX.

.... 6 Cheryl Lynn Benson b: Oct 22, 1969 in Arlington, TX.

.... +Wesley Howard Alred.

.... 7 Coty Alred b: May 29, 1989 in Fort Worth, TX.

.... 7 Ashley Nichole Alred b: June 06, 1990 in Oklahoma City, OK.

.... 7 Leslie Leana Alred b: Nov 17, 1991 in Fort Worth, TX.

.... 5 Sherry Starlett Benson b: Jan 11, 1946 in Oklahoma City, OK.

.... +Tyson D Harrison.

.... 6 Gregory D Harrison b: Jan 12, 1970 in Oklahoma City, OK.

.... +Rebecca b: April 14, 1971.

.... 7 Matthew D Harrison b: Jan 23, 1990 in Oklahoma City, OK.

.... 7 Justin Warren Harrison b: April 07, 1994 in Oklahoma City, OK.

.... 6 Valarie Cheri Harrison b: Dec 12, 1972 in Oklahoma City, OK.

.... *4th Husband of Myrtle Blanche McClard:

.... +Harry Kisten.

... 2 Albert Alexander McClard b: July 29, 1880 in Ark d: 1940

.... +Mary Myrtle Tinsley b: Aug 03, 1879 in Bonham, Fannin Co, TX m: 1903 d: 1940.

.... 3 Nellie Belle McClard b: Apr 27, 1904 in OK d: May 1987 in OK.

.... +Elmer Lee Howerton b: Mar 26, 1892 m: Nov 22, 1921 in OK d: Nov 1982 in OK.

.... 4 Betty Lou Howerton b: Feb 14, 1929 in Loco, Stephens Co, OK d: April 02, 1978 in Eugene, Lane Co, OR.

.... +Homer Dale Glover b: Jan 16, 1926 in Pontotoc Co, OK m: May 17, 1946 in Duncan, Stephens Co, OK d: Mar 31, 1992 in Springfield, Lane Co, OR. Homer Dale's parents were Joseph Leonard Glover D. 1970 in Eugene OR, and Virgy. The other children were Junior, Billy, Sonny d. 2000, Lonnie, and Ernie. They had one girl that died shortly after birth. Also had twin girls that died at whooping cough at 10 months.

.... 5 Ronnie Dale Glover b: Feb 05, 1947 in Duncan, Stephens Co, OK d: June 27, 1999 in Eugene, Lane Co, OR.

.... +Jaqueline Harris m: June 01, 1964 in Harrisburg, Linn Co, OR.

.... 6 Tommy Dale Glover b: May 1968 in Eugene, Lane Co, OR.

.... 6 Tammi Marie Glover b: April 10 1966.

.... +Ron Cash b: in Eugene, Lane Co, OR.

.... 7 Christin Cash b: in Eugene, Lane Co, OR.

.... 5 James Donald Glover b: May 27, 1948 in Duncan, Stephens Co, OK. Works for the city of Springfield.

.... +Shirley m: in Eugene, Lane Co, OR.

.... 6 Joey Glover b: Aug 24 1969, d: July 2, 1985.

.... 5 Betty Carol Glover b: Mar 09, 1951 in Duncan, Stephens Co, OK d: Apr 29, 1967 at Albany, OR.

.... 5 Nelda Louise Glover b: Apr 03, 1955 in Duncan, Stephens Co, OK. Married Feb 12, 1972 at Harrisburg OR.

.... +Stephen M. Orendorff m: in Harrisburg, Linn Co, OR.

.... 6 Stephen B. Orendorff.

.... 6 Sara J. Orendorff.

.... *2nd Husband of Nelda Louise Glover:

.... +James Fuller.

.... 5 Carl Dwayne Glover b: Dec 16, 1963 in Eugene, Lane Co, OR.

.... +Teresa Lynn Lydic m: in Reno, NV 1981.

.... 6 Jeremy Dale Glover b: May 05, 1982 in Springfield, Lane Co, OR.

.... 6 Michael Dwayne Glover b: Dec 10, 1984 in Springfield, Lane Co, OR.

.... 6 Carol Marie Glover b: Mar 05, 1986 in Springfield, Lane Co, OR.

.... *2nd Wife of Carl Dwayne Glover(common law):

.... +Laura Lawrence.

.... 6 Eric Steven Glover b: Sept 06, 1992.

.... 5 Angela Elaine Glover b: Dec 16, 1963 in Eugene, Lane Co, OR.

.... +Stony Lynn Bamford b: Jan 08, 1964 in Eugene, Lane Co, OR m: June 18, 1983 in Lane Co, OR.

.... 6 Justin Lee Bamford b: Dec 12, 1983 in Eugene, Lane Co, OR.

.... 6 Jordan Michael Bamford b: Apr 07, 1988 in Eugene, Lane Co, OR.

.... 6 Jacob Dylan Bamford b: April 03, 1990 in Eugene, Lane Co, OR.

.... *2nd Husband of Angela Elaine Glover:

.... +Patrick Edward Kaley b: Nov 11, 1968 in Cedarville, Modoc Co, CA m: May 29, 1999 at Maryhill, Klickitat Co, WA.

.... 4 Billy Ray Howerton b: Oct 26, 1922.

.... +Katherine Johnson b: Dec 15, 1928 in Waco, McLennan Co, TX m: May 31, 1946 in Texas. Lives in Bakersfield, CA.

.... 5 Randy Lee Howerton.

.... +Susan McIntyre.

.... 6 Randy Lee Howerton.

.... 6 Latisha Howerton.

.... 5 Billy Don Howerton.

.... +Carol Harries.

.... 6 Danny Howerton.

.... 6 Christy Howerton.

.... 5 Suzanne Howerton.

.... 4 Helen Marie Howerton b: in Loco, Stephens Co, OK.

.... +Archie Marion Glover b: Nov 19, 1924 m: Mar 02, 1946 in Pontotoc Co, OK d: May 11, 1993 in Springfield, Lane Co, OR.

.... 5 Archie Allen Glover b: Jan 19, 1947.

.... 5 Bobby Ray Glover b: June 06, 1948.

.... +Janice Harris.

.... 6 Tommy Joe Glover.

.... 6 Johnnie Glover.

.... 6 Dannie Glover.

.... 5 Thomas Lee Glover b: July 06, 1949.

.... 5 Onita Marie Glover b: Feb 06, 1951.

.... 5 Maryln June Glover b: July 03, 1954.

.... 5 Marion Gene Glover b: July 03, 1954.

.... 4 Jimmy Don Howerton b: in Loco, Stephens Co, OK.

.... +Sue.

.... 5 Jimmy Don Howerton.

.... 5 Susette Howerton.
.... *2nd Wife of Jimmy Don Howerton:
.... +Leslie m: in Reno, NV.
.... 5 Anne Marie Howerton.
.... 5 Tabitha Lynn Howerton.

NOTES for STEPHEN:

Religion: Protestant. Sherman Co Sheriff. Elected sheriff of Sherman Co Oregon in 1994 by almost a 2 to 1 margin in the primary election, in the general election it was 7 to 1. He took office December 1st 1994 and was sworn in by the previous sheriff Gerald Lohrey in Moro Oregon at the Sherman Co courthouse. He retired due to a heart attack in 1995. Stephen M. is a martial arts expert and has been in law enforcement since about 1977. Nicknamed "little stevie" by his brothers and sisters, also called "ornie" by his friends. Before entering law enforcement he worked in a plywood mill in Junction City, Lane Co OR and also worked at American Can Company located at Halsey, Linn Co, OR with his father and brother in Law Bruce Cobb. He was in the US army for a short time in the early 1970's. Steve had joined in an attempt to be shipped overseas to fight in Vietnam but was never sent due to the end of that conflict. As a child he had a pet lamb called "lambie" and there is a picture of him holding that lamb in the possession of his son. Also as a child he had many pet frogs and turtles he kept in an old bathtub at the house on 554 1/2 Territorial St Harrisburg or and when one would die he would have his mother give them a funeral. As a child he was also quite handy with a BB gun, as either of his sisters can attest. Once he was practicing with a target and convinced his sister Shari to go move it, as he did he shot her. She tried to run to one side of the yard and then the other but each time she did she would get hit and try to go the other way again. There are also still many bb's to be found under the paint on the outside of the house. He had a German shepherd dog that he donated to the U.S. army for use in the Vietnam War. He was married at his sister Nancy's home in Harrisburg OR, and lived in Junction City,

OR for a short time after they were first married. In high school he would ride with the local police officers. He was always interested in police work and later he pursued a career in law enforcement. First as a Reserve, and later full time, deputy in Corvallis, Benton County Oregon. Next he returned to his home town of Harrisburg to work as a resident deputy for Linn County Oegon. He also worked as a City Policeman in both Junction City and Florence in Lance county Oregon. During his years of service he investigated many major cases including homicides.

- - - - - - - - - -

561. EDDIE DAVID[13] **ORENDORFF** (521.EDDIE[12], 444.STEPHEN[11], 293.ROBERT[10], 166.WILLIAM[9], 90.JESSE[8], 65.CHRISTIAN[7], 54.CHRISTIAN[6], 48.JOHANN[5], 25.HERMANN[4], 7.STEPHEN[3], 2.HENNE[2], 1.SIMON[1]) was born 7 March 1942 in GRANITE, OK. EDDIE died 7 May 1990, at the age of 48. He married **BETTY ANN HELGET** of Austrian and Belgian decent on 30 June 1961 in HARRISBURG OR.

They had 3 children:

597.　　m　i.　　**ERIC VON ORENDORFF**, born 25 February 1971 in EUGENE OR.

Eric Von Orendorff was born Feb 25, 1971, the third child born to Eddie David Orendorff and Betty Helget Orendorff. Eric served in the Oregon National Guard.

598 .　　m　ii.　　**JEFFREY DAVID ORENDORFF**, born 17 June 1965 in EUGENE, OR.

Religion: Protestant.

Jefferey was the second child of Eddie David and Betty Helget Orendorff.

599.　　f　iii.　　**ANITA SUE ORENDORFF**, born 02-29-1963 in EUGENE OR. She married Jeffrey Benton Holmes on March 7, 1979 in Reno, NV. Jeffrey is a carpenter. The family lives in Harrisburg, OR. They had the following children: Joshua Daniel born in EUGENE, OR on 11-30-1979; Lindsay Marie born in CORVALLIS, OR on 05-26-1981; Michael Jeffery b. 07-31-83; Kayla Rachell b. 08-21-88; Kimberli Joy b.10-26-89; David Benton Steven b. 06-21-92; Aaron Jacob b. 09-13-96.

NOTES for EDDIE:

Eddie David was the first born of Eddie Dee Orendorff and Dorothy Anglin Orendorff on March 7, 1942. Called David, he began his first years of school in the small mountain town of Crow, OR. The remainder of his elementary and high school years were attended at Harrisburg. He was very interested in Indian history and enjoyed collecting war memorabilia. David also did research into family history. He was an electrician at American Can Co. in Halsey, OR.

562. NANCY LEE[13] ORENDORFF (521.EDDIE[12], 444.STEPHEN[11], 293.ROBERT[10], 166.WILLIAM[9], 90.JESSE[8], 65.CHRISTIAN[7], 54.CHRISTIAN[6], 48.JOHANN[5], 25.HERMANN[4], 7.STEPHEN[3], 2.HENNE[2], I.SIMON[1]) was born 8 December 1945 in MANGUM, OK. She married **PRESTON BRUCE COBB** 10 April 1964. He was born 12 June 1943 in MOBILE, AL. He is the son of JOHN BERRY COBB and LOU ELLA FLEMMING.

They had 1 child:

600.   f   i.   **STEPHANIE LEE COBB**, born 11 October 1967 in EUGENE, OR.

Religion: Protestant.

Stephanie is married and has two daughters. Marriage date 12-27-88. Richard Alan Murray DOB 10-19-66. Stephanie Lee DOB 10-11-67. Ashley Cheyanne DOB 5-9-94. Amber Lee DOB 12-21-95.

Notes for Preston:

Occupation: Pulp & Paper Employee.

Religion: Protestant

Bruce Preston is the only son of John Berry Cobb and Lou E. Cobb. He was born in Mobile, Alabama, on June 12, 1943. The family moved to Cottage Grove, Oregon in 1952 for a short time before moving to Junction City, Oregon. Graduate of Junction City High School.

Notes for Nancy:

Occupation: Homemaker.

Religion: Protestant.

Nancy Lee Orendorff was born December 8, 1945 in Mangum, OK. The third child of Eddie Dee Orendorff and Dorothy Anglin Orendorff. She is very interested in family history. Nancy became a member of the DAR on 10-14-1993, her paperwork was verified on 07-15-1993. Member of friends of the library. Has worked with state and local humane society organizations and is currently active in fund raising projects. Favorite pastimes include genealogy, gardening, visiting museums and historic sites.

563. SHARON ROSE[13] ORENDORFF 521.EDDIE[12], 444.STEPHEN[11], 293.ROBERT[10], 66.WILLIAM[9], 90.JESSE[8], 65.CHRISTIAN[7], 54.CHRISTIAN[6], 48.JOHANN[5], 25.HERMANN[4], 7.STEPHEN[3], 2.HENNE[2], I.SIMON[1]), born 16 May 1950 in ALBANY, OR.

Religion: Protestant.

Sharon Rose Orendorff was born in Eugene, Oregon on May 16, 1950. The fourth child born to Eddie Dee Orendorff and Dorothy Lee Anglin Orendorff. She worked for the first National Bank in Harrisburg for many years and is now an office employee for a water purification company in Junction City, Oregon. She married Raymond Halsey firstly and later married James Singletery. They are residents of Harrisburg, Oregon. Her children were born in Eugene, OR and are as follows-Carleen Halsey b. 03-28-70, Brandon Halsey b. 05-11-1973 and Heather Singletery b. 11-23-1978. Carleen has two daughters, Brandon has one son and has been in the Marine Corps, Heather is a student at Washington State University in Seattle, WA.

- - - - - - - - - - -

565. EDDIE WAYNE[13] **MORRIS** (522.EDNA[12], 444.STEPHEN[11], 293.ROBERT[10], 166.WILLIAM[9], 90.JESSE[8], 65.CHRISTIAN[7], 54.CHRISTIAN[6], 48.JOHANN[5], 25.HERMANN[4], 7.STEPHEN[3], 2.HENNE[2], 1.SIMON[1]) was born 26 April 1951 in Altus, OKLAHOMA. He married **CHRISTINE ANNE** [————?————] 10 June 1978 in La Habra, CA.

They had 2 children:

601.　　m　i.　**MATTHEW EDWARD MORRIS**, born 26 November 1973 in Kirkland, Washington. Religion: Christian.

Legally adopted.

602.　　m　ii.　**JOHN WAYNE MORRIS**, born 26 June 1975 in Whidbey Island, WASHINGTON. He married AMANDA RAE MILLER 18 July 1998 in Buena Park, CA. Notes for JOHN:

Religion: Christian. Legally adopted.

Notes for Eddie:
Education: Masters in Counseling.
Religion: Christian.

- - - - - - - - - - -

566. MARY SUE[13] **MORRIS** (522.EDNA[12], 444.STEPHEN[11], 293.ROBERT[10], 166.WILLIAM[9], 90.JESSE[8], 65.CHRISTIAN[7], 54.CHRISTIAN[6], 48.JOHANN[5], 25.HERMANN[4], 7.STEPHEN[3], 2.HENNE[2], 1.SIMON[1]) was born 5 August 1957 in Altus, OKLAHOMA. She married **GARY L. NUNNALLY** 8 September 1979 in La Habra, CALIFORNIA.

They had 2 children:

603.   m   i.   **GREGORY WAYNE NUNNALLY**, born 28 August 1983 in Upland, CALIFORNIA.

604.   f   ii.   **Heather LYNN NUNNALLY**, born 21 May 1987 in Upland, CALIFORNIA.

Notes for Mary:
Education: 2 years of college.
Religion: Christian.

- - - - - - - - - - -

567. CAROLYN SUE[13] BREWER (523.MILDRED[12], 444.STEPHEN[11], 293.ROBERT[10], 166.WILLIAM[9], 90.JESSE[8], 65.CHRISTIAN[7], 54.CHRISTIAN[6], 48.JOHANN[5], 25.HERMANN[4], 7.STEPHEN[3], 2.HENNE[2], 1.SIMON[1]) was born 15 December 1949 in MANGUM, OK. She married **EDWIN EARL HUDGINS** 29 June 1974 in EASTLAND, TX.

They had 1 child:

605.   f   i.   **AMANDA SUE HUDGINS**, born 21 May 1979 in PLAINVIEW , TX.

Notes for Carolyn:
Education: BA. Wayland Baptist Univ., MSM- Houston Baptist Univ.

Religion: Baptist

Carolyn Sue Brewer was born on Dec. 15, 1949 in Mangum, Oklahoma, the first child born to Harold Haston Brewer and Mildred Jeannette Orendorff Brewer. She married Edwin Earl Hudgins and is living in Wolforth, TX.

- - - - - - - - - - -

568. MARTHA ANN[13] BREWER (523.MILDRED[12], 444.STEPHEN[11], 293.ROBERT[10], 166.WILLIAM[9], 90.JESSE[8], 65.CHRISTIAN[7], 54.CHRISTIAN[6], 48.JOHANN[5], 25.HERMANN[4], 7.STEPHEN[3], 2.HENNE[2], 1.SIMON[1]) was born 25 March 1952 in MANGUM, OK. She married **ROCKY LOYE BUNTING** 24 August 1973 in EASTLAND, TX.

They had 2 children:

606.   f   i.   **JENNIFER ANN BUNTING**, born 21 July 1975 in STEPHENVILLE, TX. She married CLINT MARSHALL CARAWAY 17 August 1996.

607.   m   ii.   **JOHN BRADLEY BUNTING**, born 21 May 1977 in STEPHENVILLE, TX.

Notes for Martha:
Education: BS/ Business.
Religion: Baptist.

Martha Ann Brewer was born on March 25, 1952 in Mangum, Ok. The second child born to Harold Haston Brewer and Mildred Jeannette Orendorff Brewer. Martha Ann has a BS in business. She married Rocky Loye Bunting and lives in De Leon, TX.

- - - - - - - - - - -

569. JAN ELIZABETH[13] **BREWER** (523.MILDRED[12], 444.STEPHEN[11], 293.ROBERT[10], 166.WILLIAM[9], 90.JESSE[8], 65.CHRISTIAN[7], 54.CHRISTIAN[6], 48.JOHANN[5], 25.HERMANN[4], 7.STEPHEN[3], 2.HENNE[2], 1.SIMON[1]) was born 27 March 1953 in MANGUM, OK. She married **JOEL CRAIG BESKOW** 21 December 1974 in EASTLAND, TX. He was born 30 September 1952 in RANGER, TX.

They had 1 child:

608.   m   i.   **JOEL HASTON BESKOW**, born 5 October 1982 in EASTLAND, TX.

Notes for Jan:
Education: Bachelor of Science in Elm. Ed., MST. of Counsel. & Human Dev.
Religion: Baptist.

Jan Elizabeth Brewer was born on March 27, 1953 in Mangum, OK. The third child born to Harold Haston Brewer and Mildred Jeannette Orendorff Brewer. She received a Bachelor of Science in Elementary Education; Master of Education and Master of Counseling & Human Development. She married Joel Craig Beskow and lives in Cleburne, TX.

- - - - - - - - - - -

570. SARAH JEAN[13] **BREWER** (523.MILDRED[12], 444.STEPHEN[11], 293.ROBERT[10], 166.WILLIAM[9], 90.JESSE[8], 65.CHRISTIAN[7], 54.CHRISTIAN[6], 48.JOHANN[5], 25.HERMANN[4], 7.STEPHEN[3], 2.HENNE[2], 1.SIMON[1]) was born 1 June 1954 in MIDLAND, TX. She married **FRANKLIN MICHAEL KRAUSE** 22 December 1973 in EASTLAND, TX.

They had 2 children:

609.　　m　i.　**MICHAEL ANDREW KRAUSE**, born 6 July 1979 in TYLER, TX.

610.　　m　ii.　**MATTHEW HASTON KRAUSE**, born 19 August 1980 in TYLER, TX.

Notes for Sarah:

Education: Bachelor of Science in Home Eco. / Northeastern Ok. State Univ.

Religion: Baptist.

Sarah Jean Brewer was born June 1, 1954 in Mangum, Oklahoma, the fourth child born to Harold Haston Brewer and Mildred Jeannette Orendorff Brewer. She married Franklin Michael Krause and is living in San Antonio, TX. Source: book "Hayes in Virginia".

- - - - - - - - - - -

582. JOHN EDWARD (JACK) [13] **ORENDORFF** (540.VIVIAN[12], 456.VIVIAN[11], 296.JOHN[10], 166.WILLIAM[9], 90.JESSE[8], 65.CHRISTIAN[7], 54.CHRISTIAN[6], 48.JOHANN[5], 25.HERMANN[4], 7.STEPHEN[3], 2.HENNE[2], 1.SIMON[1]) was born 5 October 1918. He married **ERMA FORD**. She was born 12 April 1921.

They had 3 children:

611.　　m　i.　**JOHN EDWARD JR. ORENDORFF**.

612.   f   ii.   **JUDITH LOUISE ORENDORFF.**
613.   m   iii.   **THOMAS BYRNE ORENDORFF.**

Notes for John:

Jack and Erma are interested in family history and have had contact with Nancy Cobb (Orendorff). They live in southern CA. One of their relatives has a pistol carried in the civil war by John Hayes Orenduff. Source- Nancy Cobb (Orendorff), interview with Erma Orendorff.

Index

Anna Catharina 13

Kackley,

Amanda [1851-], 92

Kaley,

Patrick Edward 238

Kane,

Ona (Meador) 116

Kaney,

Katherine Eileen 203
Kimberly Leigh 203
Lynn Ann 203
Nancy Fay (Orendorff) 203
Nancy Louise 203
Teresa Eileen 203
Thomas Mervyn 203

Keckley,

Eliza 152

Keeler,

Ethel 130

Keller,

Ann 90
Stewart 90

Kelly,

Emma E. 125

Kelso,

Margaret 61

Kerney,

Madison 153

Kisten,

Mr. 234

Kohr,

George Kasper 28

Kramer,

Anna 15

Krause,

ABOUT GREATUNPUBLISHED.COM

www.greatunpublished.com is a website that exists to serve writers and readers, and to remove some of the commercial barriers between them. When you purchase a GreatUNpublished title, whether you order it in electronic form or in a paperback volume, the author is receiving a majority of the post-production revenue.

A GreatUNpublished book is never out of stock, and always available, because each book is printed on-demand, as it is ordered.

A portion of the site's share of profits is channeled into literacy programs.

So by purchasing this title from GreatUNpublished, you are helping to revolutionize the publishing industry for the benefit of writers and readers.

And for this we thank you.

www.ingramcontent.com/pod-product-compliance
Lightning Source LLC
Chambersburg PA
CBHW071330280526
45787CB00001B/53